Deleuze and Cinema

Dedications . . . to my loving parents

Dorothy Victoria (d. 1993) and William Charles (d. 2000) and, finally, of course . . . *to the beautiful stranger* . . .

Deleuze and Cinema

The Aesthetics of Sensation

Barbara M. Kennedy

Edinburgh University Press

© Barbara M. Kennedy, 2000

Edinburgh University Press Ltd
22 George Square, Edinburgh

Reprinted 2001

Typeset in 10.5 on 13 Sabon
by Hewer Text Ltd, Edinburgh, and
printed and bound in Great Britain by
Biddles Ltd, Guildford

A CIP record for this book is
available from the British Library

ISBN 0 7486 1134 7 (hardback)

The right of Barbara M. Kennedy
to be identified as author of this work
has been asserted in accordance with
the Copyright, Designs and Patents Act 1988.

Contents

Acknowledgements

I should like to thank the many friends and colleagues from different Deleuzian persuasions, from universities both here, in America and Australia, who have read versions of several chapters in the book. In particular I should like to thank both Helen (Chapman) and Christine (Gledhill) at Staffordshire University, who have both suffered the trials and tribulations of my writing, and my personae, and offered advice and support at all times. I also want to thank especially David (Bell) and Ian (Buchanan), both of whom saved me from 'myself' in times of sheer exasperation and at times even worse, and offered both timely and welcome words in more ways than one. Thanks too must go to Jackie Jones at Edinburgh University Press, who recognised the potential, and to Jackie Clewlow, who gave time and energy with secretarial support. Of course I should like to acknowledge the Arts and Humanities Research Board and Staffordshire University for funding and support. And, of course, to those whom I love is a heartfelt thanks for continued support through difficult times.

Art is not chaos but a composition of chaos that yields the vision or sensation, so that it constitutes, as Joyce says, a chaosmos, a composed chaos – neither forseen nor preconceived. Art transforms chaotic varia-bility into chaoid *variety, as in El Greco's black and green-gray confla-gration, for example, or Turner's golden conflagration, or de Stael's red conflagration. Art struggles with chaos but it does so in order to render it sensory, even through the most charming character, the most enchanted landscape.*

(Gilles Deleuze and Félix Guattari, *What is Philosophy?* p. 204)

Introduction

Discovering the Beautiful Stranger . . .

This book has emerged out of a deliciously dangerous, but delectable journey through the spaces of Deleuzian deterritorialisations. But there are many faces of Deleuze, and I can only engage with a selection: faces from *A Thousand Plateaus* (1987), *Francis Bacon: Logique de la sensation* (1981), *Dialogues* (1987), *What is Philosophy?* (1994) and his cinema books[1] provide the main lines of flight. I have not used his cinema books as a model for theorising cinema, but have creatively melded with a web of Deleuze's work. My own line of flight took me on a journey into the unknown, where dangers lurked, forced their way into the threshold of my 'self' – one already fractured, fragile, faltering and disembodied from too much post-structuralist destratification . . . then a return to too much phallic and Oedipal anxiety. Film had always been important to my life, my pleasures, my desires. When I encountered the philosopher of difference, new thinking and outside thought enabled creative lines of flight I had never experienced before. This book traces that processual flight; it explores the energies and intensities of 'flying' with Deleuzian thoughts and transgressing boundaries of established feminist theory . . . out of bounds! The danger is . . . can I fly forever through the paths of indifference and insouciance? Why not? Or will the phallic paths of culture and academia bring me back to the containment of 'academic theory and the rational mind . . .!'

Deleuze is a figure of many colours, tones, many intensities and many variations, his texts providing vast plateaus and canvases, presenting themselves as screenic events, lines and landscapes of volitional and dynamic concepts, brushstrokes, notes, refrains, digital configurations. His multiple texts, and multiple personae, who are also not personae, act like heteronyms, puppets or mannequins in the theatre of philosophy, each text contradicting or aligning with others in machinic assemblage, more like a factory, some have said, than a theatre.

I prefer to see him as an artist than a worker. But such a term is too insubstantial, too shallow, too narrow. As an artist myself, I have always tried to understand that intensity of feeling one has in that moment of brushstroke into canvas, or in media work, the sound into image, or in dance, the movement into muscle, or muscle into movement, the in-between energies that cannot be described. Where are they felt? Where are they subsumed? Who and what do they constitute? That is Deleuze: 'it is difficult to say where in fact the material ends and sensation begins; preparation of the canvas, the track of the brush's hair, and many other things besides are obviously part of the sensation'.[2]

But maybe that's the romantic in me . . . this I can never relinquish and maybe can never really be the true academic, certainly never a true Deleuzian . . . much too romantic for that! Such honesty and integrity are not part of the Deleuzian panoply of masquerade, discretion, disguise, deceit and delights. Perhaps I fell in love too soon with a philosopher who denied too much (certainly love – and yet at times his work is distinctly reminiscent of the romantics of the German tradition – but that's another project?), decried too much and lost his humanity to the forces of the cosmos, the forces of the real, becoming-imperceptible. Get real?

Still, in the lurking dangers of his post-human thoughts, his ideas mingle or bounce off each other, split, disperse, fracture or multiply, often colliding with great force and passion, that we feel unable to resolve any formula or stance to his work. There really is no oeuvre to formulate. The 'horror' he would exclaim, in true Conradian[3] style, that anyone should deign to try to do this, or even want to, and Foucault's suggestion that this century should be called Deleuzian is, of course, a great travesty. I am not trying to utilise his ideas in any formulaic way at all, but to encourage engagement and collusion with this difference engineer, that we might find something 'perceptible' in the imperceptible – a veritable 'Figure in the Carpet'.[4]

Outside thinking and transversality cannot produce a schemic philosophy upon which we can model our cultural, sociological, psychological, ideological or libidinal spaces. Deleuze's texts meld alongside, imbricate and collude/collide with others, for example, paintings or literature, the veritable *wasp* and *orchid*, whilst at times we find a disconcerting but delectable challenge in their seemingly contradictory stances, flying off at tangents, like shooting stars or comets, into the chaosmos of the molecular: Pollock or Klee, Mondrian or Kandinsky? But maybe there just might be a touch of Rodin somewhere, even Heron or O'Keefe, if we're lucky?

I have to acknowledge this polysemic nature of his work; work which cannot and should not, God (Goddesses or Cyborgs) forbid, present a fixed model for thinking. His language and creation of conceptual personae can often make the reader feel disorientated, lost in space, floundering in a forest of neologisms. Be patient, learn to go with the flow and the force of his ideas, for they lead to exciting pathways, new territories, vistas, landscapes of silence, solitude, but often schizophrenia. Tease, taste, and territorialise his ideas into new structures, into frameworks of film, art, music, dance, literature or the performing arts. He presents not structures, but assemblages or open systems, and it is through the openness of such systems that we might foreground some of his ideas in what might seem to the philosopher a reductionist way. My apologies but also sincere dedications go out to the beautiful stranger who taught me never to be fixed, never to be satisfied, never to say 'this is how it is'; for, of course, it never is and never should be. I can only pay homage to some of his ideas, which I here use in a multiperspectival choreography and cartography, bringing back the aesthetic through the *aesthetics of sensation*.

Why now? Why Deleuze? Why feminism? Why this meld? Contemporary visual culture has been written and theorised through a wide range of discourses, one of the predominant areas being the theatre of representation, the scopic and the specular economies of the visual. How can we understand the visual structures of desire if not through the specular economy? However, as much French theory has projected, the look and the gaze have dominated film theory. Feminist film theory has specifically utilised the theatre of psychoanalysis, replete with metaphors of castration anxiety. We need to rethink a post-semiotic space, a post-linguistic space, which provides new ways of understanding the screenic experience as a complex web of inter-relationalities. The look is never purely visual, but also tactile, sensory, material and embodied. The eye in matter. This book seeks to reconfigure corporeality and the role of the mind/brain/body within the notions of sensation, through Deleuzian philosophy.

It seems that at the dawn of a new millennium, the impact of the philosophy of Gilles Deleuze, like that of his counterpart Félix Guattari, will substantially reverberate across science, literature, politics, art and the visual media. My interest has been with reference to his significance to film studies and to an understanding of a new aesthetic paradigm through which to consider film as something 'outside' the purely representational. This has significant reverberations upon post-feminist epistemologies, which have also been offering discourses outside of binary and Western traditions of thinking, and, similarly, within those debates have problematised concepts like subjectivity. A healthy concern with the non-psychical explanations of the material world emanate from both the work of Deleuze, with resonances from Bergson, Spinoza, Nietzsche and others, and also in the work of current post-feminist pragmatics and epistemologies. Deleuze's ideas have challenged the very conception of thought which prioritises rationalist discourses that underpin our ways of thinking, writing and expression, and our understanding of aesthetics, an important concern in the realm of film studies. Bringing back the aesthetic into view, following a lapse into obscurity as a result of cultural and sociological studies of film, is a stance I wish to take; a stance which will have as its basis the ideas formulated from Deleuzian lines of creativity. He stands outside Cartesian dichotomies of Western epistemology, blowing apart the labyrinths of thinking and exploring the caverns of secrecy and indiscernibility.

Within film theory and predominantly feminist film theory, film has been theorised through debates about representation, signification, semiotics and structuralism. The concepts of 'subjectivity' and 'desire' have been theorised through a wide range of critiques. This book proposes to provide a new mind-set, which offers a way of thinking beyond the language of desire and pleasure, beyond notions of a subjectivity, through Deleuzian conceptions of affect, becoming-woman and sensation. A new mind-set where subjectivity is problematised. Desire is rethought through a different lens, a different mapping. A Deleuzian theorising of the beyond of desire has much to offer a post-feminist pragmatics, an agenda which seeks to move away from the strict binary discourses of modernist configurations.

Contemporary cultural formations have been theorised through post-modern ideas of fragmentation, distillation and a 'politics of difference' which has questioned fixed notions of identity and subjectivity. How do we begin to understand and account for the popularity, the desires and pleasures of contemporary cinema outside of these notions? Cinema impacts upon the viewer; it resonates as a material capture. The experiential characteristics of cinema cannot be totally explained through discourses of desire, pleasure and subjectivity. A neo-aesthetics of the visual encounter of cinema sees film as an 'event', as a processual engagement of duration and movement, articulated through webs of sensation across landscapes and panoramas of space, bodies and time.

Film theory to date has failed to provide an adequate understanding of how film matters, how it impacts, how it acts as a body in motion, in space and in time, with other material elements of our world. Instead film theory has been locked into formal analysis of ideology, representation and critiques of signification. Contemporary films display a wide range of effects, tonalities, reverberations, intensities, which connect at an affective level, beyond any sense of subjectivity. A new aesthetic theory, which accounts for how the affective is formulated through colour, sound, movement, force, intensity, not just through psychical mechanisms, but through material elements such as the mind/brain and body, may be possible through a collusion with a Bergsonian-influenced Deleuzian philosophy.

Through modernist discourses, cinema like literature was theorised through humanist engagement with the 'aesthetic', 'beauty' and 'feeling'. Cultural theory impinged upon the humanities providing new debates concerned with ideology, the cultural construction of gender, sexuality, desire and subjectivity – a challenge to aesthetics. Feminist theory was a significant part of a cultural studies' approach to understanding the arts and offered an explanation of the structure of desire through models adapted from psychoanalysis and engagement with the film as 'text'. This was embraced through cinepsychoanalysis with an overreliance on Freudian/Lacanian structures of desire and later through French feminist reappropriations of psychoanalysis.

This book emerges through a synthesis of Deleuzian and post-structuralist feminist philosophy and a reconceiving of the aesthetic to explain the cinematic as a 'material capture', not as a text with a meaning, but as a body which performs, as a machine, as an assemblage, as an abstract machine. It will engage with Deleuzian philosophy to conceive of a neo-aesthetic as a way of exploring the enchantment of contemporary popular movies through a post-semiotic and post-linguistic paradigm. This will provide a neo-aesthetics of the film experience as an 'event': an aesthetics of force and of sensation, where 'subjectivities' are no longer purely contained in the image, or in the spectatorial psychic spaces, but through a melding of matter, the material of film, force, and sensation as movement, the 'in-between' of those spaces. Rather than film being perceived as purely representational, with images seen and perceived through a purely specular economy, film is here explored as a mind/body/machine meld, as experience, as sensation, as a perception–consciousness formation. Perception is not premised upon the visual alone, but through the synaesthetics of sensation. Within this paradigm, images on the screen operate as movement-images, as affect, as modulation in process, dynamic and unfixed, on a plane of immanence. Film is explored as processual, not purely representational.

This book will locate Deleuze, his ideas on desire and sensation, within a new paradigm of post-feminist film theory. This will provide a move towards a post-semiotic, post-linguistic exploration of desire and move beyond a contemporary politics of difference, towards an experimental 'pragmatics of becoming', where subjectivity is subsumed through 'becoming'. The film then will be experienced, it is argued, as a complex assemblage, as an abstract machine, across visualities, bodies, apparati, energies, intensities, forces and discourse. The book offers a post-feminist reconsideration and reappropriation of a neo-aesthetics of sensation. The aesthetic experience is, to quote Brian Massumi, 'dynamogenic' and involves an 'absolute continuum of depersonalisation'.[5] An aesthetics of sensation then emerges beyond the humanist configurations of subjectivity; subjectivity is subsumed through becoming, affect – and sensation. The structure of what follows is both triptychal (Deleuzian) and linear (non-Deleuzian). The first part outlines concepts of the micropolitical, the aesthetic and the post-feminist in Chapter 1. Chapter 2 introduces a concern with film theory and its basis within the formal structures of psychoanalysis, while the second part of that chapter shows how contemporary film theory has made some inroads into alternatives to cinepsychoanalysis. The second part is an exploration of some of the ideas of Deleuze and how they might be substantively relevant to a new mind-set of film theory, with chapters on Deleuzian concepts of pleasure and desire, becoming-woman, and sensation. Part three is an exploration of several films, through Deleuzian deterritorialisations. Thus I have endeavoured to produce a work which colludes, assembles and imbricates a selection of rich and creative lines of flight to offer new directions in film theory. Its only requirement is for the reader to fly with its exuberances, its eclectic mix of writing styles, sometimes poetic and personal (subjective even – such irony!), sometimes academic, and sometimes purely outrageous in its patterns of intensity.

NOTES

1. Gilles Deleuze, *Cinema 1: The Movement–Image*; *Cinema 2: The Time-Image*.
2. Gilles Deleuze and Félix Guattari, *What is Philosophy?*, p. 166.
3. I am referring to the work of Joseph Conrad, author of *Heart of Darkness*.
4. Henry James's 'The Figure in the Carpet' is a short story which provides an intriguing comparison to the complexities of Deleuzian assemblages. Much of Henry James's work has been valorised by Deleuze. James's idea about the multiplicities and configurations of language and its meaning, as somehow only having relevance according to its fields of engagement, has intriguing links with Deleuzian ideas of multiplicity and the rhizomatic.
5. Brian Massumi, 'Deleuze, Guattari and the Philosophy of Expression', in *Canadian Review of Comparative Literature*, p. 745.

Part One

Chapter 1

From Micro-politics to Aesthetics

'[T]he work of art is a being in sensation and nothing else: it exists in itself.'[1]

FROM POLITICS TO AESTHETICS:
MICRO-POLITICS, PRAGMATICS AND AESTHETICS

As an introduction, I shall outline here how the original determinations of this project were founded within feminist politics, but moved into aesthetics. A feminist political project is one concerned to present an argument that is ultimately liberatory to the cultural, social and personal experiences of women. My initial question was to explain why feminist film theory did not explain the pleasures and desires experienced when watching certain neo-noir movies, which appeared to be politically problematic. Why are films such as *Blade Runner* (1982), *Leon* (1994) and *Romeo is Bleeding* (1993) so pleasurable, for example, despite the problematic representations of woman, films inevitably critiqued as objectifying and disempowering to women? But such political objections, premised mainly on representations and image, fail to answer or engage or try to engage with why it is that such films can still operate as pleasurable and desirable experiences. My aim was to investigate how film operates as a pleasurable and desirous experience outside frameworks of image and representation alone. In so doing the very terms *pleasure* and *desire* come under close scrutiny and it is suggested that other concepts might become more appropriate to describe the cinematic experience, the cinematic event. During the course of the debate, the concept of *sensation* is deemed more appropriate for the discussion of the filmic experience.

In traditional film theory, most analysis of desire and pleasure has been based upon signification, text, meaning, semiotics and the visual, especially in feminist film theory. This has led to a focus on debates around feminist readings of what a text 'means', connecting with some overall 'political' stance. I want to argue, through the heuristic device of philosophy, for a micro-political (see definition below) position whereby the impact of cinema is not only experienced through signification, but through film as a material as much as a psychical assemblage, which operates through the processual, force, and intensity as much as image, representation and signification. Thus there is a concern with what a text does, rather than with what it might mean. The premise is then that film is thus experiential and not just representational. Any understanding of desires, pleasures or sensations needs to be theorised within an understanding of how film works ontologically, as film, rather than merely as a mode of representation.

By critiquing psychoanalysis and offering other explanations of desire and a beyond of desire premised upon philosophical ideas within continental philosophy, specifically the work of Gilles Deleuze, I originally intended to show how feminist film theory was lacking in its explorations of desire. However, I found myself very quickly moving outside such a project, through a concern with micro-politics, pragmatics and aesthetics, developing Deleuze's theories of desire and sensation into new strategies of aesthetics and the filmic experience. The project became more one of philosophy and its interpretation through film rather than film explored through philosophy. Initially some definitions are required for my usage of certain terminology.

Micro-politics is a term which might be used instead of politics, in the sense that it advocates that meanings, social structures and lived experiences are too complex and multifaceted to be explained through the more strictly fixed positionalities of politics in the wider (macro) sense. Radical macro-political arguments are usually premised upon binary discourses, one side of which argues for the advocation of liberation of some sort. A specific voice is presented for a specific group within society, with the aim of changing conditions of experience for more liberated experiences. There is, then, a very clearly fixed binary thinking involved, for example, right and left, or masculine and feminine. Any central politics of an imbrication or consilience of voices (a middle view), a third way, is negated. However, micro-politics advocates that changes occur in smaller, less coagulated or clearly framed groups and structures, outside of any binary terminologies. Macro-political struggles are conceived as taking place in collectivised groups. But struggles occur not only in group-sized multiplicities, but *within* and across those groups as it were, rather like the patterned, molecular elements of the atom. 'Struggles occur not only in group-sized multiplicities, but also in those multiplicities internal to or functional through and across subjects, within subjects, against the control of the ego and the superego.'[2] For example, political battles such as the Tiananmen Square incident (1989) actually had reverberations which were much wider than the overly political. They concern artistic and attitudinal resonances, multifarious and not fixed within a set political view, the results of which had significant cultural and aesthetic resonances not previously set up by the main political agenda.

Pragmatics: I shall be referring to the concept 'pragmatism' as follows. Pragmatism starts out from Darwinian ideas. In other words, Darwinian naturalism. The origin of naturalism was based upon the Darwinian idea that human beings are chance products of evolution. Pragmatism provides a suspicion of the great binary oppositions which Western philosophy such as metaphysics has held important. Thus Darwinians share a concern with the notions of Platonic other-worldliness, critical of the belief of any other world than the real and the natural. Darwinian belief is further critical of distinctions such as mind/body and objective and subjective and attempts to try to reformulate such Platonic foundations through contingent thinking processes. Within pragmatism, then, based on this naturalism, everything is constituted by *relations* with or to other things, contingently, where there is no intrinsic, ineluctable nature to language or to living things. Pragmatism gets rid of dualistic or dichotomous thinking, in terms of relational thinking. Pragmatism also is suspicious of all forms of foundationalism (Platonism, metaphysics, transcendentalism and so on) and argues for the contingency of language, community and self. In my use of the term pragmatism in this project, I shall be using it along with micro-politics, as a term which might be more useful than the term politics. Rather, pragmatism is a term used to describe a process of thinking contingently and relationally.

As an example of how this relates to thinking about feminism, then, I believe that women's experiences of lived and material life are complex and highly contradictory and women cannot be given a political formulaic politic through which to make sense of their experiences. One's experience of being a mother, for example, might be situated as a complexly difficult experience to think of in relation to the critique of masculinity as it prevails in critiques of patriarchy. First-wave feminism was specifically keen to problematise phallocratic structures of living as somehow dependent upon biology. Men were seen to blame for all the problems encountered by women, for example. A simplistic rendition of first-wave feminism, maybe, but the views of writers like Catherine

McKinnon and Andrea Dworkin make no apologies for the culpability of men in women's suffering. How for example, then, does one make sense of one's relations with a son, in relation to such critiques of masculinity, if such radical and restrictive binary forms of feminism are manifested in our thinking? One's experience of emotions, love, fear, hate, jealousy, pain, grief and bereavement, does not sit so easily with how one is urged to be in terms of specific forms of feminist thinking. We are individual beings regardless of gender and the emotional and rational elements of our lives are a complex process of inter-relationalities that cannot be simplistically formulated within a 'politics'. I am not suggesting that a politics with a large P is not useful for changing the experiences of a practical, economic and lived experience of most women, and those political agendas that have made significant changes to the material, economic and lived experiences of women's lives have to be commended and continued. But what I am questioning is the use of the term politics when we are thinking of much more amorphous concepts like emotions, feelings and experiences of being in the world, and how we explore these issues through academic debates. This is especially relevant in something like film studies, where subjectivities and identities might, it is argued, be constructed via ideologically framed texts, but, nonetheless, might be created from elsewhere. Thus, I find the term *pragmatism* is a much more useful term, despite the critique that this might suggest some sort of relativism.

Aesthetics: the etymology of the word 'aesthetics' designates the 'faculty of feeling' derived from the Greek adjective 'aisthetos', which means 'perceptible to the senses'. In the arts and literature, the modernist period[3] (and here I mean the early twentieth-century movements in literature and art and should not be seen as the Frankfurt School of modernism, where art is seen as critique) was specifically concerned with the valorisation of aesthetics, where the arts were deemed modes of representation of reality and aesthetic signifiers as perceptible objects. Modernism as a period of art and literary study during the early decades of this century connected aesthetic appreciation with an ethical sense of *harmony* and the *good*, but not in any romantic sense. Aesthetic elements of good form were premised around specific stylistic structures in the content of a work of art, painting, novel or poem. Form and content were very closely theorised through modernist valorisation of certain stylistic conventions. The use of line, or tone or colour, for example, would display a universally acknowledged appreciation, a harmony of relation, which would then justify value in relation to a painting. Its form would be evaluated in terms of how it conveyed taste, beauty, pleasure, through the use of specific stylistic elements. Certain sounds and assimilations of sounds would convey a similar aesthetic in terms of poetry. Leavisite determinations of the pleasures of poetry and the novel are representative of this notion. In modernist valorisation of the aesthetic, the aesthetic message did not simply have a transitive function. It was of value in itself. Pierre Giraud has written that, 'Art is subjective, it affects the subject', that is to say, it 'touches the human organism or psyche by means of an impression or action, whereas science is objective, it structures the object'.[4]

However, I use the phrase *neo* – meaning 'new' aesthetic – throughout my project to define a newly framed definition of aesthetic, one which attempts to imbricate the artistic and the scientific, premised on the existence of a material basis rather than just a psychic basis, to the affective experience. Questions of affect are explored through different premises from those of modernist aesthetics. I want to look at how the affective is experienced through a material process. In other words *beyond* the subjective positionality premised upon psychic processes it held within the modernist movement. I am not suggesting that the psychic construction of subjectivity is not still an important factor, but rather I am looking at how subjectivity is a much more complex concept and can be re-theorised through a connection with scientific or biological sources of the materiality of the body/brain. This 'neo' (and in many ways *bio*) aesthetic will also be used in a differently framed political sense in that through an encouragement of the neo-aesthetic, new affectivities, new intensities between people might provide a mutant sensibility which could prove more significant in changing people's experiences of themselves and the world, than any macro-defined politics. Affectivity might formulate a more significant trajectory towards the transformation of our culture than politics.

It has been difficult to trace how what was originally a project on feminist film study, then, has now become a philosophical project about aesthetics and the cinematic experience. The significance of subjectivity and desire have been of intrinsic importance to all persuasions of feminist film theory and thus since my project argues for a move from thinking about the subjective/objective binaries within film experience, to present a notion of 'becoming-woman' of the affective and sensation, then to some extent it is still important to engage with some debate on feminist film theory. If I am to locate a neo-aesthetics of 'becoming-woman' which moves us beyond thinking through subjectivity, in favour of a 'beyond' of subjectivity, through to sensation, where the materiality of the brain/mind and body are more closely connected, then it is necessary to show how and why subjectivity was important in early feminist film theory. The importance of subjectivity to feminist thinking about film has blocked the way forward, because of its intractable problematising of psychic manifestations. I want to show a way out of this impasse by changing the mind-set and the thought perspectives away from subjectivity as merely a psychical process. But the engagement with feminist film is only tangential to the main premise of the project, which is to argue for a beyond of subjectivity, in sensation and affect. Consequently in Chapter 2, for the purposes of locating the project, I briefly describe how desire and pleasure were theorised in cinepsychoanalysis and then how feminist film theory began to become involved with more materialist models of the filmic process, by moving beyond psychoanalysis and initiating some concern with the materiality of bodies.

The very term 'body' will become significant as it becomes a polysemic and polyvalent term, in my premises, rather than a fixed definition of biological body. I acknowledge here that it has not been my intention to thoroughly critique the range of psychoanalytical paradigms used in the whole field of feminist film theory. (This in itself could constitute a book or thesis alone.) What I do, rather, is show how feminist film theory moved away from psychoanalytical discourses which were reductively based upon specific renditions of desire as connected to some specific subjectivity and through that subjectivity to an ontological transcendent state of being. Furthermore, within such theories, the role of the body (and definitions of what body might mean) was very much missing. The very concept of desire is important within this discussion, and provides the linchpin for newer theories of desire and what I refer to as a beyond of desire, in *sensation*.

If I am to locate a neo-aesthetics of 'becoming-woman' which moves us beyond thinking through subjectivity, and rather through a 'beyond' of subjectivity, where the materiality of the brain/body/world are explored as sensation, then it is important to show how and why subjectivity was important in early feminist film theories and to some extent in contemporary feminist film theory. This therefore provides the starting point for the project. Any suggestion of a 'becoming-woman' of the filmic experience is also going to question the use of the term 'woman' with its cultural connotations which have been critiqued through various phases of feminist theory. If my use of the term 'becoming-woman' is to have any relevance to a *neo-aesthetics* then there has to be some debate about the use of this term in the light of feminist politics.

This conjuncture between the concepts of micro-politics, pragmatics and aesthetics became focused through an exploration of contemporary movies, specifically American or at least Euro/Western centred. Indeed, I initially explored the contemporary genre neo-noir, but felt that the concepts I was developing actually needed to be explained and explored more through other movies. Thus I use a combination of genres, seeing them as paradigms for philosophical engagement, rather than as the main focus of the book itself. The aim of the project is not to focus on a set of clearly defined filmic texts for investigation, but to work through theoretical and philosophical questions and utilise film as a medium through which to explore these issues, heuristically. As an interdisciplinary project, it aims to bring together the two disciplines of philosophy and film in an experimental and creative way, as film-philosophy, which might offer up innovative questions for engagement in both fields of intellectual pursuit. Here philosophy takes on the role of the micropolitical. The project becomes film-philosophy, rather than one or the other. For example, neo-noir films such as *Romeo and Juliet* (1996), *Strange Days* (1995) and *Blade Runner* offer prime examples of movies through which to explore specifically dynamic, visually exciting and thrillingly exhilarating action. Nonetheless films like *Orlando* (1992) and *The English Patient* (1996) are much more significant in terms of my development of philosophical concepts such as 'becoming-woman' since they imbricate conceptions of the term 'affect' in a neo-aesthetic sense. These films lend themselves to philosophical engagement. Films like *Leon* offer appropriate texts through which to think about the concept of 'becoming-girl', a trajectory from 'becoming-woman' and used in an assemblage of new aesthetic regimes of thinking.

Thus I justify my use of different genres by stating that I am exploring 'affect' and 'sensation' through different experimental visual engagements, all taken from contemporary films, and generic categorisation is not prioritised as an important element in that debate. The outcome is a different theory for understanding the process of the filmic encounter, beyond notions of desire and pleasure, into sensation, where the concept of the 'body' becomes wider and more complex. It is an experience which is premised upon the materialist aesthetic of sensation, where body and mind are imbricated, rather than theories of desire or pleasure, where the body and mind are separated. Furthermore the very term 'body' takes on new and polysemic definitions in this argument.

In a project set within the parameters of a philosophy/film intersection, what began as a feminist political project, then, has emerged as a valorisation of a neo-aesthetic through resort to a philosophy of *expression* (that is, a new definition of the concept 'aesthetic' which does not have its connotations of modernism and elitism) as a way forward in transforming our cultural, political, emotional and ethical places in the world, and as a way of changing our lived experiences of the world. This is therefore a newly framed political agenda.

My original intentions were to try to explain why it is that certain films that are problematic in representational terms to a feminist politic are still nonetheless pleasurable. The debate initially was concerned with the concepts of desire, pleasure and subjectivity and how they have been articulated within feminist film theory, specifically through psychoanalytic criticism. However, what emerged was an interesting development away from the politics of representation, to a concern with how the visual experience of the cinematic encounter impinges upon the materiality of the viewer, and how affect and sensation are part of that material engagement. By materiality I mean the biological, molecular and material nature of the body and the perceptions within the brain/mind of that body. The concept materiality is *not* here used in the Marxist sense of the term.[5] The term 'body' is also differently conceived to mean more than just the flesh and blood corporeal body.

The project then began to develop into a concern with the aesthetics of the visual image, and how that impinges upon the minds/bodies of those who view, outside any psychical explanations that psychoanalysis might provide. Definitions of terms such as mind/body became significant to this debate. The whole imbrication of the corporeal body with the body of the natural world and the body of technological forms, such as film, became part of the debate. Thus an argument about gendered spectatorship developed into a wider consideration with aesthetics, an aesthetics assembled across the imbrication of bodies in a more abstract sense. The catalyst for this change in direction was the exploration of the role of subjectivity and the body and how these had been particularly important in feminist film theory. But that concept of subjectivity itself was distanciated and radically dislocated to such an extent that subjectivity was subsumed through a pragmatics of 'becoming'. 'Becoming' is a term taken from philosophy and refers to a continual processual movement in time, with no finality, no fixed positioning. 'Becoming' is pure process. The significance of this term in relation to this book is explored at length in Chapters 3 and 4. Questions which I initially proposed, then, in the light of feminist film theory, questions around pleasure and desire in relation to contemporary movies, especially neo-noir films, gradually developed into a debate about the cinematic encounter as an experience, as an 'event of material capture', rather than with any intrinsic meaning those films might have ideologically, politically, culturally or libidinally. This project argues that film is experiential: a material capture of the processual, rather than merely representational.

My call for a 'becoming-woman' of the cinematic argues that the cinematic encounter may express such material capture through its affective and aesthetic resonances and provide a micro-political manoeuvre in terms of ways of thinking and feeling. Within the 'becoming-woman' of the cinematic, desire and pleasure are rethought through a deeper level of feeling, in 'sensation'. But I use the term sensation in new ways, premised upon the work of Deleuze on affect. It is not sensation as it is used in the literal or phenomenological sense of the term. Sensation involves more than a bodily or corporeal engagement. The very terminology 'becoming-woman' is explored, in the light of the concept 'woman' and to some extent my argument repositions aesthetics, through a new concept of 'woman'. It functions in a micro-political and pragmatic way, as opposed to a political strategy within a feminist agenda.

The question of politics has been prevalent and problematic throughout. In a contemporary cultural, economic and political malaise which continues to put profit and production as the prime motivators of human actions, aesthetics might occupy, as Félix Guattari writes and explores in *Chaosmosis*,[6] a significant position for a radical ethics at the convergence of the twentieth and twenty-first centuries. It cannot be argued that aesthetics in itself is a political or a transformational paradigm. Several attempts by materialist film-makers and the avant-garde have of course experimented with the use of film for political ends.[7] But a different understanding and encouragement of a neo-aesthetics might produce a mutant mentality and encourage a rethinking, re-enchantment and engagement within our lives. It might just begin to highlight the processes of creativity, which might then impinge upon transformations of our experiences. An ethics of experimentation, an experimentation which this project itself is partly trying to engage with, in its experimental use of philosophy, may emerge which will provide different ways of thinking and feeling about our experiences at the beginning of a new millennium. By trying to imbricate the philosophical, the aesthetic and the micro-political, I am attempting to present a creative understanding of visual culture, specifically contemporary film, an understanding which might impinge upon the sensibilities and mentalities of those who view.

FROM A MICRO-POLITICS OF POST-FEMINIST THINKING TO RETHINKING THE AESTHETIC

As I am presenting a claim for a materialist aesthetic, premised on the affect and sensation, where subjectivity is rendered subjectless, I want to explore how and why 'subjectivity' has been important to feminisms, and how my definition of post-feminism moves away from a concern with subjectivity. Therefore this section of the chapter aims to explore the main points of intersection between current feminist epistemologies and post-theory (that is, theories of post-structuralism). It then shows how we might move into rethinking the aesthetic as a paradigm for a post-feminist pragmatics.

In a theoretical climate saturated with post-structuralist and post-modernist debates, contemporary feminism has become a contentious and problematic arena. I shall only provide an acknowledgement of this array of feminist discourses, and not provide an analysis of its various manifestations in detail.[8] However, I need to explain the range of feminisms, albeit tangentially, for the concept of the 'subject' and 'subjectivity' have been fundamental within these debates. It is the concept of 'subjectivity' which has been important to feminist film theory and is to become significant in my own argument on the neo-aesthetic and so I need to explain where and why subjectivity has been located within feminist theory.

I shall then distanciate that definition of subjectivity through what I will call a *post*-feminist perspective. Before exploring the concept of subjectivity then, first, how do we define feminism and post-feminism? *Feminism* is a term which describes both a cultural practice and a political position. Feminist theory is both a political practice and a discursive field that has specific epistemological bases and also particular methodological principles. I am not going to outline the history of feminist theory and I do therefore assume some knowledge of this by my reader, but it is important to highlight some of its basic concepts. Within feminist discourse, the concept of the 'subject' has been fundamental to the production of gendered identities. Cartesian and structuralist discourse have prioritised binarism, through which the process of thinking has been contained within a series of binarily formed oppositions: male/female, animal/machine, rational/intuitive, subject/object, mind/body, for example. Such oppositions serve, according to feminist theory, to position the 'subject' as fixed and intransigent, on one or other side of the binary. The sentient and fixed subject, according to feminism, is a legacy of masculinist theory, which from Cartesian origins prioritised the masculine subject in discourse, as a positive term against the feminine as negative. Along with that fixed, sentient, masculine subject has been the prioritisation of specific concepts like rationality, logic and reason. Western philosophical epistemology has created deep structures of our lives, consciousness and experiences to be representative of all humans, regardless of gender. Seyla Benhabib argues that such categorisations obliterate differences of gender, as these shape and structure the experience and subjectivity of the self.[9] Western reason has been a discourse of a self-identical subject. This of course has prevented the presence of difference and otherness. A philosophical tradition from Plato to Hegel then prioritises this subject of reason: a male, sentient and logical being. In opposition the female was perceived as emotional and irrational. Such binary categorisations have maintained an intransigent approach to theories of the subject.

Debate proliferates regarding the effects of post-structuralist[10] determinations of a fractured subject and the implications for feminist theory and practice.[11] The main contention has been that just when feminism appears to have enabled the articulation of an agentic, autonomous subject for women, post-structuralism fragments that politic. Indeed, Seyla Benhabib is suspicious of a post-theory which advocates the dissolution of the subject. The post-structuralist dissolution of the 'subject' is not, according to Benhabib, compatible with the aims of feminism. She believes that any subjectivity that is not structured by language and by the symbolic structures of narrative available in culture is unthinkable.

Most post-structuralist concerns with the fragmentation of the subject have indeed taken their lead from feminist theory in contradistinction from Seyla Benhabib. The aim of much feminist philosophy has been to provide for a locus for a new 'female subjectivity'. Feminism's political agenda has been to distanciate the sentient subject of phallocratic discourse. But the advocation of a sentient subjectivity maintains a binarist positionality across gender relationships. It still prioritises the 'subject'. It does not question the very concept of 'subjectivity'. Subjectivity is still defined as a concept which emerges from structures of psychic, social, libidinal and biological determinants. It does not offer any problematisation of the very concept itself and neither does it take into consideration the materiality of experience.

I would argue that *subjectivity* may be reconceptualised even beyond the post-structuralist notion of fluidity or multiplicity as it is explored specifically in French feminisms for example.[12] It may be subsumed through a more complex situational and contingent exploration of forces outside of the psychic, the social, the libidinal or the biological, in favour of a more complex web of processes, and intensities, through an inter-relationality of differences and repetitions within experience and the material. This argument of the book will show how this occurs and is manifested through the filmic experience.

Rosi Braidotti[13] has referred to contemporary feminist philosophy as a practice of sexual difference and claims a 'feminist female subject'. She explores the concept of the 'nomadic subject' as a way to think about subjectivity and specifically a female, feminist subjectivity beyond the phallocentricity of the dominant conceptions of the 'subject' found in traditional philosophy. Unlike Benhabib, Braidotti sees an engagement with post-structuralism as an area of new possibilities. She does not perceive a 'crisis' of values in the same way as Benhabib. Rather, Braidotti argues for a 'qualitative leap in the feminist imagination' which will adapt heterogeneity and new forms of materialism in a micro-political framework. This is precisely what this book is attempting to do. Admittedly, French feminist writers like Irigaray and Cixous have prioritised a feminism of difference which has argued for the ossification of binarism and to project a concern with multiplicity and fluid subjectivities, thus challenging Cartesian and structuralist concern with a fixed notion of gendered identity and subjectivity. (See note 13 above.)[14] Similarly Moira Gatens has positioned significant debates regarding conceptual shifts in feminist theory. Her politics of difference, drawing on Foucault, explores the micro-politics of power, and investigates the construals of bodies and power, through a politics of difference.[15] But much work still maintains either the significance of a specific subjectivity, or at the very least the continuing significance of the very term 'subjectivity' whether in the singular or the plural. Even Donna Haraway's claim for a cyborg heteroglossia,[16] whilst it has been substantially liberatory for rethinking feminist politics, has a notion of subjectivity, albeit cyborgian. Indeed, Haraway's cyberfeminism offered alternatives to Enlightenment ideas of subject, identity and selfhood.[17] A cyborgian politics is premised upon differences and affinity, not on identity and opposition. Far from appropriating phallocratic structures within culture, it breaks down those boundaries which have maintained oppositional discourses. Cyberfeminism offered new configurations of the 'subject' through thinking about identity and affinity and has proved significant in feminist deconstructions of cultural forms including film. However, subjectivity was still an important element in each of these feminist strands, despite Grosz and Gatens, and the real issue for this book is the fact that *materialism* was left out of the equation. There is no consideration of how the materiality of the body, or indeed what a 'body' might mean, whether through mind, brain or actual flesh-and-blood body had a role to play in the ways we experience the world. French feminisms did, of course, consider the body, but their uses of this inquiry maintained an essentialist perspective on the body/culture binary. Woman was equated with body and nature, man with culture. A new consideration of the concept of the *aesthetic* aims to bring materialism back into the equation and to offer experimental thinking about the nature of 'body' and 'subjectivity'.

In contrast with the contentious deliberations across feminisms of 'difference' a *post-feminist* agenda is concerned with the micrology of lived experiences, across and between the spaces of any fixed, sentient, or even fluid gendered subjectivity. How can we define post-feminism? How is this term used in this book? The media proliferate the term in articles about post-feminism, claiming that feminism as a political practice is no longer popular, or necessary, that it no longer needs to be concerned with its original principles. Debates abound each day on this topic. I have no wish to be part of this debate, since such a definition of post-feminism seeks only to look at the cultural, economic and social implications of feminism, in terms of women's lived experiences in the real world. I am not saying that this agenda is not still important. Rather I am trying to define a post-feminism, which colludes with post-theory, which is about more than the lived experience, but is about thinking processes at a fundamental level, a post-feminism which tries to bring back materiality and to understand the basis of experience as having a material and affective basis, as much as sociological, cultural or libidinal.

The restricted definitions of post-feminism that the media portray do not consider the more philosophical inquiry into the nature of the complexities of the very act of thought itself. A definition of *post-feminism*, in an academic sense, may initially be described as a theoretical set of practices within which one may speak as a 'woman'. However, that very concept of woman becomes multiple, complex and polysemic. I want to extend the term therefore to explain *post-feminism* as a desire to move outside a politics of difference or a politics of gendered subjectivities, to a micro-political pragmatics of *becoming* where subjectivity is subsumed to becoming-woman. Here the term 'becoming-woman' is, in my use of the term, synonymous with the affective forces of the material.[18]

Any call for a politics of becoming is in danger of hypostatising that very politics. Therefore, a pragmatics of becoming, instead, uses contingent assemblages of thinking processes through which to distanciate subjectivity from language. Subjectivities are simulacra, which are subsumed through a more profound engagement with the forces of 'becoming', material forces, molecular and fibrous forces, rewired across new assemblages outside of language, in the pre-discursive and the pre-personal. A post-feminist agenda, as an ethical framework, engages with thinking outside the boundaries of epistemological, Cartesian, modernist thinking. It enables a reconceptualisation of the thinking process itself. A post-feminist agenda requires a rethinking of the very foundations of thought itself. Thought needs to be emancipated, freed from the labyrinths of rational and epistemological determinations, so that terms such as 'subjectivity', 'identity' and the 'body' and, for my purposes here, their relation to filmic aesthetics may become creative and experimental. In a post-feminist discourse, aesthetics then becomes part of the contingent process of thinking. This will enable a new thinking of the cinematic experience outside of those theories premised upon structuralist definitions of language. Rather, the a-signifying elements of the filmic experience may be perceived as a molecular experience of the material, as an event, as material capture, as a processual engagement of forces, intensities and affect: as a 'becoming' rather than merely with the rhetoric of spectatorship theory, where identity and subjectivity have been prioritised.[19]

Post-feminism, then, is a concept which describes a micro-political engagement with a multiplicity of voices across the regimes of feminist political discourse. Founded within post-structuralist debates which have questioned and problematised Cartesian epistemologies, post-feminism seeks to rethink the nomadic and spatial arenas of feminist voices, to present what we can therefore refer to as a 'situational' ethics, where we need to think beyond the univocity and dual perspectives of gendered categorisations, identities and subjectivities. Judith Butler argues that there is no gender identity behind the expressions of gender; that identity is performatively constituted. She is also suspicious of the claim that any theory of politics requires a 'subject'.[20] Claims that a politics is not possible without a subject merely secures a specific formation of a politics that requires that these notions remain unproblematical features of its own definition.

Maybe a post-feminist pragmatics makes possible the abandonment of such premises. Butler would argue that to claim that politics requires a stable subject is to claim that there can therefore be no real political opposition to that claim. The very act of requiring a subject forecloses a political domain and with that foreclosure, which itself becomes an essentialist element of the 'political', comes an enforcement of particular limitations on what constitutes the political. This enforcement is thus protected from any critique. Benhabib has claimed that a politics is unthinkable without foundations, without premises such as subject and subjectivity. But to argue that a stable subject is necessary is to protest that there can be no political opposition to that claim. To challenge that *is* to present a politics. We do not have to be fixed in any substantive vision of the subject to be political. What is political is using the language, and discourse through which to challenge those ontological foundations of thought itself, within and through which a subject has been discerned as required. To offer a critique of 'subjectivity' and its substantive role within politics is to argue for a concern with materiality, not instead of but alongside, psychic formations of a subjectivity. It is thus a *pragmatics* or a *micro-politics* rather than a politics.

Thus we need to consider a *micro-political* or *pragmatic* agenda rather than a 'political' agenda. As I defined earlier, micro-politics is an engagement with thinking about how struggles occur not only in groups, but through and even beyond multiplicities of identities, subjectivities and corporealities, internal to or functional through and across individual subjects and within subjects. These multiplicities are processes which are molecular, articulated through the fibrosity of the body's corporeality and materiality, in assemblage with the cultural, the ideological, the libidinal or the social. Subjectivity is therefore subsumed to the more profound game of difference and repetition. Subjectivity itself is problematised. It is subsumed through a concern with materiality and molecularity of existence, through a machinic[21] type of assemblage, rather than psychic structures of a subject. Systems of thinking which prioritise the centrality of the 'subject' need to be rethought to engage with 'effects or consequences of processes of sedimentation, the congealing of processes, interrelations, or "machines" of disparate components, functioning in provisional alignment with each other to form a working ensemble'.[22] In unpacking this quote, I would suggest that it means subjectivity is too complex to be explained through singular concepts such as the cultural or the psychological. Subjectivity is but one element in an arsenal of components that go to make up, in a machinic way, or as an assemblage, our experiences of a lived reality. Being in the world is too complex an issue to be explained through merely the sociological, the cultural, economic or psychological determinants. And psychoanalytic or cultural explanations of subjectivity are not the only formats through which we can try to understand our experiences of cultural formations such as film. Film may be seen not only as a cultural formation, but also as a psychic, corporeal and consciousness formation which exists beyond the constraining ideologies of much feminist and indeed modernist thinking. Other frameworks which bring into focus the actual material experience might be appropriate. Where for example does the aesthetic function within such frameworks? How is the aesthetic accommodated in such restrictive explanations of subjectivity? How can we determine a material aesthetic premised upon forces outside of subjectivity? Where is the space for the a-signifying aspects of experience? Where is the concept of materiality? In explaining our sense of who we are in the world and how we experience that existence, many processes are involved in complex and inter-relational, machinic assemblages and any explanation requires more sophisticated and complex webs of understanding than those already offered through sociological or psychoanalytic paradigms. Deleuzian ideas seem to open up such territories.

BETWEEN DELEUZE AND POST-FEMINISM:
APARALLETIC EVOLUTION[23]

In this section I want to signpost some of the reasons why post-feminism, micro-politics and Deleuzian ideas seem to be in consilience. I will not be exploring these issues in detail here, merely offering reasons for their coagulation and setting up some bases for later engagement. My reasons for colluding with *L'Étranger*, the difference engineer, the philosopher of the outside and of monstrosity, is that his ideas might enable a micro-political, pragmatic and post-feminist understanding of the aesthetic experience of the cinematic. An experience that is not premised on a substantive notion of subjectivity, inherent within language and a gendered reading space, but an experience that is perceived as an event, as a processual, aesthetic event of sensation, articulated beyond subjectivity. What then are the intersections of a post-feminist pragmatics and Deleuzian ideas?

Like post-feminism, Deleuzian ideas are concerned to redefine and refigure theoretical practice. Deleuze moves beyond dualistic and binary thinking processes. His ideas challenge the centrality of binary logic and critique Platonist thinking in what has been referred to as a 'reversal of Platonism' and a delegitimation of representation within Platonist thought. Thus, systems of thought based on subject and signification (as is most film theory) are no longer prioritised. Deleuze conceives of thought as an effect or process which participates as effects or processes of what he calls 'machinic assemblages' functioning with other components, for example, space, time, bodies and texts. This therefore is relevant to my argument that film can be experienced not merely as signification or process or even a symbiosis of these, but what Deleuze refers to as an 'abstract machine': an assemblage, functioning with other components such as corporeality, the body of the viewer, other bodies, such as texts, spaces, materiality and time. The abstract machine is neither physical nor corporeal in character, but exists as *matter* in collusion, or as Deleuze refers in 'aparalletic evolution', (see Chapters 3 and 4 on Deleuze), with the matters composed within the bodies of the viewer/observer. I shall be taking Deleuzian ideas forward as a methodology for developing and reconfiguring new structures in post-feminist film theory which synthesises signification, process and embodiment in new ways, where subjectivity becomes problematised, and even subsumed, in the equation, just as post-feminism attempts to do.

As indicated, Western and Enlightenment epistemologies have prioritised the rational and have legitimated the erasure of women and their contribution from all areas of life, socially, culturally, sexually and epistemologically. Deleuzian ideas provide a powerful set of 'differences' which we might use, alongside other discourses, to experiment with a new way of thinking. I don't see his ideas as in any way confrontational, but as a web of discourses with which we might decentre, alter, disorientate and destratify the discourses of phallocentrism, prevalent within structuralist thinking: to think perspectivally, machinically and transversally, rather than structurally. Deleuzian concepts invite a rethinking of the very process of thought itself and thus enable a total re-engagement with how meaning is experienced and articulated within cultural formations such as cinema. Similarly his work questions and rearticulates 'subjectivity' enabling a desubjectified conceptualisation of experience, through an engagement with materiality. Post-feminism is also seeking to push back the boundaries of thought and politics which have maintained the significance of concepts such as 'subjectivity'.

Second, why Deleuze and film theory? I am *not* within this project offering a new theory of spectatorship, through Deleuze, nor am I critiquing or explaining Deleuze's own concepts of the cinematic as he explains them in *Cinema 1* and *Cinema 2*. I am rather thinking about how we might experimentally imbricate the philosophical with film, moving beyond film theoretical debates which have prioritised spectatorship and subjectivity. I am using his ideas to enable a move towards rethinking concepts such as 'subjectivity', its distanciation, through affect and sensation and terms like 'body' and the role of that within the filmic experience, exploring the significance of such a move to the creation of a new discipline of *film-philosophy*.

This frame of questioning allows us to bring back the 'body' into theory and into a post-feminist theory, in a different and experimental way which does not lock the definition of the 'body' into old structuralist and negative terms in relation to woman and nature. An emergent engagement of woman and body is enabled which is not biologically deterministic. The 'body' can then be conceived outside the negative connotation it has had in feminist film theory. Indeed, the very term 'body' takes on new and engaging prospects. If the 'body' is conceived outside any Cartesian epistemology, then the work of Deleuze must have relevance to a post-feminist pragmatics, within which the concept 'body' is yet another element in an assemblage of processes. Deleuze and Guattari's notion of the body as a set of continuous flows, energies, organs, processes and affects has to be of relevance to those of us who are trying to rethink 'bodies', especially women's bodies, outside any polarisations which have been placed on the body through binary structures of thinking. Deleuzian ideas on the body provide a creatively innovative perception of the body, in that there is an engagement with how bodies 'link', the relational quality of bodies, the linkages of the human body to other bodies, human and inhuman, animate and inanimate, machinic and non-machinic in a post-human trajectory. Thus the 'body' of the cinematic relates and assembles with the bodies of those viewers/observers in a web of inter-relational flows in material ways.

A theory premised on the micro-political or the pragmatic, rather than the political, allows for the contingency of such encounters. It enables a theory of film as an *event* across bodies, as a processual becoming, rather than the filmic text as a system or form of representation. Thus a post-semiotic and post-linguistic inquiry into the 'event' of the cinematic process provides a way forward in cinematic theory that questions the prioritisation of the visual or the scopic regime. It offers in its place or at least alongside it, a theory of a technologised[24] or assembled 'body', a molecular body in the process of cinematic experience. Deleuzian ideas about 'body' then might establish a post-feminist pragmatics, a pragmatics which establishes a new dimension for the 'body' engaging with a post-linguistic inquiry into the event of the cinematic.

To answer those who question the need for such a pragmatic manoeuvre, I would add that, at the dawn of a new millennium, the constraining ideologies of much feminist film theory have explored and explained the filmic text through theoretical debate, but have never been able to answer why it is that politically problematic films might also be enjoyed. A Deleuzian engagement enables us to think through the complexities of such encounters outside the containment of discourses such as psychoanalysis, premised as it is on binary constructions of language, thinking and the libidinal articulations of Freudian/Lacanian and French feminist psychoanalytic analyses.

Questions of the body and subjectivity are, within film theory, inevitably concerned and explained through structures of desire and pleasure. Deleuzian concern with desire, and his articulation of a 'beyond' of desire, can take us into different paradigms of thinking about the cinematic encounter. Rather, other issues are at stake, such as affect and sensation, instead of the concept of desire as such. Psychical depictions of desire are thus set alongside a different rendition of desire as 'process' 'aleatory' and 'cultivational of joy'. This therefore brings into focus the third element of connection between post-feminisms, Deleuzian concepts and film theory. If film theory is to move beyond a questioning of desire and the theatre of the 'visual' in terms of psychoanalytic feminist film theory, it might usefully employ Deleuzian ideas of desire as process, as an immanent sense of desire as positivity, flux and machinic assemblage, a process which has no 'subject', a destratified or at least an hystericised 'subjectivity'. The 'eye' thus is not just the 'eye in culture', the I is not just the I of the Imaginary, but the Eye/I is the embodied eye in matter. Deleuzian perspectives on desire render psychoanalysis as insufficiently effective in explaining the materiality of the filmic experience. A re-engagement with the experience of the cinematic through a post-feminist pragmatics needs to move outside the paradigms of cinema as a set of representational images, through which we can relate to the concepts of 'identity' and 'subjectivity' to a concern with experience, modulation and expression (see Chapter 3, section 'Deleuze on Pleasure and Desire'). The book's alignment with Deleuze therefore, in Part Two, will outline a range of concepts and images of thinking which are deemed appropriate to a post-feminist pragmatics, specifically in relation to bodies, sexualities, pleasures, desire and the cinematic experience as an aesthetic engagement with material forces and as an event of process.

Deleuzian terminology is richly textured and often has been critiqued as full of neologism, but there are significant terms which will be explained and utilised; these terms, which rather than be critiqued as neologistic, are used as a new vocabulary in contemporary film-philosophy. Such terms as 'becoming', specifically 'becoming-woman', 'affect' and the 'bloc of sensation' create refreshing plateaus and different vocabularies for us to think about film, beyond the more traditional notions of pleasure and desire, which have been prevalent within psychoanalysis.

RETHINKING THE AESTHETIC

[T]he forms of force which manifest themselves in art are the forms of force which manifest themselves in life.[25]

[T]he only reality in life is sensation. The only reality in art is consciousness of the sensation.[26]

Political and ideological analyses of film have overshadowed the filmic experience as one basically involving moving images of colours, tones, lines, images and sounds of all kinds which actually impinge on the body/

mind/brain in a multiplicity of ways. I argue that the visual engagement is but a pathway to other synaesthetic experiences such as tactility, or hapticity, and proprioceptivity, for example. The question of subjectivity in much feminist film theory has been confined to *political* discourses which endeavoured to maintain some sentient notion of subjectivity as existing through social, cultural, psychological or libidinal sources. I want to project a neo-aesthetic and bio-aesthetic approach to film theory which will enable a rethinking of how and why film is still enjoyed, why it still *impacts* or *resonates*, or connects, outside theories of the visual, outside psychoanalytic theories of desire, outside notions of gendered subjectivity and despite political problematics.[27]

The visual experience of the cinematic needs to be thought of as an 'experience' as a material capture, as synaesthetic experience in sensation, not merely as representation. Thus an aesthetics of some sort needs to come back into the equation, and I would deem this a post-*feminist* aesthetics because it is founded on the same basis as post-feminism: experimentation, pragmatics, transversal and perspectival thinking and contingent processes of engagement. This relationship of concepts provides a creative, experimental set of discourses. I suggest post-*feminism*, because what I am arguing for is a set of theoretical ideas which imbricate post-structuralist discourses and yet take on board previous *feminist* film ideas. I use feminist film theory as a starting point from which to develop different strategies of thinking. So in this sense I would defend my term post-*feminist*. Also this new paradigm of thinking will actually bring into question whether gender and feminism, and specifically gendered subjectivities, are necessarily the only issues at stake in the affective experiences of the visual engagement with film. If something other than subjectivity is at stake, or at least a differently conceived definition of the subjective, then maybe the very terminology *feminist* film can be distanciated. I don't of course wish to ignore the range of theory that still operates as feminist film theory, and such analyses continue to be liberating and thus politically important, but I am offering a different set of ideas premised on aesthetics, alongside such perspectives. Indeed, in a typically Deleuzian sense, it is what happens in the 'in-between', or the 'interstitial spaces', that really matters. This set of ideas is engaging with *post*-theory in ways that feminist film theory has not.

Furthermore, a post-*feminist* approach also involves what I shall refer to as 'becoming-woman', which might enable us to conceptualise a post-feminist aesthetics which re-positions and rethinks the term 'woman' in terms of technologies or assemblages of meaning. Here the very term 'woman' is distanciated from any essential or intrinsic connection to the

way in which the term has operated in feminist theory. Rather, contemporary discourse, through Deleuzian philosophy, asks us to think
about such terms as part of contingent assemblages, machinic assemblages, and not as singular, identifiable terms. 'Becoming-woman' then
has nothing to do with real, physical, lived beings. It is used as an abstract
term (see Chapter 4). This neo-aesthetics will argue that psychoanalysis in
feminist film theory has not allowed for a material aesthetic which
Deleuzian paradigms enable.

Deleuzian ideas enable an analysis of how desire and pleasure might be
theorised outside such paradigms. Maybe something more is at stake
rather than desire or pleasure. Something beyond these two terms? Here
the concept of sensation, and how sensation is premised within a discourse of a *materialist aesthetic*, that is an aesthetic which explains the
importance of affect and sensation as operating 'beyond' any subjective
experience of that feeling, as 'depth' or an 'intensity' which is felt
primordially, in the body, but beyond subjectivity, is prioritised. Through
Deleuzian ideas, as I later argue, subjectivity is subsumed in a 'becoming'.
Hegemonic formations are resisted through a flight away from subjectivity. Subjectivity is retheorised through a more complex relationship
between the concepts of *affect* and *sensation* in 'becoming'.

Rather than the subject having some coincidence with a specific
consciousness, Deleuze argues that the unconscious can be treated as a
field of 'veritable becomings' (not locked into subjectivity) but a non-
coincidence of subject and consciousness. A redefinition of thinking and
the process of thought (a pragmatics, or a micro-politics) thus allows a
vision of subjectivity which is 'subsumed' because it is accommodated
through a materiality, through the notion of affect and sensation as a
material state, not a psychic state. Subjectless subjectivity. A different
engagement with the term aesthetic. Subjectivity is subsumed through a
materiality where affects are 'becomings' encountered through a 'body'
which is both mind/brain and corporeal, flesh and blood body. This body,
however, is not the ordinary physical body, in its biological determinants,
nor a psychic body, but a complex set of intersecting forces.

How then do we bring back the aesthetic into film theory in a *post-
theoretical* climate which has challenged all the elements of modernist
conceptions of the aesthetic. In pre-modernist discourse[28] aesthetics was
defined in two ways, in dualistic ways, premised on subjectivity and
objectivity. For example, in one sense aesthetics defined a theory of
sensibility as a form of possible experience. This provides an objective
element of sensation, which is conditioned by the significant elements
such as space, time and form. The second definition of aesthetics provides

a subjective element of sensation. Here the main concern is that art is a reflection on real experience and it is expressed in the feeling of pain or pleasure. Thus an objective and a subjective definition of aesthetic. Later, modernist (modernism as an artistic movement at the beginning of the twentieth century) conceptions of the aesthetic were premised on a science of sensibilities, which encouraged a greater moral good. This conception of aesthetics has its origins in Aristotelian claims that the objective aim of art is beauty, which will produce in others 'the same impression as derives from the contemplation of beautiful things'.[29] The beautiful was defined by specific adherence to specific form. Form was a significant element in that debate and the forms of works of art, films, poetry, novels, were analysed for specific formulaic devices: use of tone, line, space, or colour, for example. Proportion, line, colour, space and tone were stylistic devices which were able to render a form 'beautiful' by virtue of the way these elements were used. The concept 'aesthetic' then seems locked into definitions within modernist and dualist discourse. The role of the artist as supreme originator of meaning because of some innate gift of ability was of course connected to 'transcendent' notions of goodness and morality, specifically within romantic discourse. This usage of the term 'beautiful', then, has its originations in romantic discourse, and is something I want to question and disorientate in the location of a neo-aesthetics.

In post-theory, the 'beautiful' is not necessarily consilient with goodness, the romantic, or transcendent notions, but to a feeling of duration, movement and continual process: what Deleuze refers to as 'haecceity'[30] or 'intensity'. Neither is it defined as it was in modernism, as 'individual spontaneity' or 'cultural imposition'. The anti-aesthetic of post-structuralism merely challenged those modernist ideas. I am not arguing here for a return to the early definitions of the aesthetic, premised upon the ideas of people like George Moore, Clive Bell and Roger Fry, in the early part of the twentieth century, but to rethink the term, through an engagement with Deleuzian philosophy, in relation to a material aesthetic (an aesthetic premised on the materiality of the body/mind/world as process, not an aesthetic premised on set standards of taste and beauty within a modernist dialectic, or on the dualism of subjectivity and objectivity).

This innovative, emergent definition of aesthetics requires a redefinition of the beautiful. Beauty, here, is not perceived in relation to good form, but to a temporal element, or *process, movement, dynamism* – a 'haecceity'. 'Beauty thus pertains to a process that takes empirical precedence over form.'[31] The beautiful, in this new definition, is a processuality, a continual movement. The determination of beauty becomes temporal, not reflective: an open-ended process, a feeling of flowing, rhythm, or 'becoming'. Indeed, a refreshing concern with sensation, rather than desire or pleasure, requires us to think about sensation as a rhythmical experience, not one of static shock of excitations on the nervous system. It is much more complex than that, as I shall explore in Chapters 3, 4 and 5.

The concept of the beautiful in classical definitions was premised on an external opposition of object and subject, between objectivity and subjectivity. A different definition of beautiful within a neo-aesthetic involves a melding of these terms as inseparable elements of 'matter'. This new conception of the 'beautiful' and sensation, then, within the neo-aesthetic is not premised upon romantic, transcendent individualism but it is based upon impersonal, biological, corporeal 'matter' in the material. What I shall later refer to as an immanence, or 'becoming-woman'. Thus 'beauty' has nothing to do with 'taste' or as a judgement of taste, but is rather a felt 'immediacy', 'force' or 'intensity' in process. A neo-aesthetic in this sense then is an aesthetic as an abiding, a manner of being in continual process, or 'becoming', where subjectivity is rendered subjectless, and the affective is a material state, as much as it is deemed a psychic state within psychoanalysis. Deleuze writes of the significance of this sense of 'immediacy' or 'force' as pertaining to all the arts, 'there is a community of the arts, a common problem. In art, and in painting as in music, it's not a question of reproducing or inventing forms, but of harnessing forces.'[32]

I am merely setting up this debate in this chapter for later analysis. In this neo-aesthetic paradigm, process then takes precedence over *form*. The 'beautiful' of the neo-aesthetic is contained in its autonomy. This autonomy is a 'subjectless subjectivity' that is expressed in the process of perception. The filmic encounter involves all aspects of the body's sensibilities, not just vision and brain: eye and cortex, but the entire body, an integrating of the materiality of film and the environment. Subject and object integrate into a larger autonomy of involvement; matter and mind meld together, as a technic or as an assemblage. This understanding of aesthetics is seen more as an empiricism than as romanticism. Here the aesthetic experience involves a whole and total engagement with molecular forces of being in the world. A complete depersonalisation is involved, where subjectivity is rendered subjectless. Barbara McClintock explains how this 'depersonalisation' feels in describing her scientific work, 'The more I worked with chromosomes the bigger and bigger they got, and when I was really working with them I wasn't outside, I was down there. I was part of the system . . . As you look at these things, they become part of you. And you forget yourself. The main thing is that you forget yourself.'[33] Rather than a feeling being felt then by some subjectivity, a feeling is not owned by a subject, but the subject is *part* of the feeling. In other words, the 'subjective encounter' is experienced within the materiality of existence. 'The world and I exist in difference, in encounter. In the feeling, being is *in* sensation.'[34] I shall explore this later in Chapter 5.

The Portuguese poet Fernando Pessoa has described this experience of impersonalisation or depersonalisation as a dynamogenic experience: one outside of subjectivity, but premised upon a real bonding with the molecularity of the world itself. This kind of depersonalisation is actually similar to the 'imagination' or is at one with the imagination. The imagination is the 'manner of subjectless subjectivity in continuity with matter, as its first effloration in expression at its "precise point of emergence" out of itself, into perception, by way of sensation'.[35] Thus in terms of arguing towards a different aesthetics of the beautiful, here in a post-feminist aesthetics, the beautiful is experienced through the processual, through movement, dynamogenic processes of the vitality of the 'material'. (Post-feminism is a term which I will use to describe a multiplicity of feminisms which imbricate and collude with post-theory, and post-structuralism. It is not necessarily something that comes 'after' feminism, as the term 'post' implies, but rather a merging with other post-theoretical discourses, to present a series of vectors of meaning.) This is an aesthetics of 'intensity' and 'becoming', not an aesthetics of good form. The reason why I think this might be defined as post-*feminist* is that it incites some interesting coagulations of woman, movement and process, which might enable a reconceptualisation of and the valorisation of other paradigms of experience outside of language. For example, how the body, dance, movement and process might be ways of articulating ideas, feelings, attitudes, experiences in ways outside of written or oral language. It is this sense in which I shall be articulating a neo-aesthetics of affect, as the processuality of the filmic process as a material capture of matter, in relation to the material experience of individual imagination, through sensation.

In conclusion to this chapter then, I am suggesting that there might be a new language, a new formation of the affective and felt experience, in the concept of *sensation*, which is beyond 'subjectivity' and that which is signified within formal structures of language formation, signification, semiotics and regimes of meaning construction such as we might find in psychoanalysis, for example. Contemporary post-feminist epistemologies, as we have seen, seek to disturb metaphysical notions such as 'identity' and 'subjectivity' and dichotomous discourses within which binary concepts such as mind/body, subject/object, rational/emotional, male/female, animal/human, human/machine have been formulated, concepts redolent of an Enlightenment and Cartesian tradition. This is extremely important for any consideration of film, since film theory to date has been formulated through languages which have clearly been premised on such dichotomies.

Much film theory over the last two decades has appropriated the logic of structuralism, semiology and the discourse of psychoanalysis for formal analysis of films and the spectatorial relations with which they engage. How can we offer, alongside such theories, a theory which engages with the new discourses of post-feminism and post-structuralism, in a neo-pragmatic turn from the political, and into the aesthetic, and in so doing delegitimating the sentient 'subject' and binary languages? Without doubt, contemporary film theory has formulated new reading practices that do profoundly transform earlier notions of film theory, but they haven't gone far enough. Connections are needed with contemporary theories or definitions of the 'body'. More contemporary conceptions of the 'body' take us away from the merely phenomenological sense of the body. Contemporary film theory needs to engage with such discourses. Newer ideas in film theory should also take into account continental philosophical analyses of the nature of materiality, and the machinic. It also needs to engage with emergent theories of aesthetics (a neo-aesthetics) premised outside any notion of sentient 'subjectivity'. The philosophy of Deleuze and Guattari is the key to these new paradigms of thought.

As David Rodowick has pointed out, 'blocked by a formal conception of text, spectator, and the relations between them, Anglo-American film theory has not engaged with the implications of the new reading positions offered within post-structuralist thinking'.[36] A neo-aesthetic turn in post-feminist film theory, in collusion with the anti-metaphysical and vitalist thinking of Deleuze, might enable us to rethink the value of the aesthetic within film theory. This may then lead to innovative conceptions of the theory of affect and sensation through the processuality of becoming, rather than pleasure and desire, thus taking us back to questions of the value of film as an art form, no longer trapped within the reductionist paradigms of sociological, semiological and psychoanalytical analyses. Film theory may thus move away from perceptions of desire or pleasure, premised on the visual and the scopic into a creative thinking of the material capture of the cinematic experience or the cinematic event. Film has suffered too much at the hands of sociological and ideological analysis. I am not denying that film does in fact provide a significant construction of ideology, but its role as an aesthetic formation, as an art form needs to be revalorised. For too long the aesthetics of film has been distanciated with sociological and empirical study. I want to reclaim film as an art form. A reclamation of film as art, but an art which is experienced through a materialist aesthetic and a bio-aesthetic is thus the main concern here.

What follows in Chapter 2 is a preparatory and basic foregrounding of the origins of the significance of desire and pleasure in film theory. In two sections, it follows an exploration of how and why subjectivity was relevant to film theory, specifically through its exploration of psychoanalysis as a framework to theorise desire and pleasure. It presents a short account of the role of subjectivity in cinepsychoanalysis and the intervention of feminist film theory. The second part of the chapter provides an explanation of newer approaches to theorising the cinematic encounter, which move beyond psychoanalysis. As such it provides a platform to take my ideas (positive and aleatory concepts) forward through the thinking of Deleuze, in relation to the concepts of pleasure, desire and the ultimate 'beyond' of pleasure, sensation, through affect and a 'becoming-woman' of the cinematic, in Part Two of the book, Chapters 3, 4 and 5 on Deleuze.[37]

NOTES

1. Gilles Deleuze and Félix Guattari, *What is Philosophy?*, p. 164.
2. Elizabeth Grosz, 'A Thousand Tiny Sexes: Feminism and Rhizomatics', in Constantin Boundas and Dorothea Olkowski (eds), *Gilles Deleuze and the Theatre of Philosophy*, p. 193.
3. I am referring to the early decades of the twentieth century when writers like George Moore and Roger Fry were concerned with 'form' as that through which an ethical sense of the 'good' is achieved. That form would be premised on balance, harmony and a relational of aesthetic characteristics producing a harmonious 'whole'. Definitions of modernism are problematic here, I acknowledge, since modernism has been used to categorise a period of art as critique, for example, the Frankfurt School, where distanciation in a work of art enabled a political and ideological critique. I am not referring to this concept of modernism.
4. Pierre Giraud, *Semiology*, p. 67.
5. Marx based his analysis of society on the materialist conception of history. According to such views, history was seen not so much as a recording of events like wars, monarchs or statesman, but a recording of the ways in which people organise themselves in order to provide and satisfy their material needs, of clothing, shelter, food, etc.
6. Félix Guattari, *Chaosmosis*, p. 20.
7. *La nouvelle vague* of course was eminent in this area of experimentation with directors such as Jean Luc Godard, and François Truffaut. Earlier directors such as Eisenstein had similarly experimented with aesthetics and film form, in terms

of politically charged meanings in film: *Strike* (1925), *Battleship Potemkin* (1925), or *October* (1928), for example.

8. For a detailed analysis of the trajectories of feminist theory see Linda Nicholson (ed.), *Feminism/Postmodernism*.

9. Seyla Benhabib, 'Feminism and Postmodernism: An Uneasy Alliance', in L. Nicholson (ed.), *Feminist Contentions: A Philosophical Exchange*, p. 17.

10. Post-structuralism is a contemporary theoretical discourse which calls for the dissolution of the fixed and sentient subject. The subject is seen as fluid, mobile, transitional and fragmentary.

11. The debate about subjectivity and its construction is an important debate within the context of this chapter, but I only tangentially position some of the main theorists on this. I urge the reader to read further with recommendations as follows. It is important, however, to acknowledge here that if subjectivity and the subject have been fundamental concepts within film theory, then any new perceptions emanating out of post-theory will have an important effect in film theory. For an explanation of the heterogeneity of subjectivity, a post-structuralist vision of subjectivity, see Félix Guattari, *Chaosmosis*, ch. 1, 'On the Productivity of Subjectivity', in which he explains that subjectivity is plural, and polyphonic, and is an amalgamation of machinic dimensions. According to Guattari, semiological elements, like the family, education, fit alongside elements constructed by the media, to the more a-signifying regimes. Here Guattari identifies the importance of current research in ethology and ecology as a requirement to understanding the complexity of 'subjectivation' as a material process, within the material formations of the cellular structures of the brain. (See also Chapter 4 on Deleuze in this book.)

12. See for example the work of Irigaray, Kristeva and Cixous, each of whom have different perspectives, but who are prioritising feminisms which articulate multiple and fluid subjectivities. Their work is, however, mostly premised on a rearticulation of psychoanalysis, specifically Lacanian. Thus their feminisms, and I acknowledge there are differences across these three, are still premised on psychoanalytic constructions of subjectivities. For a brief overview see Toril Moi, *Sexual/Textual Politics*.

13. Rosi Braidotti, *Nomadic Subjects: Embodiment and Sexual Difference in Contemporary Feminist Theory*.

14. Within contemporary feminist epistemology, the debate about the 'subject' proliferates. Writers like Irigaray and Cixous argue for a feminist subjectivity, while Moira Gatens has positioned significant debates regarding conceptual shifts in feminist thinking (M. Gatens, *Imaginary Bodies: Ethics, Power and Corporeality*). Her politics of difference, drawing upon Foucault, explores the micro-politics of power. For Gatens, the aim of feminist theory is to deconstruct the webs across embodiment, differences and power, through a politics of difference. Donna Haraway has also written on the potential of a liberatory cyborgian 'subjectivity' and Chela Sandoval offers an oppositional consciousness, which articulates a differential subjectivity. See D. Haraway, *Simians, Cyborgs and Women: the Reinvention of Nature* and C. Sandoval, 'New Sciences: Cyborg Feminism and the Methodology of the Oppressed', in B. Kennedy and D. Bell (eds), *The Cybercultures Reader*, p. 374. See also Nancy Fraser, 'False Antitheses' and 'Pragmatism, Feminism and the Linguistic Turn', Drucilla Cornell, 'What is Ethical Feminism?' and 'Rethinking the Time of Feminism', and Judith Butler 'Contingent Foundations' and 'For a Careful Reading' in L. Nicholson (ed.), *Feminist Contentions*, for a thorough discussion of the polemics of current post-feminist thinking and the contradictions across their ideas.

15. Gatens, *Imaginary Bodies*. Grosz and Gatens embrace Deleuzian materialism.
16. See Barbara Kennedy, 'Post-feminist Futures in Film Noir', in M. Aaron, *The Body's Perilous Pleasures*, pp. 126–143, in which I discuss Haraway's relevance to film.
17. Haraway, *Simians, Cyborgs and Women*.
18. The notion of 'becoming' will be explored in Chapter 4 on Deleuze in more detail. I wish to signpost it here only. The term is predicated on Nietzsche's concept of 'becoming'. For Nietzsche there is no distinction between the world in which we live and any other transcendent plane of existence. For him there is no ultimate truth, no metaphysical world to which we aspire through Being. There is only ever the processual experience of the 'real', the real forces of life and its natural existence in its germinal and viral contingencies. (Premised on Darwin) 'becoming' epitomises that process of the affirmation of the dynamic of living in the real world, an acceptance of the cruelty of life, the joy of cruelty in that existence, the sheer ineluctability of life's transience. There is no other to which we can aspire. The 'real' is all there ever is and, within that, our experience of the real; 'becoming' serves to define life's ephemerality. Deleuze expands upon this notion of 'becoming'.
19. Of course I am not suggesting that ideology and signification are not still significant discourses through which to theorise the filmic experience. I am arguing that there are other paradigms as well.
20. See Judith Butler, *Gender Trouble: Feminism and the Subversion of Identity*; *Bodies That Matter: On the Discursive Limits of Sex*.
21. I want to highlight the term 'machinic' as one which advocates creative possibilities of connection: machinic in a positive and affirmative sense, and not in any negative or entropic sense, as it might be perceived in its literal definitions. Machinic in my use of the term is meant to denote openness, connectivity and alignments of thinking, feeling and material assemblages. See also Guattari, *Chaosmosis*, for discussion of the machinic, outside conceptions of this term as a literal technological term.
22. Grosz, 'A Thousand Tiny Sexes: Feminism and Rhizomatics', in Boundas and Olkowski (eds), *Gilles Deleuze and the Theatre of Philosophy*, p. 193.
23. Deleuze and Guattari express the concept of 'aparalletic evolution' as the 'becoming' that exists between two contrasting matters. As an example, I quote from Gilles Deleuze and Claire Parnet, *Dialogues*, p. 2, 'There are no longer binary machines: question/answer, masculine/feminine, man/animal, etc. This could be what a conversation is, simply the outline of a becoming. The wasp and the orchid provide the example. The orchid seems to form a wasp image, an orchid-becoming of the wasp, a double capture, since, "what" each becomes changes no less than that which "becomes". The wasp becomes part of the orchid's reproductive organs at the same time as the orchid becomes the sexual organ of the wasp. One and the same becoming, a single bloc of becoming, "aparallel evolution" of two beings which have nothing whatsoever to do with one another.'
24. I use this term in the Harawayan sense, and not in any literal sense of the word technology. Here technology is a much more amorphous abstract concept, meaning an assemblaging of components. Thus for example we can talk of a 'technologised' intellect or a 'technologised' thought process, or a 'technologised' body. This does not necessarily mean any literal change to the body's outward appearance, but describes a set of complexities which re-constitute the body in an amalgam of different ways, physically, mentally, intellectually or emotionally, or all of these. See also Rosanne Allucquere Stone's 'Will the Real Body Please Stand Up', in Kennedy and Bell (eds), *The Cybercultures Reader*.
25. Fernando Pessoa, *A Centenary Pessoa*, p. 254.

26. Pessoa, *A Centenary Pessoa*, p. 254.
27. This of course begs the question as to how one 'enjoys' without some sense of subjectivity. I shall be exploring the idea of an existential integrity: that is, a sense of self which is not premised on a sense of consciousness, in later chapters. I merely add this here to indicate that this question is relevant to the claim of enjoyment outside of subjectivity. The use of the term 'impact' is perhaps therefore more useful than enjoyment.
28. One could trace this dualism back to philosophers such as Kant who wrote about this in the *Critique of Pure Reason* and in the *Critique of Judgement*. I do not wish to engage with these ideas here, merely to initiate the derivation of the dual conception of aesthetics.
29. Pessoa, *A Centenary Pessoa*, p. 254.
30. The word haecceity derives from the Latin form 'haec' meaning 'Thisness' and was used in the texts of Duns Scotus and later the poetry of Gerard Manley Hopkins, denoting an experience of 'Thisness', an immanent sense of becoming, nothing to do with a transcendent understanding of being.
31. Brian Massumi, 'Deleuze, Guattari and the Philosophy of Expression', in *Canadian Review of Comparative Literature*, p. 746.
32. Deleuze, *Logique de la Sensation*, p. 39, translated by Ronald Bogue, 'Gilles Deleuze: The Aesthetics of Force', in Patton (ed.), *Deleuze: A Critical Reader*, p. 257.
33. Barbara McClintock quoted in Robert Root-Bernstein, 'Art, Imagination and the Scientist', in *American Scientist*.
34. Massumi, 'Deleuze, Guattari and the Philosophy of Expression', in *Canadian Review of Comparative Literature*, p. 765.
35. Massumi, 'Deleuze, Guattari and the Philosophy of Expression', in *Canadian Review of Comparative Literature*, p. 757.
36. David Rodowick, *The Difficulty of Difference*, p. 3.
37. I emphasise the notion of tangential, since the chapter is only a brief and simplistic trajectory of some elements of cinepsychoanalysis and its relevance to feminist film theory, as a departure point for new ideas. It does not engage in debates across different readings of psychoanalysis (but still acknowledges these) and its appropriation by a wide range of different feminisms. It provides further references for a fuller account for the reader. It does not give a total account of all strands of feminist film theory, (mentioning only in passing the seminal work of Laura Mulvey) nor can it do so in the constraints and the aims of the locus of this book, which is to present a collusion between Deleuzian philosophy and the filmic experience.

Chapter 2

From Oedipal Myths . . .
to New Interventions

FROM OEDIPAL MYTHS . . .

In the context of Chapter 1, it is apparent that subjectivity, the body, pleasure and desire are critical concepts within a post-feminist pragmatics, a pragmatics which enables a re-evaluation of the aesthetic or the production of a 'neo-aesthetic' in film culture. That neo-aesthetic can then be considered as a micro-political framework which might provide creative possibilities for the transformations of consciousness, outside macro-political structures. A new set of concepts emanating from a neo-aesthetic would be productive in understanding the cinematic experience as an 'event' or as 'material capture' and a processuality which engages with the notion of the material.

FILM THEORY AND A BRIEF INTERLUDE INTO CINEPSYCHOANALYSIS

Unlike mass audience study or sociological and empirical work in film theory, cinepsychoanalysis premised the viewer as a set of conflicting and fluctuating features. 'If psychoanalysis can be said to address the problem of "interlocking subjectivities", caught up in a network of symbolic systems, psychoanalytic film theory addresses spectatorship as an integral part of this complicated wave.'[1] The construction of subjectivity and its role within desire are crucial to this debate. Film theory used psychoanalysis as a model through which to explain patterns of pleasure and desire and how these are manifested to a spectator of a film, either within the formations of the film as text, or within the cinepsychoanalytic construction of the cinema-viewing 'subject'. Cinepsychoanalysis designated the cinematic experience as a production of fantasy, identification and, most importantly, a subjectivity, created through a series of primary (that is, actually experienced by us as individuals) psychical processes. The cinema was seen to construct a psychically produced 'subject'. The relationship between screen, spectator and manifestations of desire was perceived as one involving several interlocking concepts: fantasy, the scopic, identification and subjectivity. Films thus have meaning by virtue of a fictive viewer. That 'fictive viewer' is a psychically constructed subject. His or her subjectivity and its role within the process of desire is formulated through the manifestations of the cinematic text, in an analogous relationship to the processes of the unconscious and the development of the subject. Premised upon models of Freudian and Lacanian discourse, cinepsychoanalysis argued that cinematic desire is explained as a result of the fictive viewer's relationship with the film. This was seen as analogous to the complex staging of events within the unconscious, from early primordial originations of the organism, from maternal plenitude, through to the acquisition of language within culture.

The first stage in this setting of unconscious processes is the state of 'unity' or 'plenitude'. This incorporates a desire to be united within reality and a desire for unity with those who provide a sense of identity with one's self, where of course meaning and words provide some sense of awareness of that reality. This desired state of meaning is a recuperation of that state first experienced in the pre-Oedipal stage of maternal plenitude and fullness. Cinematic desire establishes this through an illusory state where the filmic experience offers a 'womb-like' security,

> [T]he totalising, womblike effects of the film-viewing situation represent . . . the activation of an unconscious desire to return to an earlier state of psychic development, one before the formation of the ego, in which the divisions between self and other, internal and external, have not yet taken shape.[2]

The second stage for the organism is the entry into a stage of 'illusory' unity. This is an imagined unity and occurs in what Lacan refers to as the mirror stage. Here the emergent subjectivity is provided by an 'imaginary' unity with its own image reflected in the mirror. But this is a fragmented image, one first encountered by the face to face, mother/other maternal stage. (This involved scopic processes, looking and being looked at in a symbiotic relational.) The splitting of the self occurs when the ego separates from the imaginary unity and the self-image at the Lacanian mirror stage. Here, the infant has that first recognition of a distinction between self and m(other)/mirror-image (self as other). Second, there is a recognition of lack or absence, either of the mother or the gratification of those early biological needs within the pre-Oedipal state, provided by the mother. Replacing the infant's dependence on the (m)other with a self-reliance, the mirror stage becomes the place for compensation for the child's acceptance of its lack. This is however an illusory identification of the infant with its visual 'gestalt' in the mirror. It also marks those early origins of separation within notions such as inside/outside, subject/object, self and other. From now on, splitting, binary modes of thinking and lack are the modes of understanding for the infant. This causes it to seek out an identificatory image through access, first with image and later through language. The infant has thus moved from an early maternal state of plenitude, to an imaginary state, where images, doubles and 'others' are part of its visual identifications. As a result of this fragmentation and splitting, the organism seeks to find a completeness, whilst accepting its splitting. Thus the child becomes ensnared within a process of recognition and misrecognition. An image of itself is both correct and yet also illusory. An ambivalence presides within Lacan's account of subjectivity. So, the infant recognises itself at the very moment it loses itself, in the 'other'. The subject's construction of its identity is therefore locked into this dialectical model.

The significance for film theory is of course Lacan's prioritising of the visual. This is because vision, more than any of the other senses, can be split between the looked at and the looking. Tactility and the olfactory cannot so easily be split into subject and object categorisations. Lacan's mirror phase emphasises the scopic, a vision-centred mechanism, but as Elizabeth Grosz argues,

> Lacan's ocular centrism, his vision centredness, its complicity with Freud's, privileges the male body as a phallic, virile body and regards the female body as castrated . . . We should note that the female can be construed as castrated, lacking the sexual organ, only on the information provided by vision.[3]

Psychoanalytic prioritisation of the visual (at least in Lacan) becomes crucial within feminist film theory, especially in its relation to sexual difference, through the castration complex.

As we have seen then, within the organism's reality, or the 'infant's' reality, unity and identity are only 'illusions'. A third stage of events involves the notion of 'difference'. It is this crucial element of 'difference' which has caused so much debate within film studies, specifically around the notion of gendered subjectivity, and explanations of gendered desire. In this third phase, language becomes part of the complex explanations of desire. Following the mirror phase, the infant can begin to distinguish various elements of its world, people, objects, from its 'self' whilst simultaneously seeing a place of recognition of 'itself' in the world, and, at this stage, comes the notion of a sexed subjectivity, enabling a sense of gendered identity. That notion of a sexed subjectivity comes from the Oedipal complex.

This important 'concept' of difference comes out of the axiomatics of structuralist linguistics, premised on the work of Saussure, who argued that language can only ever have meaning by virtue of 'difference' but difference in terms of oppositional difference. Psychoanalysis, then, explains this first element of difference in that very sexual difference through the 'having or not' of the signifier, the phallus. Sexual difference is thus marked through a division between 'lack' or 'not lack', whereby the female equates with 'lack'. Sexual difference is equated with the notions therefore of absence or presence (of the phallus). For the emergent subject, the only way to recuperate the plenitude is to return to those pre-Oedipal moments. This is prevented by the intrusion of the third element in the Oedipal triangle, the father, who symbolically represents the Law of the Father (by virtue of the penis/phallus) takes over the mother, possesses and takes away the maternal from the infant. This traumatic experience, of sexual oppositions, establishes the castration anxiety in the infant, and establishes sexual difference. Sexual difference equates with a fear of the loss of the phallus, a loss of the signifier of power in the cultural arena. This is important as it equates with linguistic difference, as a constitution of human subjectivity.

Thus, the split subject in culture, who acquires language, through acculturation following the symbolic order and mirror phase will seek to recapture a lost plenitude of 'unity' before the split, a return to originations, oneness with primordial and teleological originations. Desire is constructed as the attempt to recapture this early stage. It is also a stage of transcendence, in the Freudian sense of a return to origins, and return to a stage of inorganic beginnings (see Chapter 3, section 'Rethinking Pleasure beyond Freud'). The subject can only do this through language; but the problem is that language is insufficient, too static, too incapable to enable this fluctuating and fluid experience. It cannot 'speak' desire, because it is restrictive and encoded in oppositional difference. So desire can never be fulfilled, satiated, encapsulated. Language is always insufficient to accommodate this. There is a continual mismatch or a constant area of the 'abyssal', an 'unsurmountable lack', which constitutes desire. Whereas Freud positions the formulae of sexual drives in ontogenesis and species survival and predetermined biological development, suggesting that drives are given, Lacan analyses sexual drives through the functioning of language and linguistics. One is innately biological, the other cultural. For Lacan, the drive is not to be seen as biological or real (as it is in Freud), but is a function of the field of the 'other'. It is based on language and the symbolic: the cultural not the physical. 'Desire', as such, comes out of the gap which lies between what Lacan refers to as 'need' (which is fulfillable) and 'demand' (which is insatiable). Desire is situated in the dependence on demand,

> which by being articulated in signifiers, leaves a metonymic remainder that runs under it, an element that is not indeterminate, which is a condition, both absolute and unapprehensible, an element necessarily lacking, unsatisfied, misconstrued, an element that is called 'desire'.[4]

The reason why I emphasise this point is that desire is here determined through processes which are negative, abyssal: a desire which is always premised on lack, a need for satiation, for finality and satisfaction. Such determinations cannot account for the viscerality and vitality of film as a processual experience, encapsulated through movement and duration, which is why we need to look for more complex accounts of cinematic desire.

Therefore, if language is incapable of fulfilling this gap, in providing this sense of desire, the image, it has been surmised in film studies, might return the subject to its state of plenitude. So, the scopic/visual processes of the cinematic encounter, argues cinepsychoanalysis, mimic early psychic formations of pleasure through these interrelationships, inter-relationships premised upon binary distinctions, and binary language. Within that binary logic the main opposition of mind/body had been clearly maintained in cinepsychoanalysis, such that the body was only considered in relation to the biological difference between male and female viewers as responsible for their psychical manifestations. Within the arena of visual representation and the image, gender is a crucial element, because of the image of woman, denoting a symbolic 'lack' through her anatomical 'body' as lack. The phallus as signifier is inherently located in the literal figure of the penis. Women have a major role in the production of the symbolic (language and culture). However, because of her 'lack' woman can only have a negative position in culture, in relation to the positive position of masculinity, premised on the symbolic signifier of the phallus/penis. Woman cannot have access to desire, in this scenario, because she represents 'lack'. Female sexuality is not allowed expression; it cannot be expressed through language, or through iconic representation. The symbolic activity of both these arenas annihilates the 'lack' woman represents. She thus has no access to her own desire; she is silenced, misplaced, out of the picture. So argues feminist film theory from the 1970s and onwards.

However, this is too simplistic a reading of Lacan, and of course his ideas do acknowledge that the phallus is but a signifier and is not in any way a literal conception of penis. He categorically removes the equation of the phallus from any anatomical or biological body, arguing that there is a constant slippage between the signifier and the signified, an oscillation that can never be fixed. This has provided the grounding for much reconstitutive work by feminists, through Lacan and beyond Lacan through French feminist psychoanalysis. Indeed, his distinction between phallus and penis had enabled Freud's biologistic account of male supremacy and women's state of 'lack' to be explained in linguistic and symbolic terms. However, there lies one of the many contradictions in Lacan, because he states,

> [T]he fact that the penis is dominant in the shaping of the body image is evidence of an autonomous, non-biological imaginary anatomy. Though this may shock the champions of the autonomy of female sexuality, such dominance is a fact, and one which cannot be put down to cultural influences alone.[5]

Thus, I want to stage the problematic ellision of the biological penis/phallus as the signifier of lack, as one which still haunts cinepsychoanalysis, and despite the wide range of feminist film theory which has reread and reappropriated psychoanalysis for women and to 'speak' women's desire, I want to move debates in film theory away from this restrictive binarist use of language, and to remove the question of desire and pleasure away from genital sexuality and a use of language which is still premised on dialectical oppositions. Why should we be constrained by a perception of 'lack' premised still on a phallus/penis equation, and by an inability to voice or have access to desire? The psychical explanation of desire does not fit so easily with how we feel, how we experience a material and aesthetic relation to the world. We can feel intense and ecstatic resonances in an array of dimensions of experience, specifically through dance, colour, tactility, movement and the rhythmical. Why then should the iconic formations such as cinema be explained through psychical constructions of desire, locked into binarist language, and genital conceptions of sexuality or through the purely visual and scopic?

Cinepsychoanalysis has tried to explain the structures of cinematic desire for several decades, and following several attempts to destroy a perceived phallocentric pleasure, as Laura Mulvey argues in 'Visual Pleasure and Narrative Cinema', feminist film theory appropriated a range of different Freudian and Lacanian texts to enable a multiplicity of readings of a pre-Oedipal subjectivity, for justifying a specific female desire and a female subjectivity.[6] Mulvey's seminal article 'Visual Pleasure and Narrative Cinema'[7] sought a destruction of film's processes of pleasure, maintaining that this construction of cinematic pleasure was formulated upon the masculine subject of desire. Woman, as we have seen from the above discussion, was missing from the processes of desire. Drawing on Lacanian psychoanalysis, feminist theories of cinematic desire were contained within a binary construction of difference in terms of opposition, through which positive terms are produced only in relation to negative terms. Sexual difference has been seen to be key to the production of subjectivity, gendered identity and structures of desire. Vision and binary oppositions are crucial to a theory of the gaze. Laura Mulvey argued that psychoanalytic theory had positioned a cine-subject which was very much a male subject and that the visual determinations of the cinematic experience presented female images as 'coded-in-to-be-looked-at-ness' whilst man was 'bearer of the look'. Such arguments as outlined in detail in 'Visual Pleasure and Narrative Cinema' are well known within the auspices of feminist film theory.

However, despite the array of post-Mulveyan discourse, some of which has reappropriated Lacanian psychoanalysis in reclaiming female desire, and moving outside of a fixed notion of gendered subjectivity, there is a crucial point which needs to be displaced and even turned around within the mapping of cinepsychoanalysis. I want to take the selection of concepts of desire, subjectivity and the body and rethink them in a different sphere from the notion of genital sexuality, or morphological notions of the body. Psychoanalysis has been too locked into the equation of processes of desire with the body and an anatomical and genital sexuality, despite Lacan's distance from Freud. It premises its whole explanation of desire through anatomical difference. Desire is locked into models which require a genitalised and specific anatomical relation to the body of woman. The fact that she represents 'lack' through a lack of a specific organ has been used to provide the basis of the whole myth of Oedipal scenarios. I want to rethink the very concepts used here, to problematise notions of an 'anatomical' body for example. Those Oedipal myths have also been locked into determinations to return to teleological inorganic plenitude, where a concern with the death instinct is connected to the notions of the erotic (see Chapter 3, section 'Rethinking Pleasure beyond Freud'). Pleasure and death become equations in a search for original unity, a transcendent notion of the subject.

What I want to do by setting up a collusion across post-feminist pragmatics, Deleuzian philosophy and film theory is to argue that the whole premise of desire need not be located within notions of transcendent states, or an 'anatomical' body, whatever that is, or with recuperations for the subject, of lost empires in the mythical, psychical lands of the inorganic. Indeed, the very language that we use, with terms such as 'body', needs to be rethought through different perceptions of language. Sexuality may also lie outside/beyond configurations of a genitalised experience, an orgasmic or blissful ecstasy of genital formulations, one which imbricates the jouissancial pleasures of death in that moment of 'le petit mort' (although it also resides deliciously there as well . . . perhaps!). Rather desire may lie beyond, in a more complex explanation of the 'body' and 'desire', beyond the anatomical and Oedipal restrictions that we find within psychoanalysis. Desire does not need to be reliant upon phallic determinations of a teleological satisfaction, premised upon such equations with the genital.

I believe that aesthetic modulations, rhythm, movement, energy, duration and intensity and a wide range of aesthetic resonations provide ennervating, vital and creative cartographies and joyous spaces to which we might look for new configurations of 'bliss' beyond desire. Aesthetics 'becomes' the new sexuality; processes of movement, ecstasy, the durational and processuality become the new dynamics, a new dance, beyond the scopic, replacing that fixed and mythical theatre of Oedipal anxieties. Desire premised upon genitality is too constrained by the binary, the dialogical and dialectics of structuralist linguistics and restrictive definitions of the body. Even French feminist discussions of a specifically feminine subjectivity and desire have premised that 'jouissance' upon a sexual relational within and through the anatomical female body, despite of course more recent explanations of their work as being located through a morphology, rather than a literal anatomical sense of the body.[8]

PROBLEMATISING AND MOVING FORWARD

If we are to locate a new mind-set which emphasises the aesthetic as 'becoming-sexuality', through sensation, in relation to cinematic desire, I want also to locate that within a further problematising of cinepsychoanalysis and restrictive structuralist language which has prevented us from using concepts in more fluid, assemblaged and machinic ways. Cinepsychoanalysis has been too tied up with exploring the text and its viewer as a cinematic process which is concerned with psychical formations of subjectivities and desire to explain a wider perception of film as an aesthetic and artistic experience. If aesthetics 'becomes' as it were the new 'sexuality', this has important implications for explaining the experience of film outside of psychical explanations of desire. Aesthetics, as a processuality of molecular sexualities, moves beyond the notion of gendered desire. Film studies has for too long been concerned with textual/sexual operations, and the idea of a psychically constructed and gendered viewer. Film is an excitingly visceral, vital and dynamic aesthetic experience, and wider frameworks of understanding are needed to explain the aesthetic resonances beyond the restrictive codings so far discussed, outside codings which locate a sexualised subjectivity. How do we begin to understand the aesthetic experience of the 'event' of the cinematic, as a processual, material capture of experience, rather than thinking of the film as a text which produces intellectual or psychical formations of subjectivity and desire. Film energises, it mobilises, it works as matter, in assemblage with other bodies of matter. It connects in amorphous ways outside the merely scopic and psychical. Cinepsychoanalysis merely accounts for psychical perceptions of the experience and it clearly locates a gendered subjectivity and a split subjectivity as part of that process, a subjectivity which is formulated through the very process of the visual/scopic experience and a subjectivity that experiences desire through Oedipalised mechanisms.

Subjectivity, as a term itself, however, is too complex a concept to be completely explained through psychoanalysis, a framework locked into binarism, and reductive accounts of the subject. If subjectivity is problematised and examined through wider philosophical discourses which I introduce through Deleuze, then this enables a more creative explanation of how the film, as an aesthetic process of sexuality, connects in more amorphous ways, through the gestural, the mimetic, and the pathic. Subjectivity and psychoanalytical explanations of desire are too limiting to address how films work, connect, impact as material 'capture', as an aesthetic. Furthermore, psychoanalytical versions of desire lock the concept into frameworks of negativity, need, demand and the scopic. This does not explain the vitality, the viscerality and the processuality of film in duration, in movement and force – an ecstatic and vital play of molecularities and intensities. A different understanding of subjectivity as 'subjectless subjectivity' which is located beyond frameworks of Lacanian desire, and Freudian determinations of pleasure, would provide some new and innovative thought about the aesthetics of the film as 'event', as a material capture of those aesthetic sexualities.

What is also problematic about Lacanian versions of desire is that they confine debates within a linguistic mise-en-scène and a language which is very clearly formulated through binarisms; difference is discerned through oppositions. This prevents any notion of desire or a beyond of desire, which operates in ways outside of linguistic structures and psychical versions of subjectivity: for example through the aesthetics of a sensation/sexuality which is a machinic assemblage of the gestural, the pathic, the affective. Within an aesthetics of sensation, the concept of 'affect' becomes a much more useful term than either pleasure or desire, as I shall explore in Chapter 3. The concept of affect becomes more relevant to the aesthetic experience than either pleasure or desire. Psychoanalysis does allow for some consideration of the term 'affect', and Elizabeth Grosz states it has been perceived as a form of psychic discharge or energy which effectuates some sort of emotional response. Writing in relation to language and the unconscious, she states, 'The quota of affect or energy of the threatening experience, which is intimately connected to the drive, is separated from the memory or image, leaving a smaller quota associated with the idea. The idea continues to strive for conscious expression and motility in the form of a *wish*. The wish is nothing but this process of striving towards consciousness and motility or *"discharge"*. The drive is thus bound up with representation or signification as soon as it is capable of psychical registration. Indeed this is its condition of psychical existence.'[9] This equates the affective as an ultimate satisfying (that is, through discharge of desire). However, desire may be explained as processual, without finality or satisfaction. Affect cannot be located only in the psychical, but exists also within the materiality of the organism's make up.

'Affect' has been seen by some versions of psychoanalysis as existing within psychic states of the Imaginary; the verbal, voice, rhythm, tone and colour are for example perceived as elements in a pre-discursivity, a pre-Oedipal realm before language acquisition. But there are whole areas of experience that lie outside the psychoanalytic model which have a major place in the experience of the cinema, which cinepsychoanalysis claims to explain. 'Affect' is not merely psychical, but may be defined as material energy, premised on a Bergsonian and Deleuzian conception. It may be defined as material energy, based upon molecular structures of matter. To argue that it is both psychical and the material enables a break of the binary across rational, scientific claims on the definitions of pleasure and humanist, idealist notions of pleasure. Affect is rather a coagulation of the two regimes. It is significant that the concept of 'Aufhebung', meaning pleasure of the tactile/visual affect, has been theorised from Hegel to Lacan as psychical, but through Deleuze, à la Bergson, as positioned within the material and the molecular.

Indeed, affectivity encompasses both the psychical and the material, and is an important factor in rethinking the aesthetic/sexual experience. The affective might occur at a deeper and more primordial level than the psychical. This involves thinking about elements other than the psychical, other assemblages outside of psychical or phenomenological formations.

The cinematic experience is more than just the scopic or the visual. The aesthetics of the experiential are encompassed across the synaesthetic, the kinaesthetic, the proprioceptive and the processuality of duration and movement. The aesthetic then in this sense might be perceived as part of a material emotion, felt at a level deeper than a psychically constructed subjectivity.

This breakdown of the binarism across the meaning of affect is also pertinent to a discussion on the concept of the 'body'. Traditional discourses of film theory and cinepsychoanalysis were premised on binary language structures which firmly demarcated a disjunction between the concepts of mind and body. The corporeal body, the flesh and blood body of the literal spectator, was left out of debates which were more concerned with the mind and its role in psychical accounts of subjectivity. The term 'body' equated with either male or female versions of human biological construction: the 'having' or not of a phallus/penis for example. Debates within film theory, specifically feminist film theory, were replete for several years with concerns with images of woman, determined purely on this binary opposition of gender and sexuality. As a result of post-structuralist discourse, post-feminist theory and cyberdiscourse, the binary construction of language, and conceptual thought, has been questioned. Thus the oppositional differences that had once been perceived, within structuralist linguistics, between the concepts of mind and body (and of course through a whole range of other binarisms, such as animal/machine, nature/human, organism/machine)[10] began to be considered. The problem with cinepsychoanalysis is that it maintained a dependence upon a link between psychical formations of desire, and the identification with a specific gendered image on the screen or a specifically gendered subject position as a psychically constructed spectator. It maintained a notion of a 'sentient' subjective vision of an image on the screen. Psychoanalysis had no role thus for the body as a lived body or for any wider conception of the term 'body'. This term was restricted to its binary opposite of the mind or to a notion of an anatomical body which has or does not have a phallus. What has been lacking in psychoanalysis has been a wider conception of the term 'body'. Post-theoretical discourse has problematised the concept to the extent that the body may now be conceived, through theory, as part of an assemblage of meaning formations. The body might be perceived as aesthetic, material, technological, biological or machinic, in the more contemporary meaning of the word machinic. Both body and mind can be 'technologised' in the abstract sense of 'fitting together as an amalgam of different elements, whether material, biological, aesthetic, pharmacological or psychical'. 'Body' itself becomes a term of much wider conceptualisations. Psychoanalysis, despite its reappropriations in multiple ways beyond early uses, did not allow for theorising this complex assemblage of meaning for the concept 'body'. What, we might begin to ask, constitutes the concept 'body'? How might newer conceptions of the term 'body' rather than 'the body' involve wider formulations than the corporeal, flesh and blood body. The body can also be conceived as an assemblage, as a machinic assemblage in connection with other assemblages. Bodies can also be defined as complex forces and intensities that coagulate, oscillate and imbricate, as machinic assemblages of the molecular. The real, flesh and blood, technologised individual, as part of this extended determination of 'body', experiences the event of the cinematic encounter in a variety of ways, outside (although as well as) psychoanalytic mechanisms.

In relation to a post-structuralist and post-feminist pragmatics, then, how can newer theories that develop the concept of the 'body' outside of its binary positionality in structuralist discourse be useful in film theory? The term 'body' might be deemed an abstract concept which describes an interstitial space of the molecular, the technologised, the material and the aesthetic, as I explore them throughout this book. A materialist aesthetic and a neo-aesthetic, through Deleuzian philosophy, which rethinks the 'event' of the cinematic, might enable us to rethink the concepts 'body' and 'sexuality' in relation to film aesthetics. I shall develop this in Chapter 4, where I discuss the idea of 'constituting bodies'. How then does 'aesthetics' become a significant concept in such post-theoretical frameworks?

As I argued in Chapter 1, film theory has for too long been concerned with sociological and empirical research that its place within our aesthetic sensibilities seems somewhat lost, confused and at times even ignored. What I want to do through my imbrication with Deleuze is to bring back debates about film as an art form, as an element in a wider understanding of an aesthetic/sexual process which incorporates the 'bodies' of our material, technological, and molecular worlds, as well as rethinking debates about the scopic and the visual. Cinepsychoanalytic notions of 'pleasure' presented a universal acceptance of what it is to be 'pleasured' and why certain images may be deemed pleasurable. Such debates were premised on the scopic configurations of the filmic experience, and that pleasure was related to structures of looking, the gaze, the visual and the psychic. But, the scopic and the visual need to be rethought across a more creative mind/body/brain and brain/body/world connection. The body is both responsible, as well as the mind/brain, for the ways in which visual elements such as colour, form, movement, rhythm are effectuated within, through and beyond our consciousness.

Considering such concepts will encourage a newer understanding of aesthetic terms such as the 'beautiful', but through a different perception and understanding of the term, as I explained in Chapter 1. Re-evaluating concepts such as the 'beautiful' and 'feeling' will incorporate different theories of the body, in relation to mind and brain, through collusion with Deleuzian thinking. This will present an understanding of film therefore as a 'material capture' occurring at levels beyond any perceivable sense of psychically constructed subjectivities. Indeed, through these different debates, desire and pleasure are dislocated from their position within film theory (although not negated) to an innovative concern with 'becoming' and 'sensation' as a landscape for a neo-aesthetics. A neo-aesthetics which effectuates a neo-sexuality.

The concepts of pleasure and desire, framed as they have been through psychoanalytic configurations, are insufficient then for explaining the aesthetic resonances of filmic experience: the processual, the affective and experiential aspects of the cinematic encounter, the cinematic event. A move to Deleuzian paradigms, through the concepts of becoming, affect and sensation and a requestioning of subjectivity, will offer different, creative and experimental frameworks which are also post-feminist as they will pragmatically enable multidiscursivity. We live in a post-theoretical cultural *élan vital* within which we are able to utilise, perspectivally and contingently, a multiplicity of discourses from which to explore and explain our experiences, to question metaphysical notions such as the 'subject' and to offer post-metaphysical and post-feminist languages which invite redefinitions of terms like 'body', 'machine' or 'sexuality'. Within those post-metaphysical languages, new explanations of the aesthetic may be explored through non-binary notions or identitarian thinking which have prioritised subjectivity. This requires thinking about the complexity of our lives, lived experiences, hopes, anxieties and relations across bodies, power and differences and how these differences are manifested within, but also beyond and outside, the cultural assemblages and other assemblages which are part of that lived experience. Such assemblages are best explored, not through the psychical, linguistic or cultural, but through what Deleuze calls the schizoanalytical. Such ideas might thus forward a 'materialist aesthetic' and a neo-aesthetic/neo-sexuality outside psychoanalytic myths and theatres of the past.

TOWARDS NEW INTERVENTIONS . . .

Contemporary feminist film theory has moved on from those early foundational and epistemological roots based within a radical feminist political arena and within a definition of film as apparatus, as it has moved on from Mulvey's early dialogue with cinepsychoanalysis. A post-feminist film critique, rather than a feminist film critique, per se, is in a position to ask different questions, but, as I do here, to use the same concepts but in different ways and thus offer debates away from foundational discourses. Those debates have fundamentally been based upon ideological, libidinal, or cultural studies paradigms. Furthermore, feminist film theory has been locked into binary systems of thought at all its stages of history. The very use of psychoanalysis during this history maintained a discourse premised on binary language. It was also premised on the equation of desire with lack and the abyssal. It is now possible to think of desire across more complex mechanisms of mind/body/matter construals. The materiality of affect and aesthetic resonances of the filmic process were obfuscated in a concern with 'texts', which have a 'meaning' discernible through an array of Freudian/Lacanian game-playing and language systems, based within Western, transcendental and Cartesian frames of reference. Confirmation of binary and rationalist use of language systems meant that theory was seen to be the territory of the mind alone, and the body was accommodated only in relation to psychic processes.

A post-structuralist and post-feminist pragmatics seeks an engagement with the filmic experience which moves from debates which theorise 'representation' and the 'image' and their concern with pleasure and desire, to theories of 'material affect' and 'sensation' and 'becoming' and a neo-aesthetics as sexuality. Such post-feminist film theory needs to question the very ontological and teleological foundations of language use and meaning, to provide a fresh approach to what it is to 'think' about ideas and concepts outside the language construction as we know it. It brings with it a refreshing return to aesthetics and a new consideration of the concept of 'body'. Subverting the primacy of any psychical interior, the mind/body meld makes possible a materialist consideration of cinema, one which had previously only been allowed to avant-garde texts.

We should be engaging with a material awareness of film, returning the observer/spectator to an awareness of the materiality of the film, to its molecular structure, in connection with the molecularity of those bodies which view. I want to offer a theory of cinema as 'becoming-woman in sensation', which conceptualises new structures of desire outside structuralist and psychoanalytic paradigms. New interventions in film theory have begun to discover the significance of the material, matter, the machinic and the embodied eye of vision. Jonathan Crary, Vivian Sobchack, Christine Gledhill and Linda Williams,[11] Miriam Hansen,

Anne Friedberg, Bracha Lichtenberg-Ettinger and Camilla Griggers[12] have prioritised post-linguistic accounts of cinematic desire. But they have not gone far enough to account for newly recognised structures of experience emanating from 'becoming' and the aesthetics of sensation, the movements and energies of the filmic experience. Subjectivity and the phenomenological 'lived body', rather than a more complex understanding of 'body' as processes of congealment, imbrication, consilience, assemblage, aesthetics and the molecular, are still prioritised in the work of these writers. Nonetheless, they have begun to engage post-structuralist ideas such as the fragmentation and the reification of identity, the ossification of subjectivity; the breakdown of binary languages and the theatre of 'representation'. As such they have paved the way for exciting and experimental avenues of thinking in film aesthetics.

Writers like Crary have begun to delegitimate apparatus theory and to proffer a concern with the 'corporeality' of vision: an engagement, in Crary's case, with a scientific interest with matter, optics and the body. Crary's work has been one of the first to offer a model in which boundaries between bodies and images, on the one hand, and the body as a machine for viewing, on the other, are connected. He argues that modernist discourses and technologies constructed 'newly corporealised bodies of observers', which have no precedent in the disembodied regime of the camera obscura.[13] Therefore, the long intellectual tradition of mind/body dualism, which treated bodily sensations provoked by images as suspect, has ended. Crary's work refuses psychoanalysis, since he prioritises material and scientific discourses from optics, physiology and neuroscience to explain specific filmic experiences.

Crary's intervention into film theory came with a move from the 'spectator' to the term 'observer'.[14] The 'camera obscura' model of the cinematic vision, a model premised on technologies of the 'gaze' and psychoanalytic configurations of desire, did not allow for the role of the corporeality of the viewer/observer, nor for the corporeality of the body of the film. Crary argues that a new model of vision began in the nineteenth century, to supplant the older model of camera obscura vision. The camera obscura model had operated between the late 1500s to the 1700s and was the dominant paradigm for a centred human subjectivity. Vision, the filmic experience and spectator were imbricated within a centred subjectivity. This has since been reinforced through psychoanalytic film theory. The nineteenth century saw the emergence of a model of vision dependent on machines (the traumatrope, the phenatistiskope, the stereoscope and the kaleidoscope). As a result, what took place was an innovatively fragmented, subjective and machinic vision which was different from that proposed by the camera obscura model. For the first time, the body of the observer, both in actuality and in theory, was significant in the overall desirous experiences afforded by the visual. The earlier camera obscura model did not allow for a corporealised or a materialised observer, or a newly corporealised viewer. The construction of a 'decorporealised observer' allowed for a vision of the world whose objective truths could only be rationally known. This model of a singular, and centred, point of view, prominent within theories of camera obscura vision, prevailed across the philosophical views of writers like Diderot, Descartes and Locke. Such a model was dependent on an act of idealised seeing, and, furthermore, that ideality also depended upon being aside the physical body of the observer. A new model of vision prioritised the importance of the body of the observer as a surface of inscriptions which has a whole range of multiplicitious and amorphous effects. With the supplanting of the camera obscura model of vision, the viewer was thrown into a connection with an immediacy of sensations. With this breakdown of the camera obscura model, there begins to appear a new model, where boundaries between bodies and the world fragment, and where bodies become 'machines' for viewing, within the overall machine of desire. Crary's adaptation, then, of a Foucauldian concern with 'technologies' and the 'body' began to provide a new understanding of bodily sensation being generated by the image. Consequently, it follows that the whole Cartesian duality that binarily opposed mind against body could be abandoned, or at least moved away from.

This then allows for more interesting models of the filmic experience to emerge, which move away from a concern with visual representation. Instead, we can move towards an 'aesthetics of sensation'. An 'aesthetics of sensation' describes the connections, the energies, the molecular connections of consciousness and nervousness within the mind/body/brains of those who experience film as a material encounter. In this perspective, texts or films, it might be argued, are also bodies. Indeed, the camera obscura model actually 'decorporealises' the viewer, as one who lives in a reality where objective truths can only be known through rationality, through the mind. 'Rationality', and Cartesian epistemological prioritisation of 'rationality', emerges as problematic to offering models of the filmic desire outside of the visual.

Whilst I acknowledge that Crary's work is insensitive to considerations of gender and sexuality, in relation to different observers, his work does begin to provide for a better understanding of bodily sensation and a 'material emotion' articulated through the filmic experience. Indeed, in his chapter on subjective vision and the separation of the senses, he explains how Goethe's 'Theory of Colours' has explored the corporeality of visual experience. Goethe wrote, 'Let the observer look steadfastly on a small coloured object and let it be taken away after a time, while his eyes remain unmoved; the spectrum of another colour will then be visible, on the white plane . . . it arises from an image which now belongs to the eye.'[15]

Goethe explored how experiences in which subjective contents of vision are disassociated from an objective world; the body itself produces elements that have no external correlates. Similarly, Maine de Biraine explores the significance of the body in perception, explaining that visual perception is inseparable from the muscular movements of the eye, and the physical effort involved in focusing on an object. The eye, like the rest of the body, requires the operation of force and energy. Reversing the classical model of apparatus theory, as a device for the transmission of images, both the viewer's sensory organs and their activity are inextricably mixed with whatever object they see. As Crary argues, through the work of writers like Goethe and de Biraine, observation is increasingly exteriorised. Thus the 'viewing body and its objects begin to constitute a single field, on which inside and outside are confounded. Subjective observation, then, is not the inspection of an inner space, or a "theatre of representations".'[16]

The corporeal aspects of an observing subjectivity, which are not considered in the concepts of 'camera obscura', now took on an important signification in which an observer is possible. The body, in its contingency, and its specificity, then produces the spectrum of another colour. The body has thus become an active producer of an optical experience. In his argument, Crary utilises the work of several nineteenth-century physiologists. One of these, George Fechner, engaged in experiments of vision and perception which demonstrated empirically a functional relationship between sensation and stimulus. Crary's work goes on to outline models of vision which establish an absence of referentiality to the visual experience.

This is a vital step to thinking new models of desire, which do not prioritise representation or the image, but process and the role of sensation within the processual. This very absence of referentiality is the beginning of a new model of filmic experience which will construct for an observer a new 'real' world, experienced through a 'materiality' of the film and a concern with the imbrication of body/mind/brain in the perceptions of the viewer/observer. It is a question of a perceiver whose nature renders identities unstable and mobile, contingent and fluid, and questions identitarianism and subjectivity.

However, it is important to state at this stage, that, despite a concern with 'bodies', I am not suggesting a phenomenological account of the cinematic experience. What I am concerned to argue for is a melding of the mind/body/brain with the image, in an assemblage of filmic sensation, where 'affect' affords the ultimate 'material emotion' which is beyond any subjective vision. The body, here, is not seen as responsible for a 'natural perception' as in Merleau-Ponty. Rather, it is profoundly assembled within a machinic configuration of image: perception-image, action-image and affection-image. So, we can see that Crary's work, because of its engagement with optics, and the materiality of perception, has already begun to disturb those fixed cinepsychoanalytic paradigms in feminist film theory, which, as I have argued, have fundamentally prioritised representation and signification, and within that have used psychoanalysis as the main method of understanding structures of desire.

Crary's work, and its concern with the role of the body, is developed in the more profoundly Merleau-Ponty-inspired phenomenological approach of Vivian Sobchack.[17] However, any connection of the human body with perception as organic is, in my argument, problematic. I shall, rather, proceed from both Crary and Sobchack as starting points to offer a model of filmic desires, outside of phenomenological premises. This model will not see the body as separate from the mind, but mind and body will be seen as part of a synthesising assemblage, an assemblage of material, matter and molecularity: a materiality of perception premised upon matter and energy.

Crary's work, then, has had profound implications for film theory. It has disturbed that overarching division of twentieth-century art, including film, into 'classical mimesis and an elite avant-garde modernism', which, 'stands alone in its capability of returning the spectator to an awareness of the effects of an apparatus'.[18] The classical model of spectatorship, in its prioritisation of ideology and psychoanalysis has always prioritised a decorporealised, distanced, monocular eye, unimplicated in the experience of an image. Crary's work has been important in disturbing this premise. The body is implicated, then, in the specular economy of all films, not just the avant-garde. That body, moreover, becomes a much more complex phenomenon in my theorising of the filmic experience.

Vivian Sobchack has also been significant in her observations of the role of the body. Like Crary, she engages with philosophy as a paradigm for thinking about film. Her critique of classical and contemporary film theory is that it has not addressed, fully, the idea of cinema as a mode of 'life-expressing life', or rather cinema as 'experience'. Neither has it sufficiently addressed the construal of perception (and the role of the body in that) and expression, since it has always prioritised one (in opposition) to the other. Thus, she argues for a semiosis of perception-expression, rather than one or the other. She pre-empts my ideas of film as experiential, then, in some ways, but she uses different paradigms of philosophical engagement. Whereas Crary uses Foucault and a philosophy of science, Sobchack turns to Merleau-Ponty as an inspiration for new regimes of filmic pleasure as an embodied experience. I move further into an imbrication with the continental and post-metaphysical philosophy of Deleuze.

However, Sobchack's work is predominantly a phenomenological explanation of the cinematic experience and whilst it provides a stepping stone in my argument, it does not go far enough because it is based on a theory of 'natural perception' (that is the body and mind being separate entities) rather than a molecular coagulation of perception and the materiality of the brain/body/mind imbrication. Sobchack does, however, break down the traditional oppositions between subject and object, mind and body, the visual and the visible object, arguing that the film has always been both a dialectical and a dialogical engagement of viewing subjects. But this still maintains a concern with subjectivity, with 'viewing subjects'. It still is locked into identitarian thinking and concern with psychic constructions of subjectivity as a fundamental element of the filmic experience. Her main argument is that in all theories of spectatorship and pleasure, especially the models I have discussed earlier, the body has been missing from debates.[19] She is in some ways offering a model which combined both perception and expression, whereas previous models have prioritised one or other of these. However, she still does not argue for a total assemblage across the machine of the cinematic, as a synthesis across the mind/body/brain meld. She argues that the film is not just an object for viewing, but that it is a 'viewing subject', with both a subjectivity that views and a view that is seen,

> [I]t possesses sense by means of its senses, and it makes sense as a 'living cohesion', as a signifying subject. It is as this signifying subject that it existentially comes to matter as a significant object, that is, it can be understood in its objective status by others as sensible and intelligible.[20]

She argues that the cinema uses modes of embodied existence, such as seeing, hearing, physical and reflective movements, as the main components of its language. However, she suggests that this has not been given attention in theory which has always prioritised ideological and psychoanalytic discourses. Film as 'experience', whereby the film as well as the viewer are embodied within the experience of cinema, represents a dynamic across a set of relational elements, all of which constitute 'lived bodies'. Nonetheless, her argument is still in danger of maintaining a prioritisation of 'signification' and 'meaning' and the fundamental importance of subjectivity. She says, for example, 'any film, however abstract or "structural-materialist" presupposes that it will be understood as signification'.[21] I want to move further away from signification to seeing film as 'event' as 'affect' or as 'becoming'. In Sobchack a logic of signification, rather than sensation, persists. This may be because her definition of signification is distinct from representation. Film, she argues, has been theorised through critiques of 'representation' and in terms of ideological and psychic formations, insufficiently theorised through signification. Signification to Sobchack lies outside of representation. In my perspective, 'signification' is inherently tied up with representation. Her critique of a transcendental determinism in film is based in an argument that signification is informed and predetermined by apparatus ideology or psychic structures. My position will go further than this, to distanciate subjectivity from the processuality of sensation, and thus distanciate subjectivity from the equation.

However, Sobchack does argue for the dialogical process of spectator and text. Through the address of our own vision, she says, 'we speak back to the cinematic expression, before us, using a visual language that is also tactile, that takes hold of and actively grasps the perceptual expression, the seeing, the direct experience of the anonymously present, sensing, and sentient "other"'.[22] However, this process had never been denied in psychoanalytic and cultural studies' film theory. They also articulated this 'dialogical process' across spectator, and text. What is new, however, is Sobchack's recognition of the 'embodiment' of the film as well as viewer. To Sobchack, the film is a 'body' which also views; it is a subject which also views; it has a subjectivity. The film itself, then, has its own locale, its own perceptual and expressive functions. It both 'represents' and 'presents', in a performative way, as a body. But her definition of the 'embodied text' still hangs on to a sense of subjectivity which is a felt experience, centred in an 'intentionality' within consciousness, whether that subjectivity is of the film or the viewer. The film becomes a sentient 'subject', a living body of expression, which 'locates its own address, its own perceptual and expressive experiences of being and becoming'.[23] Through an 'address of the eye' we speak back to the cinematic expression, by utilising both a haptic, tactile and visual language. Consequently, what happens is a 'decentring' of the cinematic experience. There is what she refers to as a 'double occupancy' of the cinematic space, which does not necessarily conflate the viewer and the film, but operates for both 'bodies'. She argues, as I have done, that classical film theory had privileged psychic and ideological structures over the signifying 'freedom of the individual viewers'.[24]

But Sobchack's argument remains teleological and does not address the ontological or correlational nature of film. If the filmic experience is more than the visual, the psychic, and the ideological, then, according to Sobchack, we need to consider film as an intersubjective performance, where the film is more than a visible object. It 'performs' as a body, as a 'viewing subject' just as much as it is a visible and 'viewed object'. This 'address of the eye' then posits an embodied, situated existence of the film and the material world.

Thus, Sobchack brings the body and matter, in some initial ways, into debates about filmic aesthetics. She does not prioritise 'meaning' in the text, as the fundamental structure of desiring processes. To be seen, the viewing subject must be a body and be 'materially in the world, sharing a similar manner and matter of existence with other viewing subjects'.[25] However, she still maintains that there are two embodied acts of vision at work, in the cinematic experience. Whilst this disturbs that monologic vision of previous film theory, it admits to only two performative processes. Sobchack argues that the cinematic vision is always doubled, it 'is always the vision of *two viewing subjects*, materially and consciously inhabiting, signifying and sharing a world in a manner at once universal and particular, a world that is mutually visible, but hermeneutically negotiable'.[26]

However, I want to argue that the filmic experience is an aesthetic, machinic structure, which operates in processual ways, beyond 'two performative processes' which entails a structure premised on binary thinking. There is another stage which Sobchack does not engage with, one which opens up explanations of the aesthetic of film beyond her restrictive formula. This is an aesthetic premised outside of intentionality, which might implicate a wider definition of the biologically constituted body, in relation to other bodies. Not only will I be concerned with the body, in its Deleuzian sense of a 'body without organs', but also the mind/brain melding process of the viewing experience as one of desire in sensation. Thus, I will be concerned in Chapters 3, 4 and 5, to present cinema as 'event'[27] as a processual experience of desire, premised on Deleuzian ideas of affect and sensation, rather than subjectivity and desire.

Sobchack, then, has at least begun to initiate a concern with the ontological nature of cinema as an 'expression of experience by experience'. Most of film theory has condemned this ontological being of cinema. If contemporary theory, influenced by post-structuralist and post-feminist discourse, is to move away from ideas based upon a transcendent consciousness, it needs to be located within a neo-aesthetic discourse of immanence, process, movement, processuality and becoming. It is in its modalities, its ontological modalities, that cinema offers us, as viewers, and theorists, an interpretation of 'sensation' rather than pleasure or desire.

Miriam Hansen has also been prominent in considering how cinema's structures of desire might function through the materiality of the filmic process. What is significant in her argument, as also Tom Gunning's, is its concern with how contemporary film is experienced in ways which are similar to experiences of early cinema. Pre-classical narrative cinematic desires were encapsulated through the 'material' of the filmic process, through its very ontology, in its ability to shock, to excite, disturb, transform, stimulate, frighten, energise, or terrify, its audience. In an article which critiques psychoanalysis, Hansen articulates a resurrection of post-modernist or what she refers to as post-classical cinema, of the film's power to shock.[28] Sensation and kinetics affect the body, of the viewer, and the observer, as much as the mind and the emotions. She locates her argument within a post-modern cultural climate, where the fragmentation of subjectivities and identities is manifested by new technological developments. Film is thus no longer experienced solely within the film theatre, but through a wider range of settings. An aesthetics of the 'gaze' which we saw in feminist film theory has then been disturbed and diffracted through new patterns of viewing, which renders the subject outside any positionality in terms of identity.

What is important to my argument, here, then, is that she highlights a concern with cinema as an 'attraction', cinema as a presentational medium and a process, rather than purely a representational medium. Like early cinema, post-classical or contemporary cinema addresses the viewer directly with an awareness of the filmic medium itself. If we are to develop conceptions in contemporary film theory which look towards a neo-aesthetics, then we need to account for this relationship between film and viewer: a relationship which is a construal of mind/ body/matter in process. Thus new theories are not necessarily bound up in reception theory or theories of subjectivity or identification. We need to think about what a film 'is' and how it 'impacts' as an aesthetic formation, and as a process of creative desire, rather than thinking of it as a narrative construction or representation, alone. I am not of course denying those realms are important, both politically and ideologically, but we need to look at all possible conceptions. There are, then, some epistemological connections here across the work of Crary, Sobchack and Hansen, to do with the material emotions of the body. Crary's scientific interrogations of the 'body' as a machine for viewing and Sobchack's concern with the film as an 'embodied subject' with its own body of materiality, expression and perception have progressed film debates. Thus, a 'body' of work is now beginning to be established which takes distance from a concern of the 1970s and 1980s with the political (ideological) and the libidinal (psychoanalytic). Instead, it might be concerned with the schizoanalytical.

Tom Gunning's[29] work describes the filmic experience as 'vertiginous', an experience produced by a mixture of pleasure and anxiety, which could be labelled 'sensation'. He defines this as an 'aesthetics of attractions'. In terms of my argument, then, 'sensation' has in many ways some connection with 'pleasure', but it is removed from psychoanalytic or text-obsessed theories. Moving beyond Gunning, sensation, affect and the film as 'body', in its materiality, is the new framework I wish to consider in relation to the 'becoming-woman' of the cinematic.

Finally, Anne Friedberg's work has also made some move towards these new theories of the filmic experience. Friedberg's work has been significant because it locates film within a post-modern context, and like Crary, she articulates the significance of the breakdown in classical centred and univocal forms of vision. She still, however, keeps the debates within the auspices of 'vision' and the 'gaze' – arguing for a matrixial gaze[30] – a mobilised gaze, thus disrupting the fixed, immobile locations in earlier feminist film theory. She does not locate this mobilised gaze within any psychoanalytical paradigm of exchange, but reappropriates both Benjamin's and Baudelaire's work on the *flâneur*.[31] She does take a 'gendered perspective' on a new post-modernist vision, within a post-feminist context. Like Hansen, she connects new critiques of film to the notion of 'experience' rather than in connection with 'mediated images'. Film experience then becomes a more pertinent term than cinematic 'spectatorship'. This experience, she argues, is part of the late twentieth-century cultural arena of virtual, electronic and mobilised gazes, incorporating video and technocultures. Subjectivity, then, can no longer be conceived through an engagement with 'specific images'. Indeed, the capacity to manipulate time/space has rendered an increasingly detemporalised viewer through a physicality of sensations.

In summation to this chapter, the important trajectory within my argument is that if we are to present a post-feminist pragmatics and a neo-aesthetic of the cinematic, then we need to move further than the work of writers like Sobchack, Crary, Williams and Friedberg. Feminist film theory prioritised psychoanalysis which could not consider the post-feminist and post-structuralist concerns with the mind/body imbrication. The current concern with 'bodies', and what they constitute, has resonances for new theories outside of those located within psychoanalytic or semiotic paradigms. We need to engage in debate which continues this move away from the role of subjectivity, or the defined positionality of a viewing subjectivity, in relation to constructions of desire.

As I outlined above the main problems with much of this theory has been in relation to the following areas: subjectivity, a limited definition of bodies, the notion of binary language, the concepts of desire and pleasure and the concept of the aesthetic. What I want to do through a Deleuzian philosophy is to present a new concern with the 'affect' to argue for the 'becoming-woman through sensation' of the cinematic, to argue for a constitution of bodies, which presents film as a processual experience, an 'haecceity', an event and material capture. A neo-aesthetic of the film as event (which will rethink some aesthetic terms such as beauty and form) and as experience will sit alongside other theories of spectatorship. Through new vocabularies emanating from Deleuzian philosophy, we might recapture some sense of a neo-aesthetic, where concepts such as beauty, movement, time, space, sensation, affect and the processual and their interrelationship might be part of a new structure of cinematic desire. This imbrication of new vocabularies will project a theory of becoming, useful for film-philosophy and for rethinking the filmic text. The concept of subjectivity will be subsumed through becoming. Within Deleuzian ideas, psychoanalytic configurations of pleasure are rendered otiose, the subject is rendered otiose, and instead notions of immanence replace a teleological concern with transcendent principles.

Within this framework, representation may be distanciated by different discourses which are concerned with the event of cinema as images in movement. Rather the image becomes part of a processual engagement. Desire is rendered processual and energic, not abyssal or negative. Rather than thinking of film theory in terms of representation, signification and semiotics and the roles of pleasure or desire, we can consider film in terms of a neo-aesthetic of sensation and becoming. A neo-aesthetics of the filmic experience will encourage resurrection of the aesthetic in film as an arena through which to imbricate a new sexuality, rather than the restrictive and reductionist concerns with ideology of semiotics or the libidinal of psychoanalysis. Film will be seen as a process of desire, as a machinic assemblage of desire, where subjectivity is subsumed to the more profound concept of sensation: a rethinking of film as aesthetic 'event'. Part Two of the book takes us into those landscapes of sensation, through the work of Deleuze.

NOTES

1. Robert Stam, Robert Burgoyne and Sandy Flitterman-Lewis (eds), *New Vocabularies in Film Semiotics, Structuralism, Post-structuralism and Beyond*, p. 141.
2. Stam, Burgoyne and Flitterman-Lewis (eds), *New Vocabularies in Film Semiotics*, p. 144.
3. Elizabeth Grosz, *Jacques Lacan: A Feminist Introduction*, p. 39.
4. Jacques Lacan, *The Four Fundamental Concepts of Psychoanalysis*, p. 154.
5. Grosz, *Jacques Lacan: A Feminist Introduction*, p. 123.
6. Writers such as Gaylyn Studlar, Joan Copjec, Constance Penley, Elizabeth Cowie, Kaja Silverman, Griselda Pollock, Bracha Lichtenberg-Ettinger have been significant in reappropriating and rethinking psychoanalysis, both Freudian and Lacanian, and through French feminisms, to accommodate the notion of female desire, and gendered subjectivity. For example, Freud's text on 'A child is being beaten' has been used to argue for multiple gendered subject positionalities in spectatorship, and Studlar's work on the masochistic aesthetic has enabled different readings of psychoanalysis from those of Mulvey. I acknowledge and pay respect to the work of such writers, but can only refer the reader to their work, an analysis of which is outside the purposes of my project here.
7. Laura Mulvey, 'Visual Pleasure and Narrative Cinema', in Laura Mulvey, *Visual and Other Pleasures*, p. 14.
8. See Toril Moi, *Sexual/Textual Politics*, for a description of Irigaray's work. *This Sex Which is Not One* argues that female pleasure, 'jouissance' is premised on the multiply sexed body of woman, her 'two lips' replacing the monologic idea of the phallus, signifier of male desire, and its unitary modelled phallic sexuality. Take the 'genitals' out of the equation, and the concept of body can be more creatively explored beyond the confines of anatomical restriction. This is of course explored, I acknowledge, through Irigaray as a morphology rather than a notion of the body as anatomical.
9. Grosz, *Jacques Lacan: A Feminist Introduction*, p. 83.
10. Donna Haraway's seminal work on cyborg consciousness, the work of Chela Sandoval and cyberdiscourse more generally have been fundamental in locating debates which problematise oppositional discourse. See articles by both Sandoval, 'New Sciences: Cyborg Feminism and the Methodology of the Oppressed', and Haraway, 'A Cyborg Manifesto: Science, Technology and Socialist Feminism in the Late Twentieth Century', in B. Kennedy and D. Bell (eds), *The Cybercultures Reader*.
11. See Christine Gledhill and Linda Williams, *Re-inventing Film Studies*.
12. See Camilla Griggers 'Goodbye America (The Bride is Walking . . .)', in Ian Buchanan and Claire Colebrook (eds), *Deleuze and Feminist Theory*.
13. Camera obscura: Crary writes that 'it has been known for at least two thousand years that when light passes through a small hole into a dark, enclosed interior, an inverted image will appear on the wall opposite. Thinkers as remote from each other as Euclid, Kepler, Roger Bacon, Leonardo, noted this phenomenon and speculated in various ways how it might or might not be analogous to the functioning of human vision. The camera obscura was not simply an inert and

neutral piece of equipment or set of technical premises to be tinkered with and improved over the years. Rather it was embedded in a much larger, denser organisation of knowledge, and of an observing subject. From the late 1500s to the end of the 1700s the structural and optical principles of the camera obscura coalesced into a dominant paradigm through which was described the status and possibilities of the observer. During the seventeenth and eighteenth centuries the camera obscura was without question, the most widely used model for explaining human vision, and for representing the relation of a perceiver and the position of a knowing subject, to an external world' (Johnathan Crary, *Techniques of the Observer*, p. 27).

14. Crary, *Techniques of the Observer*.
15. Goethe, 'Theory of Colours', in E. Cassirer (ed.), *Rousseau, Kant and Goethe*, pp. 81–2.
16. Crary, *Techniques of the Observer*, p. 73.
17. See V. Sobchack, 'Phenomenology and the Film Experience', in L. Williams, *Viewing Positions*, p. 36.
18. Williams, *Viewing Positions*, p. 7.
19. See V. Sobchack, *The Address of the Eye: A Phenomenology of the Film Experience*, p. 40.
20. V. Sobchack, quoted in Williams, *Viewing Positions*, p. 9.
21. Sobchack, 'Phenomenology and the Film Experience', in Williams, *Viewing Positions*, p. 38.
22. Sobchack, 'Phenomenology and the Film Experience', in Williams, *Viewing Positions*, p. 40.
23. Sobchack, 'Phenomenology and the Film Experience', in Williams, *Viewing Positions*, p. 41.
24. Sobchack, 'Phenomenology and the Film Experience', in Williams, *Viewing Positions*, p. 47.
25. Sobchack, 'Phenomenology and the Film Experience', in Williams, *Viewing Positions*, p. 53.
26. Sobchack, 'Phenomenology and the Film Experience', in Williams, *Viewing Positions*, p. 54.
27. Dudley Andrew notes that film theory has to date only been concerned with signifying processes in terms of textual semiotics. It has not been concerned with 'signification' in any other way. To Andrew, what needs discussing is the 'process of its congealing and the event of its mattering'. (See 'The Neglected Tradition of Phenomenology in Film Theory', in *Wide Angle*, 2.2, p. 45–6.)
28. See Miriam Hansen, 'Early Cinema, Late Cinema: Transformations of the Public Sphere', in *Screen*, 34: 3, pp. 197–210.
29. See Tom Gunning, 'An Aesthetics of Astonishment', in *Art and Text*. In 'An Aesthetics of Astonishment' Gunning shows how early cinema was one replete with visual shocks. The film–spectator relationship was specifically relevant to a pre-classical cinema, based on shock, excitement and its power to affect, its power to disturb the physical body of its audience. The cinema was a machine which produced, by its very ontology, physical sensations. One is specifically tactility. Gunning refers to cinema's power to 'warrant closer examination and the involvement of the sense of touch'. He defines the 'cinema of attraction' as the 'aesthetics of attraction' as it addresses in an experience of assault. Rather than being an involvement with narrative action, or empathy with character psychology, the cinema of attractions solicits a highly conscious awareness of the film image, engaging the viewer's curiosity. Most importantly, the 'spectator does not get lost in a fictional world and its drama – but remains aware of the act of looking, the excitement of curiosity and its fulfilment'.

30. Bracha Lichtenberg-Ettinger also locates the notion of the matrixial as a creative adaptation of Lacanian psychoanalysis in visual cultures. See Bracha Lichtenberg-Ettinger, 'Matrix and Metamorphosis', in *Differences, A Journal of Feminist Cultural Studies*, 4.3, p. 176.
31. Anne Friedberg, *Window Shopping: Cinema and the Post-Modern Condition.*

Part Two

Chapter 3

From Abstract Machines to Deleuzian Becomings

Art preserves, and it is the only thing in the world that is preserved. It preserves and is preserved in itself (*quid juris?*), although actually it lasts no longer than its support and materials – stone, canvas, chemical color, and so on (*quid facti?*). The young girl maintains the pose that she has had for five thousand years, a gesture that no longer depends on whoever made it. The air still has the turbulence, the gust of wind, and the light that it had that day last year, and it no longer depends on whoever was breathing it that morning. If art preserves, it does not do so like industry, by adding a substance to make the thing last. The thing became independent of its 'model' from the start, but it is also independent of other possible personae who are themselves artists-things, personae of painting breathing this air of painting.[1]

ABSTRACT MACHINES

Before introducing Chapters 3, 4 and 5 on desire, becoming-woman and sensation, through these three chapters on Deleuze, I want to discuss how Deleuze has been important in reconsidering the very act of thinking and thought itself. His ideas on the complexity of thinking and thought are useful in helping us to rethink some basic beliefs about language and its possibilities. We can then take such ideas forward to rethink the vocabularies of film theory in a post-feminist pragmatic framework.

This first section will look at Deleuze's ideas on thought, and his description of the 'abstract machine', which he sets up as different from structures, such as structural linguistics. I tangentially describe these elements, not as a philosophical debate (this is after all not a book about philosophy as such, more film-philosophy), but to give the reader some way into understanding the complexities of how Deleuze asks us to think about 'the very act of thinking'. Deleuze provides us with a tableau of ideas and new terminologies, which are innovatively exciting, for conceptualising 'thought' in creative ways. Deleuze conceives thought as an effect or process which participates, colludes, or collides with other processes to make up what he refers to as a 'machinic assemblage'. These processes function with other components, for example, time, space, bodies, matter. Thinking in this way takes us out of the idea that language is based in logic and can only be used in specific ways. This then might open up debate to move beyond thinking about the cinematic experience as purely focused in the image, since it might operate in other ways as well. Film functions through an array of components, in what Deleuze calls a 'machinic assemblage'. An 'abstract machine' is neither physical (a literal technological machine) nor corporeal in character, but exists in matter, in 'aparalletic evolution'[2] with other material. What this concept enables is a model of cinematic desires in which corporealised spectators/observers have a capacity for being affected by sensations that have no specific link to a referent. Such models need to be explored as a newly legitimated way of experiencing, as a newly conceived form of cinematic consciousness.

Through Deleuzian ideas we can begin to present an 'aesthetics of sensation', where the cinematic experience is not necessarily one concerned only with verisimilitude, subjectivity or with psychoanalytic configurations of desire, but one involving transversal and perspectival discourses, constructing the bodies of spectators/observers as a collection of disparate, complex and decentred perceptions. Not only can we move away from centred, unitary and disembodied models of vision, but we can move beyond the visual, and theories of subjectivity, into a theory of the cinematic which is 'machinic' in several ways. Why is the term 'machinic' significant to this?

Deleuze argues that the 'abstract machine' is a condition of existence that exceeds what is perceived through language. It functions differently from the conception of semiotics. Unlike the semiotic 'sign', the 'abstract machine' does not function to represent, but rather it constructs a 'reality' of a different order. A 'reality' premised on the material nature of experience. Writers such as Chomsky have considered language and linguistic structures as the main arena through which we can understand the world, reality, and ourselves, within that reality and within culture. However, verbal, literary, structured and organic languages are too static, fixed and immobile. They are too sedimented and not 'abstract' enough to theorise how things connect outside of 'meaning' in a wide range of ways: feelings, connections, and flows, between, across, and within bodies, the gestural and the pathic awareness within those bodies. Those bodies might be human or technological or material, or all three.

But the very term 'body' might also be explained and used differently from its definition as a corporeal body, as we shall see in Deleuze's 'body without organs' concept. Deleuze argues that language is limited to an articulate form of expression. An 'abstract machine', however, has no formal structure, in the way that language has. Thus it makes no distinctions between expression and content. If an abstract machine does not operate through semiotic mechanisms, then how does it function?

The 'abstract machine' functions as a diagrammatic system, as in systems theory, in which systems oppose structures. Similarly, the brain patterns through which perception occurs operate in non-linear dynamic systems. The abstract machine works as amorphous matter, not as a substance with a function. Therefore, we can theorise cinema as an experiential 'abstract machine' by considering how it connects, as a body, of matter, with other bodies and matter, through a consideration of processes of consciousness within which sensation becomes an important element. Because a machinic system works through syntheses and multiplicities, rather than binary ideas as we find in the axiomatics of structuralist thinking, this enables a post-feminist and pragmatic theorisation about the impact of the cinematic experience. This post-feminist and pragmatic theorisation moves away from thinking about subjectivity, identity formations and the purely visual dynamics of pleasure and desire, elements that have framed psychoanalysis and gaze theory for so long.

In theorising about language and ideas, the notion of the 'rhizome' is one of Deleuze's leading figurations. In place of the sign of semiotics, Deleuze's conception of the rhizome enables us to rethink the questions we should engage with as spectators of the cinema. Rather than think only about the sign of the cinematic, or what a film 'means', we can also debate how the film connects across a diverse arena such as the mimetic, the pathic, the gestural, the cognitive, the affective. Cinema operates in non-teleological ways, as process, as movement, immanence, through which newly configured desires are apparent that do not lock us into thinking of 'identity' or 'subjectivity' as anchored by semiotic activity.[3] Because the 'machine' offers different mechanisms of thinking outside the restrictive codings of the 'structures' of semiotics, this enables a micropolitical and pragmatic theory of the cinematic.

Deleuze suggests that it is force and intensity that establish ideas, as opposed to images. Ideas are not necessarily the product of thought. Ideas can exist without thinking. He argues that ideas are like events, lines, that take us into a fibrous web of directions, much like a map or a tuber (in terms of plant formations). Language entails not merely subjects and objects, but a set of variously informed speeds, intensities, energies and matters in molecular fusion. Language may also be visual, as well as written and verbal, and this is specifically significant to a discussion on the machinic materiality of the filmic experience. Deleuze and Guattari express a concern with the differential and evolving rhythms and affective intensities, rather than privileging identities and entities such as species and organisms. Thus the 'identity' of the cinematic might legitimately be set in parallel with a concern with its 'evolution' as a process of affectivities, intensities, rhythms, matter, speeds and movements. As a living system, the 'machine' of cinema needs to be understood in terms of its 'relations' with other machinic configurations, such as viewers. 'If living systems are "machines" then they need to be understood in terms of "relations" and not of component parts.'[4]

This provides an important development from Crary's ideas of the spectator/observer as someone who 'connects' in molecular ways, with the cinematic process, rather than merely 'seeing' the images in a specular way. Deleuze's rhizomatic style foregrounds the affective foundations of the process of thinking. It articulates a new definition of the activity of thought (and philosophy) which might be described as nomadic, and thus suited to a disjuncted 'self'. Thus the classical notion of the 'subject' inherent in metaphysical thought is capable of being considered in ways aside from identity. Consequently, this will have resonances for how we think of gendered subjectivities in filmic representation. No longer are such questions the most important frameworks to think about the cinematic experience. No longer does subjectivity frame the main arguments. If 'identity' is delegitimated in favour of 'movements' and 'intensities', then film theory based upon text as having meaning, in relation to identity and subjectivity, can be expanded through different paradigms.

For Deleuze, ideas are events: lines that point human thought towards new horizons.[5] Similarly, the desires of the cinematic experience, it may be argued, emanate from the affective, rather than identification with subjectivity or identity, sited in the image. Many contemporary thinkers use the idea of the 'affective' as a force capable of liberating us from hegemonic ways of thinking. Affectivity can be said to be the prediscursive.[6] In terms of film, then, a web of connections might be drawn not only from the film-maker's 'intention' and the viewer's reception, but through a wider, more complex set of 'machinic' interconnections.

In his early collaborative text with Claire Parnet, *Dialogues* (1987), Deleuze explains three categories across which we might possibly function as individuals or groups. He suggests we are composed of a series of lines, latitudes, lines of flight. The first line is what he refers to as a line of 'segmentarity'. This can be explained as a rigid, structured or fixed line, or rather a molar line. This is something we use as a foundation or structure to our lives. Elements such as family, class, religion, gender, sexuality are regimes of this line.

Simultaneously, suggests Deleuze, we exist or have lines of molecularisation, or lines of the molecular, which veer away from the strict rigidity of the segmentary line. Lines of molecularisation make detours: they 'sketch out rises and falls; but they are no less precise for all this, they even direct irreversible processes.'[7] There is, finally, the third line, or line of flight, the nomadic line. This line enables a move away from the segmentarity and the evanescence of the molecular into zones of experimentation. It is on this line, Deleuze suggests, that we move away from fixed positionalities. It is also the line of experimentation, excitement, creativity, volition, flight, but also danger and risk, loss and possible annihilation. Truly the line for the artist, the dancer, the thinker. But Deleuze describes the attraction of this line as follows, it is, 'the most complex of all, the most tortuous: it is the line of gravity or velocity, the line of flight and of the greatest gradient . . . this line has something exceedingly mysterious, for, according to him, it is nothing other than the progression of the soul of the dancer'.[8]

I want to take this idea of a tripartite open structure, and the metaphor of the nomadic 'dance', as a figuration for patterning my sections on Deleuze (see Chapters 3, 4 and 5). They will thus take the format of three small chapters. As a choreographed dance and in its heuristic use of philosophy, rather than an internal debate within philosophy, this pattern takes a line of flight away from the stricter, more rational linearity of the rest of the book. Instead, it offers a series of elements to be read aparalletically, in collusion, in machinic assemblage, in synchronisation, but also elements which can be seen as a pathway towards valorising the concept of sensation and the nature of sensation. The aim is to offer a neo-aesthetics of the filmic experience, outside notions of subjectivity and desire. These three lines are immanent to each other, caught up in each other, complicated and connected.

This cartography, or schizoanalysis as it has been referred to, opens up new vistas for reconceptualising processes and forms of the cinematic. As a political defence, the third line of flight is always somehow intrinsically connected to the molar line. Thus there can never be total disengagement with a search for autonomy, for example, in a feminist project. Rather, we should see a new project which seeks to synthesise the engagement of both the molar and the molecular lines of creativity, but not so much a hybridisation, rather an oscillational 'in-between' space, which has no boundary, no positionality. Therefore, whilst Part Two outlines elements of Deleuze's work which will appropriate new dimensions in aesthetics, they will also enable post-feminist, pragmatic conjunctions along the way. Furthermore, these new perspectives in film theory are not intended to negate or displace contemporary film theory which is still premised upon subjectivity, identity and ideology, but to offer other ways of understanding experiences assembled through the cinematic. The pragmatic collides with the political, but in such a way that the aesthetic line is never truly alone, never truly abstract, but functional, providing what Guattari refers to as 'assemblages of enunciation' for a newly framed political encounter.[9] Part Two of the book contains a tripartite and triptychal system: desire and pleasure . . . becoming and affect . . . to sensation . . . the three are never separate and yet they contain an autonomous element in the aparalletic[10] and evolutionary nature of their connections.

DELEUZE ON PLEASURE AND DESIRE

Desire and pleasure, as we have seen in Chapter 2, have been fundamental to psychoanalytic interpretations of the filmic experience, to explanations of subjectivity and identity as they are manifested in the cinematic. One of the main reasons for using the philosophy of Deleuze is that it offers different ways of thinking of desire and pleasure and rethinking the language around those terms. Deleuzian ideas provide ways of moving beyond the concept of desire conceived within psychoanalysis, into other vocabularies. However, it is important to establish at the outset that the terms 'pleasure' and 'desire' are not to be conflated, and indeed Deleuze has different definitions and understanding of these concepts. If we are to discover a different paradigm to explain the experiential elements of the cinematic impact, which is not premised upon transcendent notions of pleasure, as we saw in psychoanalysis, then Deleuzian ideas might be a good starting place.

Whilst 'pleasure' to Deleuze operates outside any notions of a Cartesian 'self' with a beginning in an inorganic state (a primordial death instinct – as we saw in psychoanalysis), it might seem problematic to engage with such ideas to provide new models of filmic pleasures, since, as I have shown, most film theory has been locked into definitions of self, subjectivity, identity and representation.

However, I don't feel this has to be the case and whilst Deleuze's ideas on pleasure need to be carefully thought out, they do ultimately enable a move towards rethinking the experience of the cinematic impact, beyond the idea of pleasure or desire altogether. This is because he is critical of transcendent models of pleasure and subjectivity, and is more concerned with the flux, the movement and the dynamism of immanence, and the processual. Indeed, his ideas proffer different vocabularies with which to rethink the event, the event of the cinematic, as affect, as becoming-woman, as sensation. But before exploring these newer vocabularies, I shall explain how and why his ideas on pleasure have been somewhat problematic, at times almost contradictory, and yet also systematically (openly systematic) creative and volitional.

RETHINKING 'PLEASURE' BEYOND FREUD

In *Dialogues*, Deleuze suggests that when we think of 'desire' that we should not automatically think of 'pleasure'. While agreeing that pleasure is itself an 'agreeable' state that we would obviously wish for, and that 'we move towards it with all our might', he argues that pleasure comes only as an 'interruption in the process of desire'. Rather, pleasure is he suggests, the 'attribution of the *affect*, the affection for a person or subject, it is the only means for a person to "find himself again" in the process of desire which overwhelms him'.[11] Thus, pleasure, for Deleuze, has nothing to do with an ultimate *death instinct* or ultimate desire for finality or closure as Freud exemplifies.

In *Beyond the Pleasure Principle*, Freud explains that repetitious psychical patterns within the human psychic behaviour are primary processes that 'bind' (draw together or coagulate) mobile energy into a constant state situation, which is required for pleasure.[12] Its opposite (notice the binary terminology) is 'unpleasure'. Thus he has postulated that human psychic behaviour is motivated ultimately by what he refers to as the 'pleasure principle'. By this he means that the human psyche is driven towards the state of pleasure, defined as the 'binding' (a drawing together, or a coagulation) of excitations on the ego. The level of excitations effecting the ego determines either pleasure or its opposite, unpleasure. The higher level of 'binding' of the excitations increases the amount of pleasure.

However, Freud suggests that in order to maintain the stability of the ego, to maintain some sense of stable ego formation, the pleasure principle has to be offset by a 'reality principle', an acceptance of the real, material and economic conditions of our existence in a social, cultural and psychological experience. This is required as a balance to the 'pleasure principle'. Consequently, 'pleasure' becomes relegated to the arena of wish-fulfilment. It is also bound up with a desire to return to an inorganic state, before birth, a moment of inorganic, and primordial, being. Freud relates this desire as the 'death instinct', or Thanatos. Its opposite is the life force, or Eros. Eros, or the 'life drive', serves to restore the primal unity of the inorganic state – to rediscover a lost unity.[13] In Freud's discussion of our need for repetition, or compulsion behaviour – by which we strive to repeat patterns of behaviour and to repress specifically sexual forms of behaviour – is caused by the organism's needs to go back to that ontological state of being, to an original sense of plenitude. That is, that inanimate state in death. Here, there is a final location for the human organism in its sentient being of oneness in Death; an ultimate ontological notion of a finite locus for the self/ego. Ultimately, Freud suggests, the desire to return to an inorganic state of being is what 'drives' the human organism, in terms of its psychic processes.

As Freud suggests (and he does not say these ideas are incontestable) 'a drive is a desire to return to an original state'. But the main point about this description of the basis of pleasure is that it ties pleasure into the realm of transcendence, a subjectivity that is located within a transcendent subject. It is a transcendent understanding of pleasure. By this I mean it assumes there is a final moment of being (equated with death) which is attainable, and thus pleasure is located within a transcendent formula. However, Deleuze's ideas on both pleasure and desire, and his move beyond these concepts to becoming and sensation, enable a move away from thinking through transcendent perspectives, and so enable different explanations of an aesthetic process. Film theory can benefit from such new vocabularies.

In *Difference and Repetition* (1994), Deleuze discusses, instead, what he refers to as the 'Three Syntheses of Beyond the Pleasure Principle', in response to Freud. To Deleuze, the ultimate 'beyond' of the pleasure principle is not Death, as a transcendent state of Oneness, as Freud poses it to be. Rather, Deleuze's definition of the 'beyond' of pleasure is one which determines no material, fixed or ontological state as such; rather, the beyond is simply a 'principle'. He argues that the problem with Freud's *Beyond the Pleasure Principle* is the concept of the 'death instinct'. This serves in Freud as a positive, originary explanation for the human need to repeat. Thus, its role in Freud has a transcendent function. Deleuze argues that pleasure cannot be connected to this death instinct, since death has nothing to do with a material model. There *is* no first term which can be repeated; there is no original state of being. The 'beyond' in a Deleuzian sense refers to a much more complex concern with repetition and difference. He suggests that whether pleasure is itself effected by a contraction or a relaxation, as Freud states, is not really the issue. He suggests that elements of pleasure may in fact be found in the succession of relaxations and contractions, in the sense that Freud suggests, produced by excitations. But Deleuze argues, it is actually a different question altogether to say why pleasure is not simply an element within our psychic life, but is rather a 'principle'. In other words, we do not simply receive, or attain pleasure, by returning, as Freud suggested, to an originary lost 'beyond', but by acceding to the beyond of the 'death instinct' through materiality and notions of habitual matter. Those notions of habitual matter are located within the differential relations and singularities prior to any subjectivity, as I shall explain in the following chapter.

Deleuze argues that, as humans, we are a collection of sensory and material elements. We are simply organically composed of matter, air and water and it is the repetition of different elements of our sensory-motor states which brings about pleasure, through a material emotion of the contemplation of those states 'Pleasure is a principle in so far as it is the emotion of a fulfilling contemplation which contracts in itself cases of relaxation *and* contraction.'[14]

Deleuze posits the concept of 'repetition' as a form of displacement, and disguise, as functioning as the ground of pleasure. Not a repetition in the sense of the repeating of an original state, but a repetition *in* difference. Drives, in other words, which Freud explains are 'bound excitation', according to Deleuze are accommodated through 'differenciated' forms of material elements, molecular elements of our make-up. We are simply made up from organic syntheses, which are like the sensibility of the senses. According to Deleuze, 'We are made of contracted water, light, earth, and air – not merely prior to the recognition or representation of these, but prior to their being sensed. Every organism, in its receptive and perceptual elements, but also in its viscera, is a sum of contractions, of retentions and expectations'[15] – a vital sensibility.

In his 'Three Syntheses of Beyond the Pleasure Principle', Deleuze appears to negate the fundamental and sentient ontological being of 'pleasure' as it pertains to an instinctual state within consciousness, where unbound excitations are 'delimited' to the opposite, 'unpleasure', where excitations are less bound. If Deleuze's philosophy of anti-humanism and anti-Platonic thought *is* a rejection of Freud's notion of 'pleasure' as located in a fixed transcendental locus, then there appear to be some contradictions which need to be examined.

I want to establish four points of discussion on this, which might appear to be an internal philosophical debate. This is not meant to take the argument into the bounds of philosophy, in the pure sense of the word, but it is important to follow the reasoning to understand how and why *sensation* becomes a more appropriate concept than pleasure. This will then enable different vocabularies and methodologies of enquiry into the impact, or the event of the cinematic engagement, outside notions premised upon subjectivity and psychoanalysis.

First, if Deleuzian philosophy is premised upon anti-humanism and a rejection of the concept of an essential organism, which originally has Eros and Thanatos connected through the death drive, one could ask why he therefore proclaims that 'Doubtless all desiring-production is, in and of itself, immediately consumption and consummation, and therefore, "sensual pleasure".'[16] What, we might ask, does he mean by sensual pleasure? It seems that there is after all some concern with the senses, with *feeling*. Why does he use the word 'sensual' when it has such Freudian determinates? Indeed, Freud states that the senses arise where a highly developed organism, the highly receptive cortical layer, has been withdrawn into the depths of the interior body, with only a portion left at the surface. These are the 'sense' organs. Senses and sensuality are certain specific effects of stimulation or 'feelers'.[17]

However, Deleuze's perception of pleasure is one innately bound to the materiality of the organism, felt at a level beyond any subjective sense of self, beyond traditional conceptions of subjectivity. It is rather felt at a pre-subjective level within an existential integrity, a concept which I explore in the following chapter. In tracing his understanding of sensation, I shall be distinguishing how affect and becoming trace a path away from pleasure and desire, towards sensation. Sensation might therefore be a more appropriate term to follow, in relation to the cinematic impact.

Second, Deleuze argues that 'A genuine consummation is achieved by the new machine [that is, the process of desire as production, not as lack or negativity], a pleasure that can rightly be called autoerotic, or rather automatic: the nuptial celebration of a new alliance, a new birth, a radiant ecstasy, as though the eroticism of the machine liberated other unlimited forces.'[18] This autoeroticism is experienced via intensive states, what he later refers to as 'haecceities' and not 'subjectivities'. He refers to this as an intense feeling of *transition*: 'There is a schizophrenic experience of intensive quantities in their pure state, to the point that is almost unbearable – a celibate misery and glory experienced to the fullest, like a cry suspended between life and death, an intense feeling of transition, states of pure, naked intensity stripped of all shape and form.'[19] There is no static final positionality, as we see in psychoanalysis.

Third, in exploring Deleuze's definition of 'feeling' I want to refer to his description of intensive states, which he discusses in *Anti-Oedipus*. He describes these states as 'hallucinations' and 'delirium'. 'These are often described as hallucinations and delirium, but the basic phenomenon of hallucination (*I see, I hear*) and the basic phenomenon of delirium (*I think . . .*) presupposes an *I feel* at an even deeper level, which gives hallucinations their object and thought delirium its content – an "I feel that I am becoming a woman", "that I am becoming a god", and so on.'[20] Thus, there is an acknowledgement of 'feeling'. Deleuze, as we see, refers to this 'feeling' as a state existing at a fundamentally deeper level. He even refers to this state as 'I feel that I am becoming-woman'. This is a crucial line from Deleuze which I shall later frame as part of my move towards a materialist aesthetic. I later explore how 'becoming-woman' might be used as a term to express the beyond of subjectivity, through affect towards sensation.

In talking of the eroticism of the machine, Deleuze appears to be acknowledging the presence of Eros as a life force, which, he says, liberates other forces, based upon 'feelings' at a deeper level. That 'deeper' level then may exist, not as a fixed place of plenitude, and being, or fulfilment as in psychoanalysis, but a place which is immanent, contingent, in movement and flux, not in fixity or finality. He suggests that this 'I FEEL' is only secondary to the really primary concept of emotion. This emotion is experienced across the machine of desire. So, whilst I am not entirely dispelling Deleuzian negation of finitude and transcendence as found in Freud, nonetheless, I am suggesting that there is some concern with sensuality, and the senses, and 'feeling' which provides a way forward to think beyond the subjective, into a definition of feeling as a material state, as I later exemplify.

Fourth, Deleuze is critical of Freud's ideas about the death instinct. However, Deleuze's understanding of the 'beyond', whilst rendering the subject otiose, and the notion of the death instinct as a transcendent state of the subject, nonetheless might be problematic. Deleuze's understanding of 'beyond' attests to an ontological state of 'being' in the 'habitus' and, as I stated earlier, in 'repetition'. This aesthetic, however, is reappropriated in Deleuze through the sovereign state of an aesthetic of *sensation*. Sensation then is the 'beyond' of the pleasure principle, rather than the death instinct. How sensation works is later explored in Chapter 5. As such, 'sensation', unlike pleasure, or desire, does not need any satiety or satiation. Thus, pleasure is replaced, Deleuze articulates, by a 'materiality of emotion' through sensation. The materiality of emotion is theorised through the following stages of the chapters: in affect and becoming-woman. Deleuze refers to the experience of autoeroticism as a pleasure felt within the materiality of a pre-subjective state. This autoeroticism is experienced via intensive qualities, or what he calls 'haecceities', not 'subjectivities'. The desiring machine, as Deleuze postulates in *Anti-Oedipus*, is material, not personological. He thus replaces 'pleasure' felt by any desiring subject, with a material emotion, a flux of forces and intensities, not felt by any subjectivity. This is not pleasure 'felt' by any desiring subject, but a range of forces oscillating and circulating. The circle of that range of forces completely abandons the ego/self. Deleuze argues in *Anti-Oedipus* that the emotions as such are experienced through a plane of intensities, on a plane of immanence, where pleasure is not 'felt' by any subject. Rather, a range of forces, oscillating in a circular framework produces an 'affect'. Here, Deleuze refers us to Klossowski:

> The centrifugal forces do not flee the centre forever, but approach it once again, only to retreat from it yet again: such is the nature of the violent oscillations that overwhelm an individual so long as he seeks only his own centre and is incapable of seeing the circle of which he himself is a part: for if these oscillations overwhelm him, it is because each one of them corresponds to an individual other than the one he believes himself to be, from the point of view of the unlocatable centre. As a result, an identity is essentially fortuitous, and a series of individualities must be undergone by each of these oscillations, so that as a consequence the fortuitousness of this or that particular individuality will render all of them necessary.[21]

Deleuze continues with,

> The subject spreads itself out along the entire circumference of the circle, the centre of which has been abandoned by the ego. At the centre is the desiring-machine, the celibate machine of the Eternal Return.[22]

Consequently, it might seem that the concept of 'pleasure' to some extent becomes less of an issue, in theorising the experiential elements of the cinematic. But desire, as Deleuze explores it, also has its role in offering different paradigms of subjectivity or the subject, from Freud and Lacan.

RETHINKING DESIRE, THROUGH DELEUZE

Deleuzian ideas about desire lead towards affect, sensation and a new concern with the body, but in a totally different way than we saw in phenomenological accounts of the body, used by Sobchack or Crary in their work. Deleuze is critical of the Freudian psychoanalytic configurations of desire, arguing that psychoanalysis 'talks a lot about the unconscious – it even discovered it. But in practice, it always diminishes, destroys and exorcises it. The unconscious is understood as negative, it's the enemy.'[23] He argues that what psychoanalysis calls production or formation of the unconscious are 'failures, conflicts, compromises, puns. In the case of desires, there are always too many for psychoanalysis.'[24] Psychoanalysis is replete, he argues, with 'lack', 'culture' and 'Law', and he suggests that metaphor and metonymy signify within psychoanalysis a narrative which is confined to an explanation for behaviours. This narrative always has its origins in the Oedipal scenario, in Oedipal myths and familial stories. He is thus critical of psychoanalysis in its inherent abyssal and negative connotations, failures, conflicts, compromises, and he is scathing of its exploration of sexual behaviours as somehow the outcome of pre-Oedipal scenarios of plenitude and fulfilment, satisfaction and internal drives. Instead, he argues, the unconscious is something which can be produced. Whilst of course in Freud and Lacan the unconscious is also 'produced', the nature of this production and what it contains are problematic. That is, it is only understood in terms of Oedipal structures. In Deleuze, the unconscious is not a metonymnic 'text' or a 'narrative' with specific signifieds, or referents, but is a 'production', a vitalist, and dynamic process of forces and intensities. 'The unconscious is a substance to be manufactured, to get flowing – a social and political space to be conquered. There is no subject of desire, any more than there is an object. There is no subject of enunciation. Fluxes are the only objectivity of desire itself.'[25]

If this is the case, then, there is much purchase from Deleuzian ideas of production for the aesthetics of film theory. The idea of a productive, positive and aleatory concept of desire enables a move away from the negative and abyssal psychoanalytical versions of pleasure and desire, and their relevance to construction of subjectivity. It enables different vocabularies of the filmic experience to be opened up, since it brings into focus the idea that cinema works as a rhythmical, processual and moving form; that we need not necessarily relate to it through a *subjectivity*, nor that we should have a subjectivity that is formulated through it. Subjectivity and the aesthetic process, or event, might instead be problematised and rethought, something which is also happening as I explained within a post-feminist pragmatics. Deleuzian ideas also enable thinking of the ontological nature of film itself as a 'body' which moves in connection with other bodies. But that definition of bodies is further expanded in Deleuze, offering a closeness in relation to a post-feminist pragmatics which seeks to undermine the binary of mind/body. Rhythm, process and non-fixity thus provide different lines of enquiry into the impact of cinema.

Deleuzian ideas on desire enable us to critique subjectivity and the role of the subject in the visual engagement with the screen. He argues that there is no subject of desire, any more than there is an 'object' as we see in psychoanalysis. There is no subject which enunciates, or originates, the narrative. Rather desire is an 'effectuation'; that is, something which is transiently in process, as opposed to a satisfaction. In other words, desire is something in continuum, in movement, in process, with no final satisfaction in endings. As we saw in psychoanalysis, desire was always tied up with Freudian ideas of final inorganic resolutions, in the death instinct. This created a transcendent notion of desire, rather than an immanent notion. Desire, suggests Deleuze, lies outside the coordinates of persons, subjects and objects. Rather it is seen as a process that is articulated on what he refers to as a 'plane of immanence' or a 'plane of consistency' criss-crossed by fluxes and particles which break free from subjects and objects. For the purposes of this chapter I shall define that the term 'immanence' is used in contrast with transcendence. This is a simplistic and residual explanation and is not an extensive definition which we might find in philosophy per se. But the term immanence is located within Deleuzian ideas of desire and becoming. Deleuze argues, as we have seen, against any psychoanalytic frameworks of desire. He argues that psychoanalysis is premised in Freudian notions of desire, emanating from the need to return to a lost state of plenitude, a finite sense of oneness in death. This is a transcendent model of desire, where there is a constant wish to repeat and a compulsion to move beyond death to this transcendent state. Alternatively Deleuzian debate proclaims that desire is processual, immanent, productive and energic, and has nothing to do with forces of transcendence, or a return to a lost plenitude, through death. Desire is rather aleatory, processual and constitutive of joy. Desire is produced, it does not emanate from lack. It is *immanent*. It is energic, and dynamic joy lies in its immanence, a continual process of contemplative and productive forces, 'Desire is therefore not internal to a subject, any more than it tends towards an object: it is strictly immanent to a plane which it does not pre-exist, to a plane which must be constructed, where particles are emitted and fluxes combine.'[26]

This idea of a 'plane of immanence' becomes crucial to Deleuzian ideas on the beyond of desire, through sensation. Alongside the 'plane of immanence' Deleuze posits a 'plane of organisation' (a molar line) consisting of forms, the formation of subject, object, themes, motifs, personages, structures, the Law, the State, on a structural and genetic plane. Deleuze refers to this as the 'molar' plane.[27] Such a plane is a structured, transcendent plane, a design which when deconstructed is shown to be bound up with myths of origination, finality and psychic structures of subjectivity. Immanence, what Deleuze also refers to as 'becoming', is of an entirely different nature. The plane of immanence, or becoming, 'is a question not of organisation but of composition; not of development or differentiation but of movement and rest, speed and slowness. It is a question of elements and particles.'[28]

Molecularity, matter, particles and even fibres become more pertinent to mechanisms of desire than the molar plane of psychoanalysis. It has nothing to do with 'subjectivities' but exists through 'movement, process, rhythm, forces'. The plane of immanence is replete with haecceity. 'Hecceities are simply degrees of power which combine, to which correspond a power to affect and be affected, active or passive affects, intensities.'[29] This paradigm is a different framework from psychoanalysis. Rather than Oedipal or Oedipalised notions such as the structures of school, nation, family, church, state and self, Deleuze prefers to talk about deterritorialised or molecular planes of fluxes or flows, machines rather than structures 'the flows that have not been reduced to Oedipal codes and neuroticised territorialities, the desiring-machines that escape such codes as "lines of escape" (flight, velocity) leading elsewhere'.[30]

Here, there are no forms, no subject, but there are individuations, without subjectivity. Nothing becomes subjective, but there are non-subjective powers of affect. A plane of immanence is thus defined through lines of flow, lines of longitude and latitude, and replaces the theatre of the subject, the point, the origin, the organism. Here, the line of velocity, becoming and intensity replaces the 'drives' and the 'pulsions' of Freudian/Lacanian scenarios which are embedded in lack, negativity and the teleology of the Oedipal drama. The teleological characteristics of psychoanalysis are set alongside an immanence through which desire is produced. Deleuze suggests that this plane of immanence or 'becoming' is replete with 'speed and slowness, floating affects, so that the plane itself is perceived at the same time as it allows us to perceive the imperceptible (the microplane, the molecular plane)'.[31]

This is the crucial element in terms of 'becoming'. It is this concept of 'affect', dislocated from its Freudian and psychoanalytic connotations of the 'release of psychic energies which effects emotional states' and connected, rather, with emotion and *sensation* rather than the organism's pleasure, which becomes central to this project. The foundations of Deleuze's concept of 'affect' comes from both Bergsonian and Spinozist legacies, and are located within the 'material' configurations of energy and matter, not in psychic formations. A materialist aesthetic might be premised on such foundations. It is nonetheless constitutive of an aesthetic emotion, but one premised in sensation. Sensation, and my use of this term in the book in relation to the cinematic engagement, is premised on Deleuzian ideas of affect, movement and intensity, as I explore in the proceeding chapters.

Already we can determine, then, a useful set of ideas which will address those issues earlier problematised in Chapter 2: binary thinking, desire, pleasure, subjectivity, notions of the body and rethinking the aesthetic. These new ideas enable a breakdown of the binary categorisations in which psychoanalysis framed desire and simultaneously considers a material aesthetic premised upon molecularity, and matter, an assemblage of machinic connections. This therefore opens up experimental ways of dealing with the aesthetics of film. Deleuze continues that if it is not the Oedipal scenario which is the problem, psychoanalysis is still rife with concepts of castration (a term which in film theory has been utilised to explain certain images of women, such as the femme fatale in film noir) and the death drives, and how they are connected with pleasure and desire. Psychoanalysis merely reduces sexuality to myths, argues Deleuze. Any concern with the affects of the screen thus needs to engage with forces beyond the represented image on the screen. Deleuze's *Logique de la sensation* takes up this argument. A philosophy of expression offers instead a new aesthetic paradigm, an aesthetic experience which, to quote Pessoa, is a 'dynamogenic' experience. By this he means that the experience of the filmic encounter is an absolute continuum of depersonalisation, where the cogito (I think) becomes a sentio (I feel).[32] Deleuze argues in *Logique de la sensation* that we cannot separate the two. All the aesthetic practices, including I would suggest cinema, participate in a common activity – of force and sensation. Sensation becomes a more appropriate word than either desire or pleasure, since it enables a consideration of the beyond of psychic structures found within psychoanalysis. This presents a logic of sensation which is not fixated in any death instinct, but a realm of pure force, movement and becoming. A total denial of Freud's pleasure principle.

Deleuze's ideas on desire enable a move into theories which further distanciate the subject and subjectivity. Instead, subjectivity becomes subsumed by an occurring process of difference and repetition beyond subjectivity, through affect and becoming and sensation, into what Deleuze refers to as haecceities. Such language offers a whole new paradigm through which to discuss, think about, articulate, connect and experience the aesthetics of the filmic, a paradigm which moves away from psychoanalytic descriptions of desire and beyond the phenomenological explanations we saw in Sobchack, to more contemporary philosophical trajectories – film-philosophy. This enables a re-engagement with film as an art process, as much as it is an ideological formation, bringing back the political through the aesthetic; a revalorisation of the aesthetic in a post-structuralist age. I want to explore, in Chapter 4, how Deleuze takes us from subjectivity, moving beyond subjectivity, subsuming subjectivity through the thinking of affect and becoming-woman, and beyond into sensation.

NOTES

1. Gilles Deleuze and Félix Guattari, *What is Philosophy?*, p. 163.
2. See Chapter 1, note 23, for an explanation of the term 'aparalletic evolution'.
3. Semiotics, here, is being interpreted as a theory of meaning of the sign.
4. Keith Ansell Pearson, *Viroid Life: Perspectives on Nietzsche and the Transhuman Condition*, p. 140.
5. Rosi Braidotti, *Nomadic Subjects: Embodiment and Sexual Difference in Contemporary Feminist Theory*, p. 101.
6. See discussion of affect in Chapter 4.
7. Deleuze and Parnet, *Dialogues*, p. 124.
8. Deleuze and Parnet, *Dialogues*, p. 125.
9. Guattari, *Chaosmosis*, p. 26.
10. Again, see Chapter 1, note 23, on 'aparalletic evolution'.
11. Deleuze and Parnet, *Dialogues*, p. 99.
12. Freud, *Beyond the Pleasure Principle*, in *The Standard Edition*, p. 3.
13. Brooks, *Freud's Master Plot*, pp. 290–1.
14. Deleuze, *Difference and Repetition*, p. 74.
15. Deleuze, *Difference and Repetition*, p. 74.
16. Deleuze and Guattari, *Anti-Oedipus*, p. 16.
17. Freud, *Beyond the Pleasure Principle*, in *The Standard Edition*, p. 22.
18. Deleuze and Guattari, *Anti-Oedipus*, p. 18.
19. Deleuze and Guattari, *Anti-Oedipus*, p. 18.
20. Deleuze and Guattari, *Anti-Oedipus*, p. 18.
21. See Pierre Klossowski, *Nietzsche et le circle vicieux*.
22. Deleuze and Guattari, *Anti-Oedipus*, p. 21.
23. Deleuze and Parnet, *Dialogues*, p. 77.
24. Deleuze and Parnet, *Dialogues*, p. 77.
25. Deleuze and Parnet, *Dialogues*, p. 78.
26. Deleuze and Parnet, *Dialogues*, p. 89.
27. Deleuze and Parnet, *Dialogues*, p. 128.
28. Deleuze and Guattari, *A Thousand Plateaus*, p. 255.
29. Deleuze and Parnet, *Dialogues*, p. 92.
30. Deleuze and Guattari, introduction, *Anti Oedipus*, p. xvii.
31. Deleuze and Guattari, *A Thousand Plateaus*, p. 267.
32. F. Pessoa, *A Centenary Pessoa*, quoted in Brian Massumi, 'Deleuze, Guattari and the Philosophy of Expression', in *Canadian Review of Comparative Literature*, p. 23.

Chapter 4

Constituting Bodies –
from Subjectivity and Affect
to the Becoming-woman of the Cinematic

This chapter expands upon the notion that the aesthetic experience of the cinematic encounter is felt at a level beyond that of the 'subjective', beyond a subjectivity constructed within the psychic scenarios of cine-psychoanalysis. I shall outline and explore Deleuze's concept of becoming-woman and how this is connected to the concept of affectivity and sensation. This chapter then explores how subjectivity, mind/brain and body become imbricated in the process of the cinematic encounter; how the impact of the cinematic encounter operates through the 'beyond' of subjectivity. This encounter is felt within the realms of the pre-personal, the autopoietic realms of a material state, where affect and intensity take us into a processual immanence, the 'becoming-woman' of the cinematic.

Taking a lead from a contemporary writer, Edward Wilson,[1] there is, I believe, a possible consilience across the arts and sciences, provided by plateaus of philosophical engagements. In their final collaborative text, *What is Philosophy?*, Deleuze and Guattari write that science, art and philosophy as forms of thought or creation have the brain as the junction of all three. This consilience might provide a contemporary way forward in moving beyond the boundaries of subjectivity, locked as it has been into the machinations of sociological or psychoanalytic mechanisms. The boundary that has traditionally separated the natural sciences from the humanities and social sciences needs to be rethought. A new conception of materialism, and a new concern with *matter* as it functions within the production of an emergent, pre-personal state, might help us to move into more creative considerations beyond subjectivity, into subjectless subjectivities. As I argued in my introductory chapter, new collective assemblages of enunciation are needed across the arts, sciences and philosophy, in a neo-millennial culture, a rethinking of some lost and forgotten aesthetics, but positioned in a new engagement with *post* post-structuralist thinking. In a new-world disorder that finds no answers to famine, ecological disasters, political stasis and a productivist economy, where, asks Guattari, is the potential for a re-enchantment of an aesthetic which might create a new sense of being and harmony in the world?[2]

If we cannot conceive of solutions in a macro-political sense, maybe there is a micro-political way which through a mutation of mentalities might promote a new sense of being in the world, through a neo-aesthetics? From Appollonian law to Dionysian spirit, the line between the two domains of science and art can easily be crossed back and forth. And so it is with Nietzschean[3] resonations that we can begin to work towards an integrational bio-aesthetics, through Deleuze, a bio-aesthetics which commingles the material world with the aesthetics of film theory. A 'becoming-woman' of the cinematic crosses the material nature of the 'affect' towards sensation, in enabling a reconsideration of film as material encounter, body, event, a 'haecceity' and not merely a 'representation'. Indeed, there is no representation of one world, but only the multiple worlds our brains achieve.[4]

To trace the thinking of affect, becoming and sensation, I look briefly and only tangentially at the influence of Nietzsche on Deleuze. What follows provides a tangential discussion of some philosophical terms to enable a new vocabulary for film-philosophy.

FROM NIETZSCHEAN ORIGINATIONS

[A]rt excites an affectivity or what Nietzsche calls a 'will to power' which maintains the desire to overcome the organism and unfold subjectivity in material expression.[5]

I begin with this quotation because it contextualises what is the essential core of this project: the subsuming of subjectivity, beyond any sense of desire premised within the organism, but rather beyond that in material expression. Nietzschean resonances are replete within Deleuze's work, and frame the origins of my own ideas on the beyond of affect, and becoming-woman. How then does Nietzsche have a relevance to these ideas?

Following Schopenhaurian influence, Nietzsche was concerned with the irrational and the subconscious as the source of human motivation. His anti-metaphysical claims are concerned with what cannot be expressed through language. His work provides instead a belief in the 'reality' and the sheer physicality of *natural* existence, a belief in the profundity of the natural and a belief in the sheer contingency of the natural. Thus, for him there is no state of *transcendence*, to which we all aspire. Rather, there is only the sheer transience of time and the natural forces of nature; for 'there is no transcendent order or form to the world, no law governing nature; there is no total system or any divine teleological pattern guiding activity'.[6] Only diversity and difference within the natural world. There is no wholeness or unity but a totality of different energies and forces. There is no other 'place' to which we can aspire. Belief in such metaphysical Being has only served to prevent humankind from accepting the sheer brutality, pain and transience of the 'real'.

Within our 'real' experiences, however, Nietzsche has proffered an acceptance of the sheer vitality, force, movement and dynamic of 'becoming'. All we can ever experience in life is the vitality, force and movement of transient existence, a belief in the sheer natural force of existence, and an acceptance of the 'cruelty'[7] of life's intransigence. This primordial sense of what *it is* to just be in the world has an important resonance for understanding how 'becoming' is used as a phrase to articulate the 'forces' of 'life' as opposed to the power of language. It is this concern with 'life' and the non-linguistic force of reality which are fundamental to an understanding of the concept of *becoming*.

Indeed Nietzsche suggests, as does Deleuze (we saw earlier how Deleuze refers to the abstract machine as opposed to structural linguistics), that language is too inarticulate to explain the sheer vibrance, force, intensity and creativity of life. Language distorts because of the way in which it is inextricably tied to metaphysics and presence. In Nietzsche's view, 'language and the judgements we form from language actually falsify life, whether by simplifying the complexity of living processes or by distorting and overlooking the unique character of our experiences.'[8] It transforms what are really unique experiences for us as individuals, into universal characteristics. It cannot capture the uniqueness and speciality of experience. Language does not express the sheer flux, instability and profundity of life's ineluctable chaos because it structures the world as stasis. Words can only be used to explain, in restricted logic-based formats, universally shared perceptions, and not the individual experience or encounter. What is really important in Nietzsche's scheme of things are the senses.

Linguistic means then are not sufficient to explain 'becoming'. Language, and specifically the way it is used in grammatical structures, organised by subject and predicate, explains experience through a notion of subjectivity, originating from a subject. Such thinking presupposes an agent, as *subject* of an action, some sense of '*subjectivity*' with an intentional consciousness. Language operates in a fixed grammatical form and does not allow for an understanding of the creativity of experience. Nietzsche wants to eradicate a belief in language, and to acknowledge that there is something more primordial beyond any sense of a natural or human self. Indeed, these are products of metaphysics. According to Houlgate, there is, for Nietzsche, 'no substantial being or essence beyond our reach: "the world that we have cannot be reduced to our being, our logic and our psychological prejudices, it does not exist as a world 'in itself': it is essentially a world of relationships . . . its being is essentially different at every point"'.[9]

The concept of 'becoming' is what exists as the 'real' for Nietzsche: sometimes referred to as multiplicity, change, world, life, or flux, 'becoming' exemplifies a continuum, a constant process of movement and changing volatilities and dynamisms. 'Becoming is restless primordial indetermination.' The concept of 'becoming', then, equates with a worldly, biological life. Nietzschean criticism of language and consciousness rests on intuition, sensation and feeling. 'In *On Truth and Lie in the Extra-Moral Sense*, for example, Nietzsche states that the free mind is now "guided by intuitions rather than by concepts": in passages from the Nachlass he exposes what he sees as the falseness of our conscious experience of "things" by comparing that experience directly with the formless, unformulable world of the chaos of sensations or with the "medley of sensations".'[10] Language and the intellect then are set aside in favour of the 'felt', the unformed, feeling, intuition and sensation. He believes that we can experience life at a pre-linguistic and primordial level, before language – outside of language. As Nietzsche explores in *Daybreak* and *Twilight of the Idols*,[11] this primordial level is a 'world of unworded experiences' or a 'pre-linguistic insight into life', and it is the senses through which this experience or 'becoming' is articulated. Thus, 'becoming', or 'transience', implies that sensation reveals the nature of reality in a purer way than the reflective and rational consciousness and language.[12] This world of 'becoming' is predicated upon the sensual, through the body. The body is, then, effectively a much richer arena of experience than consciousness/mind. This body, however, is not fixed in any singular identity. There is according to Nietzsche no fixed identity or form to the concept of 'body'. All we are is body, a multiplicity of changing desires, sensations, instincts, some purely physical, some sublimated. He believes that such forces operate through a multiplicity of 'selves' and 'many mortal souls' as opposed to the soul of the transcendent Being. Rather than transcendence, 'becoming' is expressed through a sense of '*immanence*' or a processual continuum of movement and flux. Consciousness and language are transfixed in a world of Being and transcendence. 'Becoming' is, by comparison, a process of *immanence*.

DELEUZIAN 'BECOMINGS' . . . THE PROCESS OF DESIRE

In exploring the concept of 'becoming', it will be necessary to try to understand some challenging philosophical ideas in Deleuze's work regarding 'subjectivities'. This section is not meant to be a philosophical debate, per se, but is required to enable a new understanding of affect, and how that understanding of affect might lie outside psychical structures.

The concept of 'becoming' is one of the most significant elements of Deleuze's work. It is connected to his aim of imaging the process of thought in different ways. His notion of 'becoming' is, like Nietzsche's, profoundly anti-Hegelian and anti-metaphysical. Thus, fixed identity and teleological order are replaced by a flux of multiple 'becomings'. The concept of 'becoming' in Deleuze's work operates somewhat differently from a Nietzschean perspective, though it has its origins in Nietzschean ideas. Deleuze's perception of desire, as we have seen in Chapter 3, is not one premised upon the psychoanalytic *subject* of desire. Rather, it is premised upon the processuality of the *affective* forces of materiality, a materiality of bodies in assemblage with each other, as molecular forces in coagulation. To Deleuze, 'becomings' are the process of desire, and the term 'becoming' cannot be explained as purely natural or biological. Deleuze suggests rather that 'becomings are molecular'. 'Becomings' are seen as 'affects' and it is the subsuming of subjectivity through the notion of a *material affect* that is central to a neo-aesthetics of the cinematic. Deleuze states:

> [A]ll becomings are already molecular. That is because becoming is not to imitate or identify with something or someone. Nor is it to proportion formal relations. Neither of these two figures of analogy is applicable to becoming: neither the imitation of a subject nor the proportionality of a form. Starting from the forms one has, the subject one is, the organs one has, or the functions one fulfills, becoming is to extract particles between which one establishes the relations of movement and rest, speed and slowness that are *closest* to what one is becoming, and through which one becomes. This is the sense in which becoming is the process of desire . . . Becoming is to emit particles that take on certain relations of movement and rest because they enter into a particular zone of proximity.[13]

> Yes, all becomings are molecular: the animal, flower, or stone one becomes are molecular collectivities, haecceities, not molar subjects, objects, or form that we know from the outside and recognize from experience, through science or by habit.[14]

How can we begin to explain the concept of the *molecular*, and the idea that subjectivity is subsumed through a materiality within the molecular?

This discussion will be based upon an analysis of a pre-personal level of experience, within a proto-subjectivity, and a realm of autoconsistency, before and beyond the 'subject' of structural linguistics or psychoanalysis. This therefore redefines the subjectivity which is part of phenomenology or psychoanalysis. Within Deleuze's work, subjectivities are part of a pre-personal state, existing outside any sense of self, and are multiplicitous. Like Guattari, Deleuze posits the existence of proto-subjectivities as a realm of autoconsistency, before and beyond any 'subject'. Rather, there exists what Deleuze calls an autopoietic state of being, before the social and cultural world of language structures, and before an emergent sense of a psychic self. The term autopoietic is used to define a state of autopoiesis or 'self-enjoyment', and comes out of Deleuze's ideas of the pre-personal where there exist what he refers to as absolute inter-iorities. This pre-personal exists as a kind of field of different forces or intensities, what C. Colwell refers to as wills to power, 'that resonate with one another, that interact in ways that produce effects on one another. Sexual drives, the surfaces of bodies, aggression, one's internal organs, emotions, experiences, sensations are all prepersonal.'[15] The pre-personal then is that which contracts a habit and is therefore a form of repetition. But these pre-personals are not experienced or 'had' by a Self, a subject or a person, but are instead constitutive of the self. The pre-personal remains an impersonal state. Pre-personal is often referred to as singularity in Deleuze. Singularities are points that produce effects of transition. The ways a painting affects us individually, for example. 'The difference in the ways that Cézanne's or Duchamps's works affect us depend not on their abilities to capture different extensive orders of reality (as would a Platonic form) but on the intensity by which they affect our sensibil-ities.'[16] Both Deleuze and Guattari suggest that there is a sense of inert 'aliveness' associated with this emergent state of being, which is felt through the materiality and molecularity of its material being, in and of itself. This emergent self is atmospheric, pathic, fusional and transitivist, ignoring any positionality of subject or object, masculine or feminine, and certainly it has no truck with Oedipal or matrixial configurations.[17] Whilst Deleuze has obfuscated the sense of subjectivity as fixed or formulated within psychic structures, nonetheless his proposal of a schizoanalytic subjectivity supposes that there is a range of strata of subjectivation which exist in a multicomponential format. This is differ-ent from that proposed by the conscious–unconscious mechanisms of Freudian psychoanalysis. But Deleuze's ideas do not actually reject individuation as such, but suggest that 'subjectivities' are formulated, produced at an earlier stage than any self, through pre-verbal intensities.

These pre-verbal intensities are called 'pathic events', or prehensive events. Rather than a unity, as in a phenomenological or Cartesian sense, these events operate as a 'multiplicity'. This notion of events occurring on multiple strata explains how experiences can occur through feeling, empathy, affective and pathic awarenesses rather than logical thought or discursive schema such as psychoanalysis. In other words, some things can only be 'felt' at a deeper level of the proto-subjective. This concept of a multiplicity is further defined by its qualitative components. Multiplicities are 'qualitative', rather than quantitative. Duration, movement and process are intrinsic to this qualitative sense of multiplicity. A *qualitative multiplicity* is therefore not an average of numerical parts, but is what Deleuze calls an 'event', a 'haecceity', and what Bains refers to as an 'actual, felt occasion of experience'.[18] A processual, transitivist and fusional intensity. The processual is determined by this qualitative multiplicity of proto-subjectivities.

For Deleuze and Guattari, human subjectivity or interiority emerges out of what they call self-referential territories. Although the individuated psyche is generated from a pre-individual autopoietic or self-referential node of 'events', these events themselves are actually subjectivities which have an existential integrity, an autonomy, an autopoietic 'realm'. This unites mind, brain and body. The actual brain, in its material and molecular structure, is part of the process. There is a level beyond and prior to any sense of subjectivity, felt at a level of proto-subjectivity, which involves the materiality of the brain in connection with both mind and body, a molecular coagulation.

In *What is Philosophy?*, Deleuze and Guattari provide the most important concept of this arena of proto-subjectivities, as existing in the intersection of mind/brain where the brain becomes a 'subject' in absolute survey, an auto-possession, or self-enjoyment, prior to the emergence of the phenomenal perceptual field. Raymond Ruyer was specifically influential in determining this sense of a subjectivity which is different from that of phenomenology or psychoanalysis or Cartesian accounts, accounts which have surfaced through film studies.[19] By utilising a different perception of subjectivities, then, we can begin to discern different vocabularies for the filmic experience. Ruyer's work has specific purchase in how visual perception is conceived as an in-itself outside of the scopic action of the eye–I relationship. Deleuze's notion of autopoiesis, the self-enjoyment of the transitivist and emergent self, the absolute interiority, is premised upon both Stern's and Ruyer's work. Deleuze's notion of a schizoanalytic subjectivity suggests there are multiple strata of subjectivation in a multicomponential cartography. This is opposed to the conscious–unconscious formations of psychoanalysis. It is not so much a total denial of subjectivity as such, rather a recognition that it exists in pre-verbal and pathic consistencies and these lie beyond the individual. These pathic events or consistencies are often referred to as multiplicities. It is of course difficult for specifically rational discourse to acknowledge a notion of a non-discursive affective or pathic awareness. But this is really crucial to understanding the 'affect' as entity, as something beyond psychic structures. Ruyer's biological philosophy proposes a connection between mind and matter which does not distinguish these as separate entities. Bains highlights Ruyer's notion of 'an absolute "true form" which is an absolute consistent form that surveys itself independently of any supplementary dimension, which does not appeal therefore to any transcendence, which has only a single side whatever the number of its dimensions, which remains co-present to all its determinations without proximity or distance, traverses them at speed, without limit-speed'.[20] The main point about this is that Deleuze's work proposes an ideality that is a dimension of matter. All things are material. He says, 'I see no reason to refuse the existence of the equivalent of a subjectivity or proto-subjectivity to material and living assemblages.'[21] Deleuze seems to be looking for a sense of subjectivities which is not based on a subject, or intentionality, or psychoanalytic perceptions of subject/object coordinates. He is suggesting, and this can be seen in *Cinema 1* and *Cinema 2* and in the final chapter of *What is Philosophy?*, that there is an auto-possession, an autopoiesis or self-enjoyment felt through the brain/body, prior to any emergence of a phenomenal field. In other words, the brain is the 'mind'. All we ever are is brain/mind meld. Images thus exist within this brain/mind/body meld, not outside in the world itself. Obviously, such ideas enable different definitions of the concept of affect, and allow us to rethink the visual experience of the cinematic as effecting different experiential modes of existence. Rather the pathic and the felt can be theorised outside of phenomenological accounts of subjectivity.

An entire meld of brain/mind and body is thus pertinent to an understanding of the molecularity of 'becoming'. Thus images which we experience or see and affects that we feel are not out there in the world as such but exist within our brains' formations, within the primary true forms of an emergent and transitivist existential integrity.

BECOMING-WOMAN

Deleuzian ontology, I think, presupposes an 'in-between' of subjects and objects. His work along with Guattari poses the notion of an autopoietic or self-referential production of subjectivity. This existence of an existential integrity has its own endo-consistency,[22] in and of itself. Subjectivity is not just in flux, and in multiplicity, but is displaced through immanence, through a pragmatics of 'becoming'. Molecularity is the key to this definition of 'becoming'. To Deleuze and Guattari it is the process of what they call 'becoming-woman', which is key to all other becomings. The process of 'becoming-woman', for both men and women, is perceived as a molecular process, releasing minoritarian fragments or particles of sexuality (but a sexuality that is no longer on the level of unified and genitalised sexed body) which break down the binary aggregations. The process of 'becoming-woman' is not based upon any recognition or identification with an actual entity, as a 'molar' entity of woman. The process of 'becoming-woman', for men and women, is a destabilisation of the molar identity and as such is a marker for a more *general* kind of transformation of process, through processes of the molecular:

> What we term molar entity is, for example, the woman as defined by her form, endowed with organs and functions and assigned a subject. Becoming-woman is not imitating this entity or even transforming oneself into it . . . but emitting particles that enter the relation of movement and rest, or the zone of proximity, of a micro-femininity, in other words, that produces in us a molecular woman.[23]

However, if we are to engage with these ideas within a post-feminist pragmatics, it is important to understand the problems for feminist discourse. What has been problematic for feminist discourse has been this generalised use of the word 'woman' within a process of transformation. It has been argued that it seems to be locked into essentialist categorisations of woman determined by cultural and ideological significations of the term 'woman'.[24] According to traditional feminist thinking, the term 'woman' through Enlightenment epistemology has been equated with 'other', man being firmly located as the norm, the Law or the locus of thought and culture. 'Woman' as a term has been encoded as 'essence' or 'bodily zone of transfiguration', a defining of woman as nurturer, or carer and 'woman' as nature rather than culture. This definition has been criticised for implying that woman's bodily essence is responsible for her creative, nurturing and thus transformational properties. However, if the radical democratic principles of a feminist politics are not to be sacrificed then the very category 'woman' itself needs to be rethought and understood in different and creative ways, providing a new site for political contest. Furthermore a rethinking of the term in a Deleuzian sense will provide a post-feminist pragmatic account of 'woman'.

It could be argued, as Jardine and Braidotti[25] do, that Deleuze's use of 'becoming-woman' is in danger of using the term 'woman' in its essentialist categorisation of woman as 'body' and woman as nature, in contrast with man as mind and man as culture. Why, for example, is 'becoming-woman' privileged in the idea of becoming? This suggests that in order to 'become' one must first of all take on board the categories of womanhood associated with that binarily opposed position within phallogocentric thinking: that to 'become-woman' requires of men an appropriation of the 'body' of woman, or the idea of woman. This position does not offer any criticism of a patriarchal subject position of woman from the dualistic structures that oppose it to the masculine norm. Why does Deleuze not simply explain his ideas in terms of merely 'becoming' without the resource to the term 'woman'?

But to be concerned with such questions is to maintain *binarily* constructed debates, which do not take into account molecular, rhizomatic, or assemblages, contingent thinking or transversal processes of thinking. A more pragmatic, post-feminist account considers the wider question of abstract machines, assemblages and perspectival thinking. 'Woman' thus might be perceived as part of a molecular process, within a machinic assemblage of technological, material, social and other forces, not just the cultural or biological.

Deleuze articulates these ideas in his use of the term 'becoming-woman'. His ideas are useful in presenting a pragmatics, then, as opposed to a politics, and also, by extension, in presenting a new paradigm shift in rethinking aesthetics in contemporary film theory. This is because he is arguing for a desubjectivication of the gendered 'entity' of woman. Deleuze does not display 'becoming-woman' as a concept within a feminist political theory, as a theory of 'woman'. He uses the concept in a rhizomatic way, within a pragmatics, not a politics. The 'subject' is not the point in question. If women's history has been connected with their relation to a 'subject' then we need to change the elements in relation to how the term 'woman' is understood for it to have any significance outside of a teleological political position in a molar politics of feminist theory.

Following on from Nietzschean originations of 'becoming', Deleuzian 'becomings' are desubjectified *affects*, not subjectified stages towards any positioning of an autonomous subject or agent. Becomings are *desubjectified affects*. 'Becoming-woman' has nothing to do with real women, or the entity of 'woman' in any biological, cultural or psychoanalytical definition of the term. The idea of 'body' is denaturalised and instead reconceived as a series of flows, particles, in assemblage with other bodies. The question of a gendered subjectivity in each stage of a 'becoming' is not the issue. Subjectivity is replaced by a pragmatics of becoming. Becomings are molecular, traversing molar unities. The processes of becoming-woman involve a series of movements outside or beyond the fixity of subjectivity and stable unities. It is different from the systems of binary polarisation that privileges men over women.

Using the term 'woman' then in Deleuze is not to maintain essentialist definitions of the term 'woman', but is used in new ways to rewire the term in molecular rhizomatic assemblage, not as a literal definition of the molar 'woman'. Camilla Griggers provides an example of the social and machinic assemblages of 'becoming-woman' when she describes how woman's lived experiences of the 1990s are rewired as assemblages of body/mind/matter – and the molecular. In her work *Becoming-Woman*, she introduces the preface as follows,

> This book is about what woman is 'becoming' in US culture at the end of the twentieth century. She is becoming predatory (in 1991, Aileen Wournos became America's first female 'serial killer'); she is becoming depredatory (by 1985, US women were aborting 1.5 million fetuses per year). She is becoming militarized (in 1990, Linda Bray became America's first woman in combat). She has synthetically altered personalities (6 million Americans were on the neurochemical Prozac by 1993 – the majority women); she has prosthetically altered body parts (some 2 million American women had received breast implants by 1994). She has had her biological functions exchanged on the open market (in 1992, there were 4,000 surrogate births in New York state alone). She is becoming publicly lesbian (lesbian chic is in vogue in fashion). She is becoming despotic (black men dragging the face of white femininity are the US media's darlings while images of white women are exported around the globe for mass consumption). And she is becoming at the cellular level a toxic site, ripe for neoplasty (by the end of the millennium, an estimated one in three American women will be diagnozed with some form of cancer).[26]

In terms of a molar politics for feminist theory, it is no longer possible to define the concept 'woman' as having any universal value, or having any essential values. If we are to take on board the philosophical premise of assemblage, of molecularity, then the term 'woman' can no longer be conceived through binary terminology. 'Woman' cannot merely be described as part of a binary, but a part of an assemblage of processes connecting and forming in new alignments within culture, across the social, the libidinal, the material, the psychological, the biological, and personal spaces of our existences, as Griggers exemplifies.

Deleuzian use of the term 'becoming-woman', then, is part of a rhizomatic conception of thought which does not premise definitions in fixed and binary ways. Such rhizomatics, even though they may not directly support feminist political struggles, in a molar sense, nonetheless help to open up possibilities of thinking in new ways. This is not a denial of the political category of 'woman' altogether. The term 'becoming-woman' is used as a molecular way of thinking, a part of a micro-politics, not a molar way of thinking. 'Becoming-woman' involves a series of movements and processes which are outside the fixity of molar concepts like 'subjectivity'. Instead it is a term which is connected to that beyond subjectivity, in the materiality of an asexual, a non-human primordial and existential integrity, within the pre-personal. It is thus an escape from binary concepts that privilege issues like gender. 'Becoming-woman means going beyond identity and subjectivity, fragmenting and freeing up lines of flight, "liberating" a thousand tiny sexes that identity subsumes under the One.'[27] It is rather a neo-pragmatic turn on subjectivity. Subjectless subjectivity. The 'becoming-woman' is the realm of the pre-personal, the affective, the transitivist and the fusional.

'Becoming-woman' is a tracking of woman as a 'function' of a series of processes which have no referent to transcendent entities or agency. Rather, these processes function or operate at a molecular level, at the level of material production, in the realm of the proto-subjective and pre-personal. Braidotti's critique that Deleuzian 'becomings' offer no space for a specifically feminist subjectivity might then be answered with the argument that Deleuze's work is to explore those very mechanisms which produce such transcendent notions. His aim is to rewire and deploy the concept of 'becoming-woman' as particles or as fibres, as an element within a critical neo-pragmatics.

If women's history has been concerned with feminine agency and subjectivity, and feminist film theory has been concerned with a *molar* sense of 'woman', Deleuzian ideas enable a rethinking of the very elements in relation to which woman is understood. This questioning and relocation of subjectivity enables a fresh approach to film theory where subjectivity, as we saw in Chapter 2, has dominated debates. The cinematic experience might be theorised through different vocabularies, which try to explain the impact, the resonance, the modulations of the cinematic outside any notion of, or at least a 'fixed', subjectivity and certainly any gendered subjectivity. Affect and becoming-woman move into the beyond of sensation, as I explain in Chapter 5. Thus a 'becoming-woman' will enable a move away from all those reductive and static concerns with subjectivity and agency maintained in a macro-political dialectic.

The position of woman in relation to the 'subject' has remained fairly consistent. Philosophy has reflected woman as 'other' through a wide array of discourses. Irigaray has specifically referred to the notion of an abstract immanent principle of woman in *This Sex Which is Not One*, in which she describes woman's subjectivity as multiple, diffracted, modelled on the very physicality of her sexual corporeal body. However, such a view of 'woman' consistently sees woman in the position of 'other' and as a function of subjectivity. What 'becoming-woman' in Deleuzian terms does is enable a view of woman in relation to the elemental, the material, the local, forces (matter, passion, chaos, affection and affect) where subjectivity is replaced through a materiality and a molecularity of 'becoming', in a Nietzschean sense.

This materiality, however, requires a new conception of the term 'body' which is beyond those defined by binary discourse (body and nature as female, mind and culture as male). Deleuzian conceptions of the body, based on Spinozist ideas, rethink the body outside of its configurations in such binary discourse. Spinoza states that 'bodies are distinguished from one another by reason of motion and rest, speed and slownesses, and not by reason of their substance'.[28] According to Deleuze, following Spinoza, the 'body' is perceived as a set of forces, intensities, processes, molecular and fibrous particles in connection with other forces and in consilience with the materiality of the brain. Nature, matter, affection and passion are not here perceived as static or negative terms, but flowing and relational, changing and creative, and so their connotations in relation to 'woman' no longer have the earlier connotations of 'otherness'.

Deleuze and Guattari's idea of 'becoming-woman' provides those materials for a reformulation of the 'body' itself and, with that, a rethinking of the 'body' in relation to aesthetics and the cinematic. Woman is not conceived as a 'concept' or an 'image' but part of a set of relations in process and assemblage. This is a philosophical turn on the definition of 'woman' away from transcendent definitions. Here, 'woman' functions differently. A new philosophical positioning of 'woman' is definable as the processes and orders into which she is installed, just as Griggers shows in *Becoming-Woman*. The critical question then for feminism and post-feminism, now, is not whether this is a politically transgressive or liberatory trope of 'woman' in representational terms, but what processes are involved in the production of 'woman'.

The history of feminism has been to analyse the problems of a political positioning of woman, and so it continues to repeat binary debates by trying to appropriate 'agency' and 'subjectivity' for women. But Deleuze's notion of 'becoming-woman' implies a relation between material processes and woman as she functions outside of any notion of subjectivity or agency. Instead, woman is part of an arsenal of pragmatics in rethinking 'becoming' instead of subjectivity. Thus 'becoming-woman' is not captured or restricted within a specific physical form. It is not chromosomally, psychoanalytically, biologically, culturally, libidinally or socially defined. Neither is the concept part of gender politics, or gender theorising. Gender politics is specifically concerned with formations of sociopolitical and cultural areas which may or may not be articulated through an idea of biological femaleness. 'Becoming-woman' is nothing to do with a *politics*. It transforms concepts of 'femaleness' and 'gender' into new sets of relations, into material flows of molecularity. Griggers explains how the pharmacological industry and its use of drugs has created a field of 'becomings' which is molecular, machinic and assembled, outside the categories of gender, class or other molar categories. This rewiring of processes is therefore *immanent* to material flows. Such flows are not *conceptually* driven, but *affectively* driven. If we take this idea into thinking of the cinematic, as I have been arguing, then we have a new set of vocabularies, where affectivity/feeling/intensity become pertinent as processes of molecular, and material, flows. Such vocabularies enable different ways of thinking, outside the conceptual, or the representational, of the cinematic experience. The term 'becoming-woman' is a process of *affectivity*, not a phrase which describes a move towards a political agency or subjectivity.

BODIES WITHOUT ORGANS

To explore how Deleuze and Guattari connect this concept of 'becoming-woman' to affectivity, it is important to consider their idea of 'bodies without organs'. As I explained in Chapter 2, one of the problems with current thinking in film theory, and structuralist thinking, has been the fixed positionality of the term 'body', versus mind, in critical theory. Within post-structuralist thinking, this binary is rethought, and criticised. Rather, there is a more complex imbrication across the two terms. Deleuzian thinking about the 'body' opens up new definitions of the term itself, and these newer definitions help us to think about what we might mean by the term, *body*, rather than *a body*, in a much more complex, situational, and contingent form. Bodies are no longer perceived as just corporeal, flesh and blood bodies, but the concept takes on a more complex, technologised and assemblaged notion. Therefore, we can move away from the phenomenological accounts of film and the body, which we saw in the work of Sobchack into much more experimental avenues of thinking.[29] The formulation of 'body' in Deleuze takes it outside its definition as a set of organs, blood, bones, and so on, and in opposition to mind and consciousness. In Deleuzian terms 'body' is conceived differently.

The concept of 'body without organs' is an attempt to denaturalise the body. Rather than see the body as a corporeal element, Deleuze and Guattari describe the body as a set of variously informed 'speeds' and 'intensities'. It is conceived in relation to other bodies, particles of other bodies or entities. In an interesting recent documentary, film-maker David Lynch talks about his concern with the speeds of the body and the speeds of space. He explains that a person can be fast or slow, just as a space can be fast or slow, or a range of perspectives in-between. That person will then interact with the space and time around him or her, a space and time which also have different 'speeds'. He then locates that metaphor to his visual language of film, and explores this interrelationality within the diegesis of his texts. He suggests that this relationship of speeds between 'bodies' is what gives specific scenes in films that 'unexplainable' intensity. An example he uses is the song sequence 'In Dreams' in *Blue Velvet* (1986).

Within Deleuzian conceptions, bodies might be technological, material, organic, cultural, sociological or molecular. 'Body' becomes a more composite, machinic, technologised term, dissolved from any formulaic interpretation based upon biological terms. This is premised upon Spinozist conceptions of the univocity of being: that everything has the same ontological status. In terms of particles, and fibres, and molecularities, all the world is composed of similar matter, a combination of atoms, particles and fibres, but in different formations and patterns or equations. Therefore the body and mind are 'modifications' of the same substance. Thus, all of life, in a sense, becomes 'body' in material and molecular connection. Therefore the body without organs refers to all bodies: animate, inanimate, human, inhuman, textual, social, and cultural as well as biological. The body without organs is a body which is disinvested of any psychical fantasies as we see in psychoanalysis. Again, this enables us to create new ways of thinking how the term 'body' has been used in film theory, and opens up refreshing, neo-pragmatic turns on that definition, suggesting 'bodies' of the filmic process, in the way in which David Lynch uses the term. This body without organs is an abstract notion, then, a concept or thinking of the body as a limit, or a tendency –

a becoming. As Liz Grosz indicates, 'It is the body before and in excess of the coalescence of its intensities and their sedimentation into meaningful, functional, organised, transcendent totalities . . . a point or process to which all bodies, through their stratifications, tend; a becoming that resists the processes of overcoding and organisation according to the three great strata or identities it opposes: the union of the *organism*, the unification of the *subject*, and the structure of *significance*.'[30]

This body without organs is not a place, or a scene or an actual 'body'. The body without organs is a field for the *production* of the process of desire. It is what Deleuze calls the 'plane of consistency' or 'plane of immanence' as opposed to the plane of organisation. The plane of organisation is that area of our lives through which we are structured into behavioural roles, through specific moralities and principles; the molar line – the family, law, the state, education – where things have specific values and a specific place. The plane of consistency operates alongside the plane of organisation, in a molecular coagulation with it, melding and in collusion. If the body without organs is the space of 'becomings' it is important to see it in this abstract way, not as a defined expression about the physical, lived 'body' of phenomenology.

Bodies, then, are not stable units, but become elements in assemblage, fluid and mutable, constituting life through 'becoming'. This is an abstract level of description from the body as perceived in binary discourses or phenomenology. Deleuzian conceptions of body convey the main features of 'bodies' as openness, change, mutability, fluidity, feedback, complexity. Through the 'body' then an immanent self-organisation replaces transcendent principles, determining the value of 'body' as distinct from binary divisions. Thus, 'becoming-woman', in relation to the body without organs, is not an expression of 'real biological bodies'. 'Becoming-woman' is a *process of immanence*, a description of a processual experience of the affect, as opposed to the subject. Becomings are always specific movements, forms of rest, motion, speed, and slownesses, points and flows of intensity. Such flows of intensity operate outside subjectivity and gendered subjectivity through *affect*. Those affective processes at work in the experience of the cinematic are thus effectuated through an 'unthought', through the plane of consistency, through the material of the body/brain at a deeper level than the subjective. This other realm operates through the deeper level of the proto-subjective, in the affective realms of becoming. The unthought is felt, at this level, as intensity, as becoming in a molecular connection, beyond any notion of an individuated 'body'. I think what Lynch is trying to explain is that there are certain moments in certain sequences in films which have a specific intensity and an effect on the viewer that is almost inexplicable; indeed to explain it is to take something from it. A feeling resonates and reverberates between the viewer and the text in ways which cannot be articulated through speech or verbal language. They are felt within a pre-personal state. The effects of such sequences are usually triggered by a specific equation of sounds, textures, spaces, rhythms and movements across that specific frame or series of frames in question. Again, the *Dreams* example is perhaps the most well known.

Deleuze writes in *Cinema 2*,

> 'Give me a body, then': this is the formula of philosophical reversal. The body is no longer the obstacle that separates thought from itself, that which it has to overcome to reach thinking. It is on the contrary that which it plunges into or must plunge into, in order to reach the unthought, that is life. Not that the body thinks, but, obstinate and stubborn, it forces us to think, and forces us to think what is concealed from thought, life. Life will no longer be made to appear before the categories of thought; thought will be thrown into the categories of life. The categories of life are precisely the attitudes of the body, its postures . . . It is through the body (and no longer through the intermediary of the body) that cinema forms its alliance with the spirit, with thought.[31]

This almost appears to be a contradiction in terms. I have argued so far, that the 'body' in Deleuzian conceptions is not the phenomenological, corporeal lived body, but is an assemblage of forces, intensities and so on. And yet in *Cinema 2* he talks of the 'body' being the space where the felt and unthought are experienced. I understand this apparent contradiction as an exemplification of Deleuze's ideas of the 'interstitial' or the 'in-between'. So that this definition of 'body' is really no longer seen in either singular categorisation, but a complex of both and more. The body is the unknown space of the molecular; it incorporates the mind and the brain. It is not definable as a singular entity. It cannot be constrained to the individuated body of flesh and blood, as opposed to mind/brain. Rather it is an amalgam, but not necessarily a 'whole' notion of all these. 'Body' in this sense has a new and fluid dimension which encompasses all individuated, social, cultural and affective spaces. This is a reformulation of life as 'body' – body as life. It is 'intensity' and 'affect' which molecularly constitute this Body of life.

Through Deleuzian ideas we can offer a pragmatics of becoming with which to replace the concept of subjectivity. Any call for a politics of becoming is, I acknowledge, in danger of hypostatising that very politics. But a pragmatics of 'becoming', instead, uses contingent assemblages of thinking processes through which to distanciate the concept of 'subjectivity'. Subjectivities can be determined as merely simulacra, which are subsumed to a more profound engagement with forces of 'becoming', material, molecular and fibrous forces, rewired, as I indicated earlier, across new assemblages outside of language construction. A post-feminist agenda in film theory, as a political and ethical framework, engages with thinking 'outside' the boundaries of epistemological, Cartesian thought, through a pragmatics of becoming.

This engagement with cinematic experience thus proposes to consider cinema as 'affect', as 'body' (see Chapter 5), where affect operates beyond subjectivity within the materiality of the film itself, through an immanence of movement, duration, force, and intensity, not through a semiotic regime of signification and representation, but in sensation. Questions of desire are relocated or rather dislocated from sentient identification within semiotic signification, psychoanalytic or subjective, and gendered reading positions. Rather desire is rendered processual, immanent, created through a modulational and vibrational expression of the *affect in sensation*.

It is difficult to explain the concept of affect, since there is no cultural paradigm or vocabulary that is specific to affect. Texts, visual or literary, have until most recently been explained, explored, theorised and critiqued through theories of 'signification'. How can we begin to explain how affect has become more significant to visual cultures than theories of signification, if we are constrained to work within structural linguistics? Affect has been defined or loosely seen to describe emotion. But there is a discernible difference between these two terms. Affect and emotion are not synonymous, although they may be conjoined. They have different orders of being. An emotion has a 'subjective' content . . . a subject operates as the experiencer at an individuated level, of the emotion . . . a personal experience. It is thus owned by an agent, by a subject. It is crucial to a Deleuzian semantics, to theorise the difference between emotion and affect. Affect is not ownable, by an individuated agent, in the same way as emotion.

The question one might argue, then, is how can we critique affect if it is indiscernible to an agent, to a subject? Deleuze uses Spinoza's 'Ethics' to ground the term affect. Spinoza's philosophy explores the difference between affect and emotion. He explains that affect has an irreducible bodily and autonomic nature. (Autonomic here is defined as purely a physical response to something: sensual responses, for example, the skin getting warmer, or the heart beating faster.)[32] Affect is a suspension of action–reaction circuits and linear temporality into what might be called 'passion'. This distinguishes it from passivity or activity.

Furthermore, Ruyer's work, as I explained earlier, gives us an understanding of affect as a state of subjectless subjectivity. The affect exists, according to Ruyer, in the materiality of the brain/body consilience at a molecular level. At this level of the non-human, proto-subjectivity, the molecular describes a state which has an understanding of its own existence, what Ruyer refers to as 'equipotentiality'. Quantum physics is currently looking into the existence of what are called 'microtubules', which exist within the emergent sense of all organisms. These microtubules determine within molecular organisms a sense of 'aliveness', an existential integrity, or being in the world, outside any sense of intentional consciousness.[33] Thus affect is an emotionless state, but still a state of 'feeling'. Rather there is a pathic, proto-subjective state which is not owned by the subject. Therefore we can argue that aesthetic desires are 'becomings' and they cannot be fixed or positioned in terms of extrinsic systems of reference. Rather, they can be articulated through an appreciation of transitivist, transversal and pathic consistencies. As Guattari writes, 'one gets to know them not through representation, but through *affective* contamination'.[34]

In his ideas on thought and cinema, Deleuze explains the difference between classical and modern cinema. The so-called classical cinema works, according to Deleuze, through the linkage of images, and subordinates edits and cuts to this linkage. The harmony of classical cinema is achieved by rational cuts, edits which always produce logical relations between images. Modern cinema, or what I would see as post-classical, on the other hand, provides a reversal. Images are not always linked; cuts and edits have little significance in themselves. What emerges is often a kind of 'non-commensurability' of relations between images. Images are not totally abandoned, but relinkages are subject to techniques of cutting, thus producing irrational cuts. 'There is thus no longer association through metaphor or metonymy, but relinkage on the literal image; there is no longer linkage of associated images, but only relinkages of independent images.'[35] The filmic experience has evolved through a whole new idea of the processuality, the rhythm of the film as a set of bodies, in motion, producing a new cartography of the visual. The film does not record images, or convey representation. It acts, it performs, as a 'body' with other bodies, in a constituted body, a molecular body, through the affective.

FROM BECOMINGS . . . TO AFFECTS . . . AND THE BECOMING-WOMAN OF THE CINEMATIC

In his ideas on modern cinema Deleuze explains how modern cinema is concerned with three major elements: the image, the concept and the affect. But they function contingently, pragmatically, to produce a creative and mutational element in the visual experience. This tripartite relationship constitutes a harmonics, a 'whole' system of harmonics which creates a nervous 'vibration' (see Chapter 5). In this way, the I SEE and the I HEAR are actually subsumed across the concept of the I FEEL in the affect. An I FEEL, a totally physiological sensation, one felt beyond or prior to subjectivity, in the pre-subjective level, in which body and world cannot be distinguished separately, is experienced through a 'malleable mass' of images. If cinema is a 'belief in a world' accommodated across a relationship of image–concept–affect, then that movement is experienced before language, before discourse.

In this sense, Deleuze follows Artaud's belief in the ineluctability and insufficiency of 'language' to articulate the experience of 'reality'. Deleuze says,

> Because the point is to discover and restore belief in the world, before or beyond words . . . It is only, it is simply believing in the body. It is giving discourse to the body, and, for this purpose, reaching the body before discourses, before words, before things that are named: the 'first name', and even before the first name.[36]

The 'depth' of that primordial body becomes a significant element within a trajectory of 'becoming-woman' where woman's body is rewired, reconfigured and rethought beyond discourse, through the affective and outside any gendered subjectivity.

The belief in the 'body' is fundamental to Deleuzian aspects of post-classical cinema. By dislocating discourse, semiosis, metonymy and metaphor, a 'deeper' level of engagement is proffered, which articulates a profound relation of body–brain–world connection. The relationship then of image–concept–affect is rethought through a new perception of the 'whole', which incorporates the role of 'body' and the 'body' as the 'whole'. The question is no longer that of an association of images. What matters is the 'interstices' or the 'in-between':

> It is not a matter of following a chain of images, even across voids, but of getting out of the chain or the association. Film ceases to be 'images in a chain . . . It is the method of BETWEEN, 'between two images', which does away with all cinema of the One. It is a method of AND, 'this and

then that', which does away with all the cinema of Being = is. Between two actions, between two affections, between two perceptions, between two visual images, between two sound images, between the sound and the visual: make the indiscernible, that is the frontier, visible . . . (*six fois deux*) . . . The whole thus merges with what Blanchot calls the force of 'dispersal of the Outside'.[37]

Thus various interstitial elements become 'bodies' which make up a new perception of the cinematic body. Generic characteristics no longer hold the only validity. Instead, categories, words, sounds, refrains, colours, tones, fill the in-between spaces of the filmic text. The 'body' is perceived as fundamental to this affective and aesthetic process, and equally this process constitutes a 'body'. The 'becoming-woman' of cinema is this process of the affective . . . towards sensation.

The 'becoming-woman' of the cinematic is a phrase which I wish to foreground as part of the *aesthetics of sensation*. It operates in post-feminist film theory and generates from a synthesis of Deleuzian ideas on 'becoming', 'affect' and sensation. It enables a move towards thinking beyond gendered subjectivities, through a corporeal and material sense of connection with the movements of the filmic body. Desire is experienced through the molecular, material emotion, through the processuality of the affects of the film as body, with other bodies: the ways in which colours vibrate, clash, coincide, resonate; the dimensions of their tones; the blurring of their boundaries; the linearity across and within the frames; the rhythms and movements felt across the screens; the role of sound within this experience. Not in any psychic or libidinal way as we saw in psychoanalysis, for example, but through the materiality of the film, its compositional elements, connecting with other bodies, corporeal, mate-rial, molecular: bodies as life, bodies constituting life. Such bodies are made of 'water, air and matter' as Deleuze indicates in his *Three Syntheses of the Beyond*.[38]

The 'becoming-woman' of cinema entails processes beyond corporea-lised vision into a concern with movement-image, affect, haecceity, synaesthesia and kinaesthetics: a coagulation of cinema as machine, as a body of sensation. For Nietzsche as we saw earlier, there is no distinction between the world in which we live and any other 'transcen-dent' world. There is no ultimate truth, no other metaphysical world to which we can aspire. Rather there is only ever the processual of the real, in time, the real forces of life's natural existence in its germinal and viral contingencies. 'Becoming' epitomises that process of affirmation of the dynamic of living in the real world: an acceptance of the cruelty of life, the joy of the cruelty of that existence, the acceptance of the ineluctability of life's transience. There is no other to which we aspire – all there is is the real, and within our experience of the real, the concept of 'becoming' serves to define life's ephemerality, life's ineluctability and sheer vibrance of rhythmic movement, force and dynamism. Thus 'becoming' in Deleuze may be described as an affirmation of the positivity of life's 'differences'. Consequently identity is never singular, and does not exist as a determinate factor in our existence. Identity is in constant flux and process, continually swirling through a vortex of molecularity. With this emphasis on processes, affirmation and movement, Deleuze's notion of 'becoming-woman' offers the existence of fluid boundaries in a materialist and vitalist sense of immanence as opposed to transcendence.

A 'becoming-woman' of the cinematic, then, is an exploration of the affective, processual, the dynamic and the aleatory vitalism of the forces felt across a variety of bodies. If we can move away from thinking about 'becoming-woman' as a description of an entity, then the term enables a transformation from image, or concept, to affect. The 'becoming-woman' of cinema describes the affective process of the cinematic experience where the affective is constituted through a materiality of emotion, a material sense of depth and process, through affect and sensation.

NOTES

1. See Edward Wilson, *Consilience*. Wilson writes that there needs to be a new understanding across paradigms of knowledge, of a 'consilience' across the sciences, humanities and social sciences. His work seeks to provide a coherent thesis premised upon a bio-aesthetic conception of knowledge, within the arts, one which takes its foundations from genetic and genetico-cultural foundations.
2. Félix Guattari, *Chaosmosis*, pp. 99–118.
3. See Paul Valadier, 'Dionysus versus the Crucified', in D. B. Allison (ed.), *The New Nietzsche*. I mention Nietzsche here since his ideas have had a profound influence upon Deleuze, and to some extent we need to see from where those ideas originate, in order to understand the nature of 'becoming' in Deleuze's work.
4. See Paul Bains, 'Subjectless Subjectivities', in Massumi, *Canadian Review of Comparative Literature*, p. 519.
5. See Stephen O'Connell, 'Aesthetics: A Place I've Never Seen', in *Canadian Review of Comparative Literature*, p. 486.
6. Stephen Houlgate, *Hegel, Nietzsche and the Criticism of Metaphysics*, p. 42.
7. The word 'cruelty' is not to be seen in the sense of physical or emotional cruelty to humanity, but is used here as a word which defines a flux, a dynamism, a sheer ineluctability about the natural world that can only be sensed and not described. Cruelty as a term takes on a different definition, and I emphasise it is *not* to be defined here as cruel in the sense of hurt, pain or torture. Cruelty here is more akin to a kind of excitement, creativity, indetermination. It is of course to some extent tied up with the kind of 'pain' one receives in experiencing the sublime or

that which cannot be described: the forces of nature for example in storms, earthquakes, etc, where the imagination is not able to comprehend the reality, so that what is felt *is* a kind of cruelty or pain, but is also a beauty which is indescribable. Of course any discussion on the sublime is, purposefully, outside the parameters of this project and will not be part of my discussion. Cruelty, then, in my sense of the word, is meant to explain this indescribable sense of vitalism and dynamism.

8. Houlgate, *Hegel, Nietzsche and the Criticism of Metaphysics*, p. 45. See specifically ch. 3, where Houlgate refers us on p. 46 to Nietzsche's essay, 'On Truth and Lie in the Extra-Moral Sense', as an exploration of the ideas of the falsity of language.
9. M. Haar, 'Nietzsche and Metaphysical Language', in Allison (ed.), *The New Nietzsche*, p. 11.
10. Houlgate, *Hegel, Nietzsche and the Criticism of Metaphysics*, p. 51.
11. See also Houlgate, *Hegel, Nietzsche and the Criticism of Metaphysics*, p. 51.
12. See Houlgate, *Hegel, Nietzsche and the Criticism of Metaphysics*, p. 51.
13. Deleuze and Guattari, *A Thousand Plateaus*, p. 272.
14. Deleuze and Guattari, *A Thousand Plateaus*, p. 275.
15. C. Colwell, 'Deleuze and the Prepersonal', in *Philosophy Today*, p. 18.
16. C. Colwell, 'Deleuze and the Prepersonal', in *Philosophy Today*, p. 19.
17. Deleuze and Guattari based these ideas upon the work of Daniel Stern's *The Interpersonal World of the Infant*. This explores in detail the existence of a transitivist and fusional emergent self, a self which ignores oppositions such as subject/object, and masculine/feminine. See also Brian Massumi, 'The Autonomy of Affect', in Patton (ed.), *Deleuze: A Critical Reader*, p. 217–39, where similarly he describes the sense of 'aliveness' as being a continuous non-conscious self-perception. It is the perception of this state that enables 'affect' to be analysed, as something which is outside the psychic and lies within the material and the molecular. See also Chapter 2, note 29, on the matrixial and Lichtenberg-Ettinger's work in relation to Lacan.
18. Bains, 'Subjectless Subjectivities', in Massumi, *Canadian Review of Comparative Literature*, p. 514.
19. On the survey, subjectivity and absolute surfaces, see Raymond Ruyer, *Neo-Finalisme*.
20. See Bains, 'Subjectless Subjectivities', in *Canadian Review of Comparative Literature*, pp. 519–24.
21. Deleuze quoted in Bains, 'Subjectless Subjectivities', in *Canadian Review of Comparative Literature*, p. 516.
22. An endo-consistency describes a state which has no vortex, or end state. It can only be understood or defined as relational, or fluid . . . in connection with surrounding particles.
23. Deleuze and Guattari, *A Thousand Plateaus*, p. 275.
24. See Rosi Braidotti, 'Toward a New Nomadism: Feminist Deleuzian Tracks; or, Metaphysics and Metabolism' and Elizabeth Grosz, 'A Thousand Tiny Sexes: Feminism and Rhizomatics', in Boundas and Olkowski (eds), *Gilles Deleuze and the Theatre of Philosophy*, also, Alice Jardine, *Gynesis: Configurations of Woman and Modernity*.
25. For Rosi Braidotti, the problem for feminists is how to free woman from the 'subjugated position of annexed other, so as to make her expressive of a different difference, of pure difference, of an entirely new plane of becoming'. See Braidotti Toward a New Nomadism', in Boundas and Olkowski (eds), *Deleuze and the Theatre of Philosophy*, pp. 159–82.
26. Camilla Griggers, Preface, *Becoming-Woman*, p. ix.

27. Grosz, 'A Thousand Tiny Sexes: Feminism and Rhizomatics', in Boundas and Olkowski (eds), *Gilles Deleuze and the Theatre of Philosophy*, p. 207
28. Jonathan Bennett, *A Study of Spinoza's Ethics*, p. 109.
29. See for example the work of Stephen Shaviro, *The Cinematic Body*.
30. Grosz, 'A Thousand Tiny Sexes: Feminism and Rhizomatics', in Boundas and Olkowski (eds), *Gilles Deleuze and the Theatre of Philosophy*, p. 201.
31. Deleuze, *Cinema 2*, p. 189.
32. See Brian Massumi, 'The Autonomy of Affect', in Paul Patton (ed.), *Deleuze: A Critical Reader*, p. 217.
33. R. Penrose, *The Large, the Small and the Human Mind*, p. 128.
34. Guattari, *Chaosmosis*, p. 92.
35. Deleuze, *Cinema 2*, p. 214.
36. Deleuze, *Cinema 2*, p. 172.
37. Deleuze, *Cinema 2*, p. 180.
38. See Deleuze, *Difference and Repetition*, p. 73.

Chapter 5

Towards an Aesthetics of Sensation

Affect goes beyond affections.

[A]ffect is not the passage from one lived state to another, but man's nonhuman becoming.

Becoming is neither an imitation, nor an experienced sympathy, nor even an imaginary identification. It is not resemblance, although there is a resemblance. But it is only produced resemblance. Rather, becoming is an extreme contiguity within a coupling of two sensations without resemblance.[1]

Artists are presenters of affects, inventors and creators of affects. They not only create them in their work, they give them to us, and make us become with them . . . whether through words, colours, sounds, stone, art is the language of sensations. Art does not have opinions. Art undoes the triple organisation of perceptions, affections and opinions, in order to substitute a monument composed of percepts, affects and blocs of sensation that takes the place of language. The writer uses words, but by creating a syntax that makes them pass into sensation, that makes the standard language stammer, tremble, cry, or even sing: this is the style, the 'tone', the language of sensations.[2]

Sensation operates as the beyond of subjectivity, through 'becoming-woman'. Its being lies in the beyond of any fixed subjective positionality. If film is an art form which resonates as experience, as a pure form of 'becoming-woman', then Deleuze's ideas on art and the aesthetic, in terms of the concept of 'sensation', are a significant development in thinking about the cinematic impact through affect. They enable us to conceptualise a theory of aesthetics which is outside of representation, and is premised upon the intensity of sensation.

Deleuze's theory of sensation brings together previous and more binary perceptions of sensation.[3] Deleuze initially describes sensation as having a subjective and an objective element, as perceived in the work of writers like Kant but also, 'it has no sides at all, it is both things, indissolubly, it is being-in-the-world as the phenomenologists say: at the same time I *become* in sensation and something *arrives* through sensation, one through the other, one in the other. And finally, it is the same body that gives and receives sensation, that is at the same time subject and object.'[4] It is a fusional world-body of sensation.[5] Any discussion of an aesthetic must take into account two types of sensation. The first, premised upon Plato's original conception of sensation, suggests that sensations are recognisable and objective. Common sense tells us that when we look at a hand, for example, we acknowledge its objective functions. We recognise some form of action and objectivity to the sensation of looking at a hand. But there exists (according to Plato) a second form of sensation which is to do with the *relations* into which that form merges. For example, a hand is either larger or smaller, fatter or thinner, and therefore the sensation actually forces the perceiver to think about other elements in the equation.

DELEUZE'S THEORY OF SENSATION

Daniel Smith writes that, 'The most general aim of art, according to Deleuze, is to produce a sensation, to create a pure "being of sensation", a sign. The work of art is, as it were, a "machine", or "apparatus" that utilizes these passive syntheses of sensation to produce effects of its own.'[6] Deleuze's theory is premised on this second type of sensation, on what he refers to as 'signs'. He sees signs, not as semiotic tropes, but as forces of encounter, or objects of fundamental encounter. An encountered sign has no fixity or objective form of recognition, which can be imagined, reconceived or remembered. Rather an encountered sign exists in pure movement, duration and rhythm. Thus sensation in Deleuzian argument exists outside any form of recognition or common sense, but in a realm of force, rhythm and encounter. In contrast to the phenomenologists' account of sensation, Deleuze's definition is one which removes sensation from any presupposition of common sense or recognition, where subjectivity is transcended. Indeed sensation operates beyond any subjective position-ality. As Daniel Smith states, 'By taking the encountered sign as the primary element of sensation, Deleuze is pointing, objectively, to a science of the sensible, freed from the model of recognition and subjectively, to a use of the faculties freed from the ideal of common sense.'[7] Our faculties of sensibility, memory, imagination, reason and cognition are not necessarily linked in any perception we might have of a specific object. These faculties operate, according to Deleuze, as *differential* elements, which do not need to have a conjunction in order to have meaning. Each faculty has a differential limit or tendency. Something might be communicated from one faculty (for example, imagination or cognition) to another, but does not necessarily constitute common sense. This sensibility is one which perceives signs, in the Deleuzian sense of an 'encounter' rather than a 'meaning'. Therefore, the sign in Deleuzian ideas suggests an aesthetic which is not dependent upon recognition or common sense. It operates as a 'force' and as an 'intensity' in a differential relationship.[8] A sign then is an intensity which is produced by differential relations. Sensations, therefore, refer to a whole range of differences of perceptions of consciousness, at a level beyond subjectivity. These intensive forces cannot be understood by any empirical senses. With the notion of intensity, sensation ceases to be representative and becomes 'real'.

This has significant resonance for thinking of the cinematic encounter. What we see on the screen may not operate merely as 'representation' but as signs of material encounter, as sensation. The cinematic experience becomes 'event' as well as representation. To explain this more thoroughly Deleuze's work on *Francis Bacon: Logique de la sensation* is illuminating. Deleuze indicates in *Logique de la sensation* how Bacon's paintings evince pure movement, force, modulation and process, because of the nature of their multiple images. The images are formulated across a triptychal structure.[9] They function as material forces, rather than as singular representational paintings. They are material forces, not figurative images. Deleuze takes from Lyotard[10] the notion of the 'figural' as opposed to figuration. Figuration, or representation, has meant an image which is both representational and narrative. It relates the image to a particular object of recognition. It thus loses any intensity in sensation. However, Deleuze differs from Lyotard, in his belief in the role of psychoanalysis as the framework of understanding this Dionysian anti-art form, of the visual engagement. Lyotard's psychoanalytic interpretation is too dependent upon transgression, deformation and the negativity of unconscious processes as perceived in Freudian formulae. Deleuze utilises the figural without the Freudian apparatus that Lyotard employs. In Deleuze, the figural, is the concept of an immanent process of forces. Sensation operates on a plane of immanence, through the processual, and intensity. According to Deleuze, Bacon defigures representation and breaks the figure away from representation, with the aim of rendering 'sensation' as more significant. This method of defiguration is used to achieve pure force and intensity, through the figural. In discussing Bacon's paintings, Deleuze argues that the represented image of the body in pain and torture need not be read as that. Rather the images on the canvas exist, not as 'figuration' but as the figural of rhythmic movement. The prostheses and the mutilations that the body undergoes in Bacon's paintings are not read as a 'trope' of horror (although they may of course operate as such a metaphor) but as transitions, pulses, elements that allow variations into paintings to thus allow endlessly changing 'locomotions': the body in 'locomotion' rather than as a representational image. Polan writing in his article on 'Francis Bacon: The Logic of Sensation' quotes Deleuze: 'What is painted in the tableau, [or, as I would say, what we see on the cinematic screen] is the body, not insofar as it is represented as "object" but in so far as it is lived as experiencing sensation.'[11] This has significant reverberations for how we interpret the 'image', say, of 'woman' on the screen. She may exist as figural, not as figuration, and thus the 'image' of woman might function as force, intensity.

How can the figural then epitomise force, and intensity, whereas figuration is manifested through representation? To Deleuze, the figural is the space of intensity. Deleuze explains how both abstract art, for example, with artists such as Mondrian, and expressionist art, with the work of Pollock, tried to refine sensation, by dematerialising it to a specific optical format. Pollock, for example, in his work dissolves all forms through a kind of fluid mixture of lines and colours. Such artists have moved 'beyond representation' by breaking with what was known as a hylomorphic code. This is the code which explains how art is about the imposition of *form* upon *matter*. But abstract art was about freeing up form, while expressionist artists wanted to free up matter through chaotic use of colours and lines (Pollock). But, what is missing from this model is that form and matter are in fact not so easily separable: they are more interestingly connected. They cannot just be isolated as separate terms. Matter is not just a simple, and singular, substance that can be 'formed' into something. It is something which is mutable, kinetic, moving, malleable and never fixed. In other words matter has 'singularities' (see Chapter 4). The materials that artists use in forms, whether in art or in film, are actually complexly mutable (for example, iron might melt at specific temperatures; water will change states from liquid to solid). This exemplifies Deleuze's notion of 'intensity'; all matter exists in modulation with the forms imposed upon it. 'Beyond prepared matter lies an energetic materiality in continuous variation and beyond fixed form lie qualitative processes of deformation and transformation in continuous development.'[12]

In summary, the artistic venture, whether painting or film-making, is no longer just a matter–form relation. What is significant in the event of this process is a material–force relationship. Sensation, says Deleuze, 'is not realized in the material without the material passing completely into the sensation, into the percept or affect'.[13] 'So long as the material lasts, the sensation enjoys an eternity in those very moments.'[14] The artist or the film-maker takes a specific type of material, which has energetic elements, or molecular elements, and synthesises the disparate elements in such a way that the form captures these intensities. Film may equally capture this modulation of material–force.

Polan states in his article that 'Beyond figuration and representation, then, sensation comes from a pure power that overflows all domains and traverses them. This power is that of Rhythm, which is deeper than vision, audition, etc. . . . "A logic of the senses," Cézanne said, "that is non-rational, non-cerebral."'[15] This is of course a major overturning of phenomenology's emphasis on subjectivity. If I were using Merleau-Ponty and phenomenology to explain the cinematic text and how it impacts, as Vivian Sobchack does,[16] then there would be an engagement with the subject as centred and fully formed and integrated with a 'body' of text. I prefer to use Deleuzian ideas on intensity and sensation, through which the subject is subsumed in the beyond, through becoming and sensation. The subject is, as it were, 'hystericised' or subsumed through intensities, rhythms, flows and energies. The visual act of seeing with a physical eye ceases to be a merely organic activity. As Deleuze says, 'our eye ceases to be organic to become a polyvalent and transitory organ; objectively it holds before us the reality of a body of lines, of colours, liberated from organic representations'.[17] All the modern and post-modern arts, and especially cinema, can share in this search for a discourse of sensation where representation is not necessarily the only framework through which to explain the event, impact, or resonance. Sensation is the climactic, but processually climactic, element of *desire in process*. The beyond of desire and affect lies in sensation.

Within sensation, vibration and rhythm come together to produce a 'vibratory facticity'.

> Sensation is no less brain than the concept. If we consider the nervous connections of excitation-reaction and the integrations of perception-action we need not ask at what stage on the path or at what level sensation appears, for it is presupposed and withdrawn . . . Sensation is excitation itself, not insofar as it is gradually prolonged and passes into the reaction but insofar as it is preserved or preserves its vibrations. Sensation contracts the vibrations of the stimulant on a nervous surface or in a cerebral volume: what comes before has not yet disappeared when what follows appears.[18]

Sensation passes through different stages, under the action of the forces of the material. When there is a confrontation of sensations, then their respective communications and intensities produce vibration and ultimately resonance. Deleuze discusses sensation through three specific stages.

In stating that the aim of all art is to 'wrest the percept from perceptions, and the affect from affections, to extract a bloc of sensations'; Deleuze describes three varieties of sensations, where the sensation take place at a pre-subjective level, at the engagement of body, brain and world. As I argued earlier, it is through the body without organs that sensation is accessible, through the pre-subjective state of materiality. The essence of sensation is rhythm, and the three compounds of sensation are imbricated through rhythm.

First, Deleuze refers to the '*Vibration*'. This characterises a simple sensation, which 'follows an invisible thread that is more nervous than cerebral'.[19] This synthesis is a simple sensation. But it is nonetheless also composite in that it is determined by a difference in intensity that either falls or rises, decreases or not, a 'pulsation' that is more 'nervous' than cerebral. An example of this is in a Bacon painting (evident also in the film *Romeo and Juliet* – see Chapter 8), where the various colours and their intensities 'vibrate' in a complex format, thus creating a sensation which is felt at a nervous level, a level of excitation upon the nervous system. 'Vibration' is created by the rhythmical oscillation of different colours. For example, grass which has a variety of colours in it other than green: red, blue, violet, even yellow, will be part of the final 'green' of the painted grass. This modulation of colours creates the 'vibration'. 'Vibration' is the ultimate molecular image.

Second is '*Resonance*', or what Deleuze terms the embrace, the clinch, when two sensations resonate together, by tight embracing as if in a state of symbiotic energies. Two simple sensations then come together almost like wrestlers in combat and they resonate off each other, in a molecular way. Their singularities, their intensities energise. Bacon's paintings very clearly exemplify this, as do several films under scrutiny in Part Three. For example, if we look at the way Bacon uses two human bodies in a painting, they very often are commingled in some mutated fashion, entangled, embroiled, resonating off each other, and not offering singular identities.

Third is the synthesis of '*Forced movement*', or as Deleuze states in *What is Philosophy?*, withdrawal, distension, division, 'when on the contrary two sensations draw apart, release themselves, but also now to be brought together by the light, the air, or the void that sinks between them'.[20] To explain this it is useful to draw on Bacon's use of the triptych as a form for his painting. A triptych incorporates three separate canvases, placed and viewed together and experienced as a synthetic unit. But within the triptych individual vibrations seem to undergo a type of *movement* which creates a rhythm across the entire three canvases as one. Sensation is therefore not necessarily dependent upon one element, but a set of elements across the whole: the Figure. The rhythm works across the entire triptych. The interstitial elements of light, air, colour, tones (in the case of film, we might add, sound, music, point and counterpoint) between the three canvases become rhythmical forces that connect the triptych as a unit. It is as if the air itself becomes a molecular element in their connections. In this way, Bacon was able to produce a work of art which is more than a representational image. Rather, art here functions as vibration, resonance, force: as sensation. A 'pure being of sensation'. In other words, the work of art functions as a machine, a machine which produces effects of vibration, resonance and movement. This therefore elicits the quest which has predominated the book so far: we can theorise the experience of the cinematic; we can think of the visual experience of the cinematic, not only as a representation of something with a 'meaning', but also as an aesthetic assemblage, which moves, modulates and resonates with its audience or spectator through processes of molecularity. It connects. It works through affect, intensity and becoming – and ultimately through sensation, not necessarily through subjectivity, identity and representation.

TOWARDS A NEO-AESTHETICS OF SENSATION

It is through *style*, through elements such as consonance, dissonance, harmonies of tone, line, light, colour, sound and rhythm that sensation is manifested. Visual and aural affects, like the cinematic, involve a certain style, through which sensation is accommodated. In each case (in art) argues Deleuze, 'style is needed – the writer's syntax, the musician's modes and rhythms, the painter's lines and colours'.[21] Even characters within a specific narrative, whether in literature or in film, become as it were elements in the compound of sensation, a figural, rather than existing as representatives of a specific dialogue within a narrative. An example of this is perhaps the novel *Mrs Dalloway* by Virginia Woolf. In this novel Clarissa walks through the town, and passes into the town 'like a knife through everything' and becomes imperceptible herself. As Deleuze indicates, '*Affects are precisely these nonhuman becomings of man,* just as percepts – including the town – are *nonhuman landscapes of nature.*'[22] This exemplifies the molecularity of the experiential. 'We are not in the world, but we become with the world, we become by contemplating it. Everything is vision, becoming. We become universes. Becoming plant, animal, molecular, becoming zero.'[23] How do the elements of style articulate the three compounds of sensation?

In discussing style I suggest that what we can present through Deleuze is a neo-aesthetics and a bio-aesthetics premised upon sensation and affect, rather than on subjectivity: a sensation which is based upon the molecularity of matter, and functions through the materiality of the body of work in relation to other bodies. If we take this logic of sensation we can construct a theory of communication that would respect gradations of signification (Deleuze does not argue for a complete deterritorialisation from the molar: that is, the line on which ideology functions), which would not limit meaning but would present a different semiotics from the structural semiotics which we find operative in formal film theory. More innovatively, we can begin to think about the film as an aesthetic experience, but not in terms of the aestheticism of modernist or romantic traditions. Here a neo-aesthetics is taking into consideration a biological element within the aesthetic experience. Rather, Deleuze offers a kind of 'fluid semiotics', concerned less with signification or distinct elements, than with tonalities, rhythms, shifts of force and energy, movement and the materialism of a cinematic body that exists as matter. In this model, a 'becoming-woman' of the cinematic, where sensation replaces desire, the image can 'vibrate' with layers of intensity, since the image is not a single unit, but a graded richness, resolute with modulations across a time-scale from past, present and future. Modulation replaces representation. Film can be seen to impact, as an aesthetic form, not as an encoder of experience but as a modulator of experience. Within the modulation, the following, molecular elements function to signify and produce a specific *style*.

Colour functions as the main modulator of sensation. The colour green acts as the prime spectrum for the eye–brain. This is because the human eye–brain's genetic structure evolved around energy conserving processes with respect to an environment dominated by the reflection of green wavelengths. In connection with green, other colours enter different fields within the eye–brain activity and will cause different affects. This change in the semiotic state requires an energy expenditure. Affect, then, becomes energy, force, modulation and sensation. '*Within the green fields of Deleuzian grasses the white butterfly's movement captures: aparalletic evolution, the wasp and the orchid.*' The visual experiences of the cinematic are not necessarily prioritised through visual energies, but other modulators, other energies, other captures. There is more than colour that causes a sensation. The eye will also engage with other processes. The first of these is motion, process, movement. The eye will connect across several distinct, but overlapping fields of view. These are basically a central focus, with left/right edges, and top/bottom thresholds. Anything, any object, force, energy, that crosses these areas will be detected by the eye–brain and this causes an instant cerebellum–efferent motor response. Thus the eye can trigger, instantly, a response without a thought . . . an intensity, an energy. Response can be evoked without image, without representation. Bergson indicated that afferent nerves transmit a disturbance to the nerve centre. 'The efferent nerves which start from the centre conduct the disturbance to the periphery, and set in motion parts of the body or the body as a whole.'[24] If the body is also an 'image' as we might find in film for example, then external images influence the body in synaesthetic ways, through the efferent nerves, and they thus transmit movement to it. Thus the body simultaneously influences the external images; it gives back movement to them. Bergson writes that, 'here are external images, then my body, and lastly, the changes brought about by my body in the surrounding images. I see plainly how external image influence the image that I call my body: they transmit movement to it. And I also see how this body influences external images: it gives back movement to them. My body is, then, in the aggregate of the material world, an image which acts like other images, receiving and giving back movement, with, perhaps, this difference only, that my body appears to choose, within certain limits, the manner in which it shall restore what it receives.'[25] Through this process of movement, the 'beautiful' can be newly discerned as a notion of duration and brain formations. How is the beautiful accommodated through movement and motion? Various forms of 'motion' are thus more appealing, more alluring, more beautiful to the eye–brain.

For example, the pathways of the flight of a butterfly will produce the most invigorating, beautiful and captivating pathways of motion, a cartography of visionary dance across the eye–brain, but also an amorphous fragility within the tactility of the image. The highly variable trajectory of the butterfly will make the brain continually break and form, break and form, breaking any symmetry, thus engaging all three fields of view of the eye. The 'eternal return' of the eye–brain activity (and the butterfly) creates the kinaesthetics, wherein the brain's activities are beyond the merely visual, but become tactile, fluid, in process.[26] (As Massumi argues, 'beauty pertains to a process, not to a form'.) Other forms of motion that break, lock and entrain the brain are spinning, the flowing of water, rolling motion – wheels of any kind and explosions. Filmic experience offers a whole range of such forces on our efferent nervous systems. The borders of sunlight and shadow, for example, will cause the eyes to flicker, to blink and cause the same tensing of the efferent pathways as actual motion – an ecliptic. (At the time of writing, the total eclipse has caused such experiences for those brave enough to view.) So in filmic experience, specifically in some of the films I discuss, such as *Strange Days* and *Romeo and Juliet*, the sensation is felt through such a mind/body/brain assemblage, a veritable 'becoming-woman'.

Movement is also connected to colour. Deleuze explains that colour operates as force. Each tone or modulation of colour exercises a force upon a corresponding body, both in and outside of any text. It is colour and the 'relations' of colour that provide a 'haptic'[27] world and meaning. This haptic world is felt as a function of hot and cold, of expansion and contraction, through the hapticity of eye into hand. According to Deleuze,

> It is color, it is relations of color that constitute a haptic world and meaning, as a function of hot and cold, of expansion and contraction.[28]

He refers to the intense force and connection of the visual and the tactile sensations, the synthesis of the optical and the tactile as a 'haptic' sense of vision. This hapticity[29] is simultaneously optic and tactile. The visual becomes 'felt'. The felt connection between eye and hand is felt, in coagulation, an evolution of hand into eye – into an Hegelian '*Aufhebung*' or '*dépassement*'. Deleuze explains this hapticity as follows,

> To characterise the connection of eye and hand, it is certainly not enough to say that the eye is infinitely richer and passes through dynamic tensions, logical reversals, organic exchanges and vicariancies . . . we will speak of 'haptic' each time there is no longer strict subordination in one direction or another . . . but when sight discovers in itself a 'function' of touching that belongs to it alone, and which is independent of its optical function.[30]

It follows from these ideas that Deleuze presents an aesthetics of sensation which is premised upon a pedagogy of the image, but a pedagogy which is formulated on *movement*, and process, on machinic connections of film as assemblage, an assemblage of new formulations and new vocabularies, or a semiotics outside of structuralist semiotics. This pedagogy of the image pares down the representational into sensation, as we have seen through a processual effect of different elements. Within this pedagogy of the image, movement, then, is an essential element of sensation (forced movement, vibration and synthesis all involve movement). In theorising the filmic experience, images that might be deemed representational are in fact 'movement-images'. They do not exist as static forms in themselves, but are experienced as images-in-movement, in process, in sensation. Images do not exist in isolation, in the filmic experience. Rather they are poses and become an ordered set of poses, with movement, relating to change over time. As Bergson indicates in *Matter and Memory* (1988), there are not only instantaneous images, and immobile sections of movement, but a coagulation of the two, into movement-images. This perceptual movement happens in the glance, or the eye. The 'eye' is not the 'too immobile human eye': it is the eye of the camera, in matter. This is because of the nature of the 'shot'. Movement has two elements. The shot acts like consciousness. However, the sole cinematographic consciousness is not us, the spectator, nor the image on the screen. It is the 'camera', which, Deleuze argues, is human, sometimes inhuman, even superhuman. The shot, in other words, traces movement. It is movement itself which is decomposed and reorganised into movement-image. As Deleuze indicates, Epstein has poetically compared the shot as pure movement, with a cubist painting or a simultaneist painting. Here 'all the surfaces are divided, truncated, decomposed, broken, as one imagines they are in a thousand faceted eyes of the insect . . . descriptive geometry whose canvas is the limit shot'.[31] Bergson indicates, 'image equals movement and every image is indistinguishable from its actions and reactions: this is universal variation'.[32] We can consider images, then as matter, in the same way that the body is both matter and image:

> My body is an image, hence a set of actions and reactions. My eye, my brain, are images, parts of my body. How could my brain contain images since it is one image among others? External images act upon me, transmit movement to me and return movement: how could images be in my consciousness, since I am myself image . . . that is . . . movement.[33]

If *movement* is the prime element of sensation, how is movement connected to the materiality of bodies? Bergson argues we cannot separate the 'ego' from the eye, the brain or the body, since all are a complex gaseous state of matter. Rather, the body is a 'set of molecules and atoms which are constantly renewed'.[34] In a construality with this body, external objects make a disturbance in the afferent nerves. This disturbance passes on to the centres of the body/mind/brain, into the centres of the body that are molecular, as Bergson says, 'the theatre of the very varied and molecular movements'.[35] Perception, then, becomes dependent upon the relation of external objects and representation to the body. 'Change the objects, or modify their relation to my body, and everything is changed in the interior movements of my perception centres. But everything is also changed in "my perception". My perception is, then, a function of these molecular movements.'[36] It actually depends on the molecular movements of cerebral substance. The perceptive faculty of the brain exists through the spinal cord. This in turn transforms into movements, the stimulations received from images. Therefore, any perception of the universe appears to be dependent upon internal movements of the cerebral substances, fibrous, energic and fluid substances: material of molecular matter. Perception, then, and within this I refer to visual perception of the cinematic experience, is a molecular *vibration* of cortical substance.

However, such perception does not only depend upon molecular movements of cerebral mass of atoms. Perceptions 'vary' with other molecular substances of the material world. If atoms are condensed into continuous fluids and movements, then the centres can only be determined in relation to some form of 'touch' or impulsion. Our nervous systems interpose between the objects which affect our bodies and those which our bodies can influence. The body becomes a conductor for transmitting movements. As a composition of fibrous threads, stretched across the universe of space, time and duration, the 'bodies' of filmic texts and the 'bodies' of those who view are a series of affections, which, through a becoming-woman of the cinematic, are experienced as sensation. The sensations are not images perceived by us 'outside' of our body; but rather affections localised within the body.

Images in movement constitute what Deleuze refers to as a plane of consistency, or immanence. On this plane of immanence, the image exists as matter, image and movement together. On the plane of immanence, perception is defined in two ways. First, what can be described as liquid perception. This describes a perception that is subjective, and in which images vary in relation to a central image and privileged image. The second is an objective perception, where all the images vary in relation to one another. Liquid perception is so defined because of the metaphor of water. Water, according to Deleuze, is the most perfect environment in which movement can be extracted from the thing moved. This is why water is so important to research on rhythm. The liquidity of the perceived image is diffused in all directions, into vibrations, just like the ever-increasing circles in a pool into which a pebble is thrown. Thus, the perception-image is split into two, liquid perception, or the molecular and the solid perception, the molar. An image on screen then can be said to become 'liquid' through the molecularised use of the shot. The filmmaker Vertov has been significant to these ideas. For Vertov, the idea of liquid perception did not go far enough. He said we should also think of gaseous perception. The liquid image is inadequate as it fails to reach a particle of 'matter'. Instead, Deleuze says, 'Movement must go beyond itself, but to its material, energic element.'[37] Therefore, logically, if we determine a perception which is no longer liquid, but gaseous, if we start from a solid state, where the molecules are not free to jostle, around (molar) we can then move to a liquid state, where molecules can move around and even merge together. Ultimately, by this logic, we reach a final gaseous state of the image, this being defined by the 'free movement of each molecule'. Consequently, the flickering, luminous, vibrational elements behind the image produce vibration, and rhythm, a stage beyond movement. This determines that we can argue for the formation of the 'image' defined by molecularity, not by visual figuration. Sensation is accommodated through such molecularity.

In the proceeding chapters, I want to explore a range of films across such Deleuzian ideas, to explain how we might bring to film theory a reconsideration of aesthetics but a materialist neo-aesthetic: an aesthetics of sensation. These ideas are not premised upon structuralist semiotics, linguistics, and psychoanalytical interpretations of desire. The filmic experience involves a much wider range of forces, oscillations, intensities and energies. Furthermore, subjectivity is not necessarily the issue at stake in determining the 'felt' experience of the cinematic. Deleuzian ideas enable us to offer a different set of vocabularies with which to formulate an aesthetics of sensation of the filmic event, and enable us to offer possible solutions to questions of the body, the machinic, desire and aesthetics, which were problematised in Chapter 2.

NOTES

1. Deleuze and Guattari, *What is Philosophy?*, p. 173.
2. Deleuze and Guattari, *What is Philosophy?*, p. 175.
3. Theories of aesthetics have traditionally been couched in binary languages as we saw in Chapter 1. Aesthetics since Kant has been described, first, either as a theory of sensibility as the form of possible experience, or, second, it has been seen as a reflection on real experience. The first of these elements composed a subjective element of sensation, governed by specific forms of time and space coordinates. The second is more of a 'subjective' element, created through feelings of pleasure or pain. Deleuzian ideas on aesthetics attempt to merge or overthrow these ideas. For a sustained argument see Daniel Smith, 'Deleuze's Theory of Sensation: Overcoming the Kantian Duality', in Paul Patton (ed.), *Deleuze: A Critical Reader*, p. 29.
4. Deleuze, *Francis Bacon: Logique de la sensation*, p. 27, trans. Ronald Bogue, 'Gilles Deleuze: The Aesthetics of Force', in Patton (ed.), *Deleuze: A Critical Reader*, p. 260.
5. It was phenomenologists such as Merleau-Ponty, Maldiney and Erwin Stauss

who had originally developed theories of sensation which were distanciated from any presupposition of recognition. Sensation was in their perspective inevitably tied up with the physicality of the body, and an intentional consciousness of a 'lived body'.

6. Daniel Smith, 'Deleuze's Theory of Sensation: Overcoming the Kantian Duality', in Patton (ed.), *Deleuze: A Critical Reader*, p. 39.

7. Smith, 'Deleuze's Theory of Sensation: Overcoming the Kantian Duality', in Patton (ed.), *Deleuze: A Critical Reader*, p. 33.

8. Deleuze's theory of difference and repetition is beyond the scope of this book, but to understand the notion of differential relations is perhaps pertinent to this understanding of the encountered sign of 'sensation'. For example, a differential relation is that which provides two different elements, e.g. the colour green is made up of the differential relations of blue and yellow. The point where they become indiscernible, in the colour green, is the point of differential relation. They are made up from different molecular structures, and yet come together in the colour green. As Smith relates it, 'a clear perception green is actualised when certain virtual elements (yellow and blue) enter into a differential relation as a function of our body, and draws these obscure perceptions into clarity': Smith, 'Deleuze's Theory of Sensation: Overcoming the Kantian Duality', in Patton (ed.), *Deleuze: A Critical Reader*, p. 35.

9. The word 'triptych' denotes a three-part form of painting, where each part is separate, but still is relevant to the whole piece of work. It was a common form of art in Byzantine and Early Renaissance religious painting, which were formed into three separate units, which could actually be folded together. This was so the work could be carried, opened up and used when required for prayer and contemplation. The word is used in Deleuze to explain a 'three'-part relationship across elements.

10. Ronald Bogue writes, 'According to Lyotard conventional visual representation represses the anomalies of sensation, the deformations and violations of "good form" that disturb the eye. In undoing the good form of representation, however, the artist also engages with invisible forces that never become directly visible, those of the unconscious, which are fundamentally forces of deformation. The "space of the invisible of the possible" then is an invented space traversed by unconscious forces that render visual what Lyotard calls the "figural" – a domain of Dionysian art-form that can play through the images of figurative and abstract art alike.' Bogue, in Patton (ed.), *Deleuze: A Critical Reader*, p. 259.

11. See Dana Polan, 'Francis Bacon: The Logic of Sensation', in Boundas and Olkowski (eds), *Gilles Deleuze and the Theatre of Philosophy*, p. 239.

12. Smith, 'Deleuze's Theory of Sensation: Overcoming the Kantian Duality', in Patton (ed.), *Deleuze: A Critical Reader*, p. 43.

13. Deleuze and Guattari, *What is Philosophy?*, p. 167.

14. Deleuze and Guattari, *What is Philosophy?*, p. 166.

15. See Dana Polan, 'Francis Bacon: The Logic of Sensation', in Boundas and Olkowski (eds), *Gilles Deleuze and the Theatre of Philosophy*, p. 240.

16. See Vivian Sobchack, *The Address of the Eye*.

17. Deleuze quoted in Polan, 'Francis Bacon: The Logic of Sensation', in Boundas and Olkowski (eds), *Gilles Deleuze and the Theatre of Philosophy*, p. 241.

18. Deleuze and Guattari, *What is Philosophy?*, p. 211.

19. Deleuze and Guattari, *What is Philosophy?*, p. 168.

20. Deleuze and Guattari, *What is Philosophy?*, p. 168.

21. Deleuze and Guattari, *What is Philosophy?*, p. 180.

22. Deleuze and Guattari, *What is Philosophy?*, p. 169.

23. Deleuze and Guattari, *What is Philosophy?*, p. 169.

24. Bergson, *Matter and Memory*, p. 18.
25. Bergson, *Matter and Memory*, p. 19.
26. John D. Norseen, 'Images of Mind: The Semiotic Alphabet', *American Computer Scientists' Association*.
27. Haptic: this term describes the collusion between the seen and the felt, an imbrication of experience across the two senses.
28. See Polan, 'Francis Bacon. The Logic of Sensation', in Boundas and Olkowski (eds), *Gilles Deleuze and the Theatre of Philosophy*, p. 250.
29. Thus, even though from Bergson we can deduce that cinema is matter and material, nonetheless, the connection between the material and the spiritual is evidenced in this hapticity. This haptic sense of feeling is part of the 'perceptual semiotics' that Deleuze expresses. Within a perceptual semiotics, a haptic sense of feeling is 'immanent' and not 'transcendent'; what Deleuze refers to as a 'haecceity' or as an 'event'. 'An haecceity can last as long as and even longer than the time required for the development of a form and the evolution of a subject . . . Haecceities are simply degrees of power which combine and to which correspond a power to affect or be affected, active or passive affects, intensities' (Deleuze and Parnet, *Dialogues*, p. 92).
30. Polan, 'Francis Bacon. The Logic of Sensation', in Boundas and Olkowski (eds), *Gilles Deleuze and the Theatre of Philosophy*, p. 252.
31. Deleuze, *Cinema 1*, p. 23
32. Bergson, *Matter and Memory*, ch. 1, quoted in Deleuze, *Cinema 1*, p. 58.
33. Deleuze, *Cinema 1*, p. 58, quoting Bergson, *Matter and Memory*, p. 31.
34. Deleuze, *Cinema 1*, p. 58.
35. Bergson, *Matter and Memory*, pp. 22, 31.
36. Bergson, *Matter and Memory*, p. 22.
37. Deleuze, *Cinema 1*, p. 84.

Part Three

Chapter 6

Orlando –
Deleuzian Landscapes of Immanence

There is a pure plane of immanence, univocality composition, upon which everything is given, upon which unformed elements and materials dance that are distinguished from one another only by their speed and that enter into this or that individuated assemblage, depending on . . . their relations of movement.[1]

Orlando . . . does not operate by memories, but by blocks of ages, blocks of epochs, blocks of the kingdoms of nature, blocks of sexes, forming so many becomings between things, or so many lines of deterritorialisation.[2]

Sally Potter's film of Virginia Woolf's novel *Orlando*, which narrates the historical account of Orlando's journey through time, as both male and female, is well documented in feminist film theory. But Potter's intentions it seems, as argued in feminist film theory, in terms of avant-garde cinema, were to present a feminist text which exemplified the constructions and patriarchal constrictions of societies across generational boundaries, cultures, time zones – a historical account of the strictures faced by the female sex. In choosing to use this film here, I want to explore the film in a different way, to present a pragmatic and post-feminist formulation of the aesthetics of the film through a Deleuzian framework; this framework is certainly not constrained by ideological and political readings of a text.

However, there still remains a plane upon which the significatory cannot be denied. The structural semiotics of Metzian film theory[3] meld between and across different assemblages of enunciation. Consequently, the reader will find reference to 'image' and to 'representation' but only as part of a newer, fluid approach which is more concerned with the processuality of the film as an assemblage, as a becoming-woman.

DEATH

Structurally, the film is divided into sections, each section indicated by the titles: Death, Love, Poetry, Politics, Society, Sex and Birth. The main protagonist in the film, *Orlando* (Tilda Swinton), is presented as an androgyne: in the first half of the film as a male and the second half as a female. So much is simplistic in the extreme; in terms of traditional film theory, using paradigms of representation, subjectivity and identity, the film might be read, and has been read, as a feminist tract, across a series of concepts, through which the political, personal and cultural resonances of specific periods of historical and cultural zones are explored through the textuality of the film's 'aesthetic', visually and aurally.

The sections present a form or structure to the narrative, while the time/space trajectory is complexly fractured and non-linear. Certainly the film utilises all the conventions of avant-garde cinema in its break from the normal patterns of linearity, narrative structure and characterisation. Each of the tableaus of Death, Love and so on has Orlando as the main character as part of a social, cultural and libidinal process. Using formal film theory which prioritises reading spaces for gendered subjectivities, desire and pleasures might be explained through a series of theoretical, psychoanalytic and structural conventions. The subjective pleasure of the female audience for example might arise from 'identifying' with the ideological meanings read through the imagery within the film's visual format. (For example, the entire sequence entitled 'Society' is a wonderfully parodic version of the 'problems' of being female.) And certainly there is no shortage of possible psychoanalytic interpretations of desire throughout the film, most specifically in the tableau entitled 'Sex' (for example, the cliché of the romantic hero, Shelmerdine (Billy Zane), the symbolic and psychoanalytic interpretations of romantic tropes: the horse, the mists of time and the transcendent nature of romantic love). Such motifs which might be amenable to psychoanalytic readings (and I don't intend to give detailed versions of these here) limit the film as a plane of organisation, through which transcendent notions of desire are encapsulated.

If we read *Orlando* through motifs within a psychoanalytic framework, then we can see a trajectory of Freudian ideas on originations, repetition–compulsion strategies, the death instinct and its allegiance to desire as the need for a return to lost plenitude; the entire film has reversed the process from birth to death, and so establishes some identification with the formal processes of a linear time-scale of existence. There may be a reversal of the states, but this still nonetheless constrains the film's diegesis within the bounds of transcendent notions of being, of journeys to origins. Desire entrapped within a trajectory towards fulfilment, endings, satisfaction. The entire film is about a journey, life's journey from birth to death, and the major life 'events' (ironically) on that journey. But here, 'death' opens up the film with birth as the end state . . . a neat reversal of the Freudian scenario, but still the same scenario . . . originations, familial connections . . . daddy, mummy . . . me! I exist, therefore I am. *Cogito ergo sum.* (We see in the final sequence the small child, significantly a female child, who is both woman and man in terms of life's journey.)

However, such readings of the film are too reductive to explain the forces which impact, or resonate, as event or as haecceity. Such readings are concerned with the molar plane of organisation in a film, as opposed to the molecular plane of immanence, or the perceptual and fluid semiotics from Deleuzian philosophy. The film is not only a semiotic, or metaphorical, account of the complexities of gendered subjectivities or the role of psychoanalysis in gendered accounts of sexuality. If we think of the film as an assemblage, as a becoming-woman, as a processual state of immanence, then we can discern a different mind-set of the aesthetics of the film through a wider range of vocabularies which might explain the resonances outside signification, semiotic or psychoanalytic explanations. If we remind ourselves of Deleuzian words, in comparison with the plane of organisation, the plane of immanence has 'only relations of movement and rest, speed and slowness between unformed elements',[4] then we can begin to detect different and more creative pragmatic interpretations of the film as event, as 'haecceity', as 'becoming-woman'. If we think of this quotation in terms of *Orlando* as a film, then molecularity, particles, fibres become more relevant to the resonances generating across the bodies/mind/brains of those who view the film. Subjectivity is distanciated, or subsumed, through a process of flux and oscillation of forces, rhythms, movements and intensities. It is not located in the singular regime of a gendered psyche, fluctuating though that may be, as we see in psychoanalysis. Haecceities proliferate the totality of the filmic event of *Orlando*. The most significant haecceities emerge as specific moments of intensity.

We are introduced to *Orlando* through an opening sequence which has Orlando sitting reading poetry; a voice-over follows the words of his text; the diegetic music, violas, cellos, Elizabethan harpsichord tonalities, pervades the scene. The camera pans slowly from left to right, echoing the frontal gaze at Orlando, thus distanciating the audience from the scene. The very objectification of the scene through the use of this obvious camera movement creates an almost Brechtian distanciation. The camera moves purposively, slowly, delicately, calmly, with precision, but with a gentle, direct and precise balanced movement. Camera set-ups and movements are important throughout the entire film in terms of how they impinge upon the efferent nerves of the viewer; calm, linear, balanced, controlled and harmonious panning movements are reassuring, quieting, and balancing to the brain/body/mind connections. A close-up of Orlando indicates the period, style and narrative context of the film: that is, sixteenth-century Elizabethan England. Close-ups figure significantly throughout the film, especially close-ups of faces in shot-reverse-shot positions. Jimmy Somerville's voice reverberates through his song 'Eliza': a gentle, melodic, and fluid accompaniment to the visuals. The sequence evinces a series of parallels and symmetries through the tableauesque frames: almost like a sequence of still paintings, ordered, and fixed in contrapuntal relationship with the music to create a sequence of harmony, order, reason and serenity. The lighting, again symmetrically evoked, uses candles to provide the soft-focus low-key lighting, which predominates much of the movie. Close-up shots of the oars in water – fluidity, liquid, glistening – echo the candles as they flicker in movement to the sound of the rain. This contrasts with the earlier slow, precise panned camera movements, now changed to multiple angles and a complexity of different camera positions. This change of positionalities and the pace of the cutting and duration creates a different intensity. With the change in camera movements and cuts in duration come a feeling of nervousness, tension, volatility and tense excitement, in contrast with the slow, meandering shots of the river. Elizabeth is presented, grandiose and royal, majestically floating into view from right centre frame, the camera panning across the screen to echo the movements and intensities of the water itself. The 'beautiful' resides in the processuality of the water's movements, much like the way in which a butterfly's flight impinges upon the efferent nerves within the body which 'views'. Beauty thus pertains to a process, and is explained through a materiality of body/brain and mind consilience, across molecularity. Similarly, in terms of the auditory senses, sound impinges on specific nerves of the cerebral chords. The music of violas, and harpsichords creates a mood of quiet elegance, insouciance, incipience and delicate anticipation – the regal, the majestic, the stated. The flickering of the lights along the shoreline contrasts in dissonance with the verticals and horizontals of the oars as they are carefully positioned. The static nature of that movement is set in contrapuntal distinction with the movements of water and lights. Vibration, forced movement (see Chapter 5) and synthesis are all modulated within this sequence. Semiotically of course, the aesthetic resonance is enhanced through a specific style: through the tactility of the richly textured clothes, the reds, golds and plums of regal costume and sensuous brocades. Ironies abound, of course, in that Elizabeth is played by Quentin Crisp, whilst in contrast, Orlando, here as a man, is in fact played by a woman; a quietly ironic reminder of the exigencies of Elizabethan drama and its acknowledgement is an intellectual pleasure. This juxtapositioning of sexualities is ironically counterpointed throughout the film and especially has significance in a later scene where Orlando comes upon a sequence from *Othello*. In this scene, men are both women and men in terms of the play's characterisations. This paradoxical gender boundary crossing might of course be part of a gendered reading of the film but it also points to Deleuzian complexities about the multiplicity of sexualities, the molecularity of sexuality, outside of gender. Indeed, Orlando is the veritable 'trickster': 'the trickster is of indeterminate sex and changeable gender who continually alters his/her body, creates and recreates a personality . . . and floats across time from period to period, and place to place'.[5]

As the 'trickster' Orlando figures throughout the film as the veritable 'figure' or figural in a Deleuzian sense. Rather than perceive her/him/it as a character, s/he/it functions as a 'figural', in terms of bringing together a set of movements, colours, tones, resonances across the canvas of the screen. This is evident in the first sequence, when Orlando rushes down to be greeted by Elizabeth. The force and rhythm of his steps, the facial expressions, lines, gestures and body movements function as a force, as an intensity of 'feeling' which resonates within the mise-en-scène as a rhythmical movement. This is encapsulated by specific types of camera movements and angles. No longer the controlled right to left panning of the earlier sequence, the camera editing is now disjointed, dynamic, fluctuating and rhythmical, creating a dissonance with the still, lingering shots of the river earlier.

We cut to Elizabeth, bathing her hands in a bowl of water – reminiscent of the oars of the river sequence. Water functions to bring together the resonances set up by Orlando the 'figural'. The resonances of this sequence are further stylised through the use of chiaroscuro lighting, dark shadows and low-key lighting. Elizabeth at the banquet is the central image and figure of the scene, in that the close-up of her face is juxtaposed in shot-reverse-shot sequence with Orlando. Such is the effect that we feel an intensity of something 'in-between' the figures of both Orlando and Elizabeth. This intensity is of course translated into the concept of death, decay, ageing and loss, through the dialogue which fixes and positions the dynamics of the visuals. 'Do not fade, do not wither, do not grow old . . .' says Elizabeth. Ageing, decay, withering and death are effectuated as the opening aegis of the film; but of course such concepts are redolent of Freudian paradigms of finality, and returns to states of originality. A notion of transcendence is set alongside a plane of immanence, through the movements of the film's aesthetic resonances. The dialogue is almost parodied through the beauty of the aesthetic resonance, so that the film itself is nowhere near a death-like metaphor, but rather an 'event' of the beautiful, and the immanent. The shot-reverse-shot mechanism from Elizabeth to Orlando juxtaposes a dream-like beauty and serenity through the faciality of those images. But this is perhaps too restrictive a reading. Rather the sequence enables a questioning of the binaries of life–death, beauty–sterility, where life and beauty are part of a processual element of immanence. The immanence of 'becoming-woman' of life's events, the event of the experience. To quote Virginia Woolf, 'life is not a series of gig lamps symmetrically arranged; life is a luminous halo, a semi-transparent envelope, surrounding us from the beginning of conscious-ness to the end'.[6]

It is, in other words, rich at every moment of being, in its evanescence, and evanescence is correlative to a 'becoming-woman'. Sterility, death, fixity, urbanity are effectuated through the style of the geometric and coordinated symmetrical lines across the screen in certain frames. For example, the central shot of Elizabeth is always centre frame. Elizabeth and Orlando become mutable 'figures' in this sequence through fluctuat-ing, heterogeneous shots, so that rather than identifying with a 'char-acter', we experience the resonances of the film through its immanence, an aesthetics of 'becoming-woman', where the characters perform as 'figurals'.

Elizabeth's boudoir, darkly lit with flickering candles and chiaroscuro has shot-reverse-shot of close-ups of faces. The whole mise-en-scène flickers: gestures, silent gestures, slow pulsating, lugubrious and loqua-cious body language; delicate, gracious movements are captured by the camera and so display a delicacy and evanescence of movement, as perception, in collusion with each other. Harmony, as Deleuze indicates, harmony of music with the close-up of Orlando and gentle camera movements, creates the intensity of this frame. Elizabeth recounts 'Do not fade, do not wither, do not grow old . . .' This ironic juxtaposition enables us to move away from thinking about the film's 'meaning' to enjoy the film's 'connections'. This is of course exemplified in the rest of the film.

Death and decay continue into the following sequence: the burial scene. We cut to a very stylised frame, almost a freeze frame, given the stillness and serenity of the mise-en-scène. The panning camera crosses the canvas, or screen-scape, as though the scene were a pastiche of tableaus from any one of a series of paintings (Gustave Courbet's *The Burial of Ornans* (1849–50) comes to mind). It is as if we ourselves are part of the funereal cortege. A pattern is choreographed across the landscape of the entire film from this cortege. Here, the pattern is initiated into motion through a range of lines of longitude and latitude. Latitudes of camera movements, tracking shots from right centre frame, from right to left, echoing and thus patterning, function like lines on a Mondrian painting: an ordered and punctuated dynamic which is also static. This 'motionless' movement is articulated through colours, as much as the angles and lighting. Black and white exude, with textures of delicate satin, lace and soft velvets, inducing the hapticity of the 'felt' immediacy of this framed shot.

Figures of mourners appear like black dots on a white canvas. The beauty of their being lies in the meandering delicacy and pace of their movement. The characters again 'figure' as lines in a painting, rather than people in a narrative. It is almost as if they are floating in thin air across the snow-scape. Their clothes, rich, black velvety hues, and awesome, heavy shapes contrast in dissonance with the crisp, white snow, echoing the linearity of the trees; people becoming-trees, becoming-landscape. The characters function as lines across the canvas, producing a landscape of silence, which evokes the death-knell of its context. But 'meaning' need not necessarily be discerned at the expense of 'connection'. Such scenes as this connect amorphously, as gestural, aleatory, pathic and haptic consistencies, with other similar sequences from other movies. I am thinking for example of the desert scenes in *The English Patient* and of course Bertolucci's scintillatingly beautiful *The Sheltering Sky* (1990). Something grand, intangible and molecular is emitted across the gestural movements of the screenic event. The emptiness and solitude of the landscape enable a connection of intensities which are about process, continuums, becoming, and ironically are far removed from transcendent notions of inorganic origins, death and fixity. Art becoming-nature: nature becoming-art.

The intensities of this specific sequence are articulated through the dynamics of camera actions, movements, planes, together with the use of black and white cinematography. A strange, ethereal and iridescent calm is experienced through the plane of consistency here encapsulated through shots, movement-images and sound molecules, in collusion. How does this impinge upon or connect as assemblage, as 'body' with other bodies, and those who view?

First, the delicate, slow, almost static and profound eloquence is articulated through a tragic and resonant stillness – art becoming-nature. Intensity and becoming are felt at a level beyond subjectivity, through the affective. The sequence exudes a frozen and disconsolate frigidity, a starkness and yet beautifully amorphous fragility of landscapes of silence. Silence breathes an air of acceptance, acknowledgement and tender cruelty, through the stillness of the camera shots, through a hapticity of 'image' into movement. But this image is rendered tactile by virtue of the effect on the efferent nervous system of those who view. We literally want to reach out and suffocate within the snow (later echoed in the final sequence with beautiful sail-like billows of canvas on the lawn of Orlando's modern-day home). So that what we see is not represented as 'image' but snow as it is evoked as a 'modulation of image'. It is not a represented image, but movement-image, on the verge of existence, fragments and fugitive thoughts. Landscapes of silence are the becoming-woman of this film. A silence which is also a void, but not only a void, but a space, an emptiness, a void which is replete with molecular resonance, resonance of material emotion. To quote Cioran, 'Nothingness does not have the rather grim signification we attribute to it. It is identified with a limit-experience of light, or, if you like, with a state of luminous absence, an ever-lasting radiant void.'[7]

The camera pans across the funeral scene to the isolation of Orlando's grief. This scene of death's finality is counterpointed, in rhythmic counterpoint, with the tableau 'Love (1610)', both of course part of the same tragedy of nihilistic encounter.

LOVE

The complexities of love are experienced through various levels in the film. Here, the 'becoming-woman' is the beyond of desire at a subjective level; the forces felt at a primordial level are a form of love in this sense. So whilst the sequence explores the finer contradictions of definitions of love – sexual, romantic, idealistic (wrapped up within a construction of patriarchal versions of female/male dynamics) – in fact the sequence works on a more abstract level. Here, love is encompassed as the processual rhythms of nature, forces of the seasons, temperatures, where love is outside gendered or genital sexuality, but functions through multiplicitous molecular connections, 'knowing how to love does not mean remaining a man or a woman; it means extracting from one's sex the particles, the speeds, the slownesses, the flows, the n sexes that constitute the girl of *that* sexuality'.[8]

These sexualities are evinced across the dynamics and energies of the natural, material world. Love moves beyond the binary boundaries of gendered subjectivities or sexualities. Sexuality becomes an abstract and aesthetic phenomenon, through the sheer vibrance, contingency, energetics, molecularity of the natural: snow, ice, heat, warmth, flowing rhythms, a natural flow of sexual exorbitances beyond anything to do with gender. The way the snow is depicted evokes both a liquid and molecular perception, and is reminiscent of the chase sequence of the replicant Zhora in *Blade Runner* by Deckard, and more recent films such as *The Winter Guest* (1997), a film where love is experienced through the vibrational and desolate landscapes of a frost-bitten Northumbrian village. The coldness and cruelty of a masochism premised upon the sheer viscerality of temperatures. 'Love' therefore might be the linguistic and structuralist concept depicting this sequence, but a 'becoming-woman' of this sequence opens up the 'event' of that visual experience into the realm of nature becoming-sexuality. Molecular, fibrous and transversal connections.

Love, death and melancholy are encapsulated in the image of the child, frozen in time, in space, in being by the cold cruelty of the winter's ravages. That fixed moment of death again recalls the final moments of a desire fixed in finality, reconstituted through a final moment of death. But here that image performs as part of a trajectory towards an understanding of life's processuality and ephemerality; nothing is fixed, nothing is finite. The child is captured by nature's cruelty, locked into the fixed moment of death within the water's icy fragments, beneath a surface which is both mirror, and enclosure. The shock of realisation impinges upon the nervous system of the viewer, as excitation–reaction. This takes us into the sequence on the contingencies and inconsistencies of love, in contrast with the previous sequence on death. Love is here in contrast with, but also collusion with, death. Love is part of the same panoply of desire, an unfulfilled desire which psychoanalysis might read as a need–demand equation.

However, the sequence does not have to 'mean' but perhaps it connects. It also operates outside any positionality with regards to metaphor, allusion, or semiotics in a Metzian sense. It can be understood through more aleatory trajectories, through desire as processuality, as 'becoming-woman'. Here, love is not relegated to the same paradigm as death, but is part of the same intransigence of life's primordial duration and intensities. As a sequence, a literal reading might evince a tale of the foreboding, negativity and sickly claustrophobic tenacity of romantic love, replete with melancholic effusions of jealousy, enduring obsession and misery in its masochistic maladies. Orlando falls 'in love' with Sasha – any feminist reading detects a critique of patriarchal, cultural values which have encouraged masculine notions of possession, ownership and sovereignty over the female. Such a discourse is locked into the trajectory of monogamy, marriage and the claustrophobia of Western transcendent idealism: man and woman bound together through the chords of matrimonial law, law of the Father, phallic possession and a repudiation of the freedom and liberty of the individual. Later, of course, Orlando is replaced through Shelmerdine, romantic hero, but also signifier of freedom, emancipation and individual liberty.

The sequence begins with a close-up shot of a child trapped in the frozen waters. From the icy entrapment of the infantile image, locked into fixity within the fluidity of the ice, the camera tilts upwards, revealing the frivolities of a Muscovite welcoming party. Delicate snowflakes waft across the screen, again reminiscent of sequences in *Bladerunner*. Such connections provide in a Deleuzian sense assemblages of 'becoming'. Something connects across the dynamics of different texts, different films in this case. Specific speeds and movements coerce and collide. Such connections provide an intensity and assemblage across the bodies of both films and those who view. The mise-en-scène is pervasively gloomy, dull, overcast and grey. The danger here of course is to resort to semiotic description of the 'meaning'. Character, dialogue, narrative read through a molar structure. What about the line of molecularity, the lines of flight which take us into the plane of consistency and immanence? How might these be discernible across the experience of this sequence?

The depths of winter (following the death sequence) are oppressively modulated through the perception-images and movement-images: right to left camera movements echo earlier patterns of linearity. Slow, lugubrious, heavy and awesome movements articulate a sterility in Orlando's 'being'. Here, movement, dynamism, volatility and viscerality introduce Sasha, who enters from left frame, through a delightful, delicious and delirious circularity of skating movements. Such movements echo the flight path of the butterfly, entrapping and entraining the brain's cerebral pathways through a discernible beauty. She swirls, sways and seduces her pathway across the plane of sterility. Such intensities and energies are 'felt' across the 'body' of the film, through perception-image and movement-image and their imbrication with the bodies of those who view; brain/body/image are coagulated into a malleable set of images, into a materiality of emotion. What is felt is not necessarily a subjective or gendered positionality, but an affective 'contagion', a material response to energies and a dynamics of processuality. The body in motion, in locomotion, connects with the bodies/minds/brains of those who view the film. It is almost as though we want to echo that joyful becoming of the dance: exuberance, vitality, embraced through the 'figure' of Sasha, not the character of Sasha. She is simply a delight. But that delight emanates from the 'figurality' not the characterisation. Of course, on a semiotic and narrative level, her sincerity, serendipity and seductiveness are embraced by Orlando; he is truly smitten! The traumatic romanticism of love is pervasive through the context of the dialogue. French is spoken only by Sasha and Orlando, excluding lady Euphrosyne to the point of rejection. Within the panorama of romantic and arranged love (Sasha and Euphrosyne) we are constantly reminded of the fragility, the evanescence and ephemerality of life. Talk of a young girl having been turned to 'powder' by the winter's ravages, the fragility of the body in collusion with the natural world echoes in ironic and parodic detachment the uncertainty and fragility of romantic love, love which is not given a chance to develop, fluctuate, resonate or flourish. The semiotics of representation meld with the fluid semiotics of Deleuzian 'affect'. The affective is modulated through a complexity of resonance, dissipation and forced movements.

In terms of the technicalities of filming, the sequence again uses left to right panning devices, echoing earlier sequences and providing a rhythmical effect of linearity in terms of organised movements. This organised movement is broken up, traversed, by a cut to the following day, when skating is the main activity: courtship rituals are part of the 'content' of this mise-en-scène. But in terms of 'action', 'passion' and 'intensities', this scene is intensified by the correlation of both Sasha and Orlando functioning 'outside' the constructs and strictures of an organised, sterile, fixed community. This is evinced through their movements, conveyed by the camera mobility and montage. Both Orlando and Sasha ('She's a foreigner', shouts one person, indicating Sasha) resemble a line of flight, a line of velocity or becoming, beyond the segmentary. They function in terms of what Deleuze calls the 'anomalous' or the outsider: *l'étranger*. Sasha floats in, through and beyond the proclivities of an ordered culture and society, evincing a delicate dream-like sensuality on all around, especially Orlando. For, as Deleuze indicates,

> It is evident that the Anomalous, the Outsider, has several functions: not only does it border each multiplicity, of which it determines the temporary or local stability (with the highest number of dimensions possible under

the circumstances), not only is it the precondition for the alliance necessary to becoming, but it also carries the transformations of becoming, or crossings of multiplicities always farther down the line of flight.[9]

The entire sequence then is an assemblage of haecceities. Deleuze indicates that such haecceities are 'degrees of power which combine, to which correspond a power to affect and be affected, active or passive affects, intensities'.[10] Becoming-woman is this process of immanence, where becomings are specific movements, forms of rest, motion, speed, slownesses, points and flows of intensity. Such is experienced in this sequence. Such flows of intensity work outside any notion of gendered subjectivities or identity. They work through a materiality of the brain/body at a deeper level, in the proto-subjective, in the affective realms. The film's style articulates those 'affective intensities' in the ways it moves and vibrates. It works as molecular assemblage. Sasha, then, rather than being 'read' as a character, with a narrative trajectory and function, works as a 'figural' by means of which she brings together different elements of the material process of the film. She functions in locomotion, not as fixed locus of identity, as an abstract force, just like the Baconian figures in his paintings (see Chapter 3).

This is most poignantly effectuated in the seduction sequences. Sasha operates not only as the 'anomalous' but also as the 'figural' across the body of the screen. Through attitudes, gestures, postures, rhythmical sways, dissonant movements and consonant assemblage with other 'figural' elements such as the 'Orlando' character, she figures as 'life'. She presents a 'feeling' of vitality and dynamism through the joyousness of her movements. A truly passionate exemplification (in a Spinozist sense). In this way, the 'image' of Sasha becomes a 'movement-image' which functions as a performer, a body, a constituted body of molecularity which functions through the 'affective'. Indeed, a 'malleable mass of images' provides a harmonics which creates a nervous vibration through the visual and the aural. A totally physiological sensation, outside of subjectivity. Thus by dislocating, but not necessarily ignoring, semiotics, metonymy and metaphor, a 'deeper' level of experience or impact is proffered which articulates a profound relation of a brain–body–world connection. As we saw in Part Two, what happens in the filmic experience, as I have just described, is a perception of whole, a totality which incorporates the 'body'. The question is no longer one of association of images. The film leaves the scenario of 'image-formation' and functions as 'states' in motion. What matters is the interstices of those states, the interstitial, 'It is a method of between . . . it is a method of AND . . .

between two perceptions, between sound and image . . . the whole thus merges with what Blanchot calls the forces of the Outside.'[11]

Consequently, within this 'body', or cinematic body, what matters is not so much generic elements, characters, events, narrative, place, and so on, but, instead, words, tones, sounds, colours and refrains: the 'in-between' spaces of the film as text. Within this sequence, dancing provides a range of mobilised gazes, through mobilised camera angling. This range of lines projects lines of longitude and latitude, which echo the lines of flight taken by the 'figural' of Sasha. Through the geometrical and symmetrical sterility of the English courtiers, the dancing evokes different types of energy. There is a definite left to right symmetry in the courtiers' dancing, with a definite camera symmetry of left to right action. In contrast, Sasha's 'figural' or 'movement-image' encircles the sterility with lively, energetic and vivacious beauty, exhilarating and dynamic, epitomised by Orlando's words, 'I'm only interested in love.' This is evoked of course by the 'passional' energies of Sasha's vitality. Her 'spirit' and 'fire' are set in dissonance with the static dance of Euphrosyne, Orlando's betrothed. On a narrative level, Sasha functions as an emblem of freedom, spirit, and liberty – a freedom which cannot be contained, cajoled or won over by the auspices of romantic love and the possessiveness of patriarchal order. Sasha's skating evokes the figural as opposed to the character, in that her movements contrast and collide with the static movements, the horizontals and the verticals of the orderly dancing. The meandering, chaotic pathways of the skater provide a collusion of lines of intensity across the screen. These lines contrast in dissonance with the sterility evoked by the courtiers, and Orlando's dance. Such movements are experienced through the eye–brain and emit specific resonance to the nervous system, such that different levels of excitation are felt at a molecular level. Sasha joins the dance, with Orlando, who is warned, 'You are in danger of becoming a fool.' The fool and the lover are only too closely connected, as Deleuze writes,

> Make consciousness an experimentation in life, and passion a field of continuous intensities, an emission of particle-signs. Make the body without organs of consciousness and love. Use love and consciousness to abolish subjectification: 'To become the great lover, the magnetiser and catalyser . . . one has to first experience the profound wisdom of being an utter fool.'[12]

Glances, eye movements, body language, heads, faces and arms waft through a textured scene of velvety fabrics, furs, silks, rich and dusky chromatic tones, creating a tactility of the image, a hapticity. 'A man must follow his heart,' says Orlando, in complete parody of course, given that Tilda Swinton is 'playing both the fool and the man' here. But of course she is later to 'become-woman'.

Cut to Orlando and Sasha on a sleigh journey to Orlando's home. Once again the mise-en-scène repeats former sequences through the scintillating snow-scapes, evoking similar resonances for the viewer. A soft, muffled snow-scape evokes landscapes of silence, stillness and serenity within a dangerously lurking coldness; the coldness and cruelty of a love which is to be spurned. The intensity of the cold is evoked through the molecularity of the perception-image, not in any phenomenological sense, but through a molecularity of perception across atoms, fibres, molecules. A rich and crystallised sensuality is articulated, which 'melts' into narrative romanticism, when Orlando peels away Sasha's glove to imprint a delicate kiss (much resonant of Daniel Day-Lewis's similar sensual moment of kissing hands, in Scorsese's *Age of Innocence* (1993)) the lingering intensity of a desire unfulfilled, the intensity pervades through this lack of fulfillment, which if consummated would lose its immanence, its passional intensity. Sensuality pervades the sequence, specifically where Orlando reaches for Sasha's delicate and porcelain-like hand. The texture of the glove against the fleshy fragility of her skin is encompassed through a multiplicity of aesthetic resonances: the warmth of flesh against the coldness of the snow; tones, colours and perceptions impose upon the senses, in collusion with the gentle movements of face into hand. He kisses her hand, her cheek . . . her mouth.

> *What is it to kiss . . . In* Blade Runner, *Deckard kisses Rachel . . . The kiss . . . butterfly kiss, kiss of death, eternal kiss, kiss of . . . the spiderwoman? Spider, insect . . . insectoid . . . viroid . . . mantis religiosa . . . mantis-machine . . . Rodin's kiss? The kiss testifies to the integral unity of the face/mask and inspires within it the rest of the body . . . that facialised body. Rachel says, 'Kiss me . . . put your hands on me . . .' The tactility and sensuality of his kiss are facialised through her body, outside of the mask, beyond the simulacrum of her face, a contamination of erotogenic zones, aparalletic evolution. Desire disperses from the Metropolis, but there is no becoming without the wasp and the orchid.*

Such eroticism and sensuality are cruelly knocked back into the 'real' through the image of a beggar carrying wood across the lake semiotically depicting a foreboding doom and melancholy. Orlando prophetically announces, 'Nothing separates melancholy from happiness.'

The jealousy that Orlando feels is part of romantic and idealistic love, which is also wrapped into a transcendent idea of being: the soul being connected to another person's identity in some way is possibly a romantic love which is not liberating to the autonomy and autopoiesis of the individual in any way. In contrast love might be encompassed within an immanence, through a becoming-woman, where processuality and intensity of the moment are intrinsically more joyful than a possessive grasp of the innately jealous and transcendent notion of monogamous, Christian versions of love. Eastern perspectives on love in a wider sense encompass love of others outside such restrictive formulae. Western versus Eastern philosophies specifically illustrate this idea. Orlando says to Sasha, 'But I love you. Our destinies are joined.' Any notion of 'destiny' replete with Freudian determinations of origins and beginnings delimits the durational and vital joy of becoming. This is finely exemplified by the dramatic act from *Othello*, witnessed by Orlando. This is an act of death, melancholy, negativity, and all that is constitutive of death: stillness, void, loss of volition and creativity. In his murderous fit of jealousy, Othello cries over the body of Desdemona, 'of one who loved not wisely but too well, and in so doing threw a pearl away worth more than all his tribe'. Orlando speaks to camera 'terrific play'. An ironic comment on the problems with jealousy, but also a sincere remark on the pain involved in such egotistical and restrictive notions of love.

The 'Love' sequence is finalised with negative imagery: rain, harsh images of glaring faces, against a landscape of death, the death of romantic love. Lightning, rain, the cold, and thunder are conventional tropes of romantic narrativity. If we take these outside of the context of representation, such imagery works as vibration, resonance and forced movements, through specific perceptions. Liquid and gaseous perceptions accommodate a 'feeling' felt at a primordial level beyond subjectivity, emphasising the sterility of love which is not joyous and free in its energic, creative alignments with nature. Thus, we read nature as it epitomises in a Freudian sense negativity, lack, the crack-up. (The ice literally cracks up under Orlando.) Sasha, however, is not going to succumb to the pressure of an emotionally charged romantic love, a possessive and jealous manifestation of obsession. Orlando states, 'Sasha, I cannot think of a life without you. We're linked, our destinies are linked. You're mine. Because I adore you.' The aesthetic resonances of this sequence articulate an affectivity replete with despair, melancholy and trauma: the chiaroscuro lighting, the crack-up in the river flow, the camera-movements across the icy river, to the close-up of Orlando's face, which is a realisation of loss, as Orlando recognises the death of romantic love and the treachery of women/men. Orlando sleeps for seven days.

CUT TO 1650 – POETRY

The poetry sequence functions as a comic and parodic piece, parodying the nature of romantic love, whilst also functioning in dissonance with both the previous and the following tableaus. Most of the sequence is a narrative about poetry, its role in language, and its usefulness as a vehicle of expression. Visually, the sequence exudes irony through the use of performance styles, acting and directional techniques which provide humour. Orlando's pursuit of Greene through the gardens is a visual delight. Orlando's awkwardness is epitomised in the clumsiness of his gait and the sense of helplessness and anticipation in his body language also adds to the irony. Here, movement and rhythm operate to expose fickleness, distanciation and irony. The music, in its light-hearted and gentle delicacy, works with the movement-images, to create ironic distanciation. The sequence functions then as dissonance in counterpoint with both previous and following sections. The most enjoyable (purely 'subjective' in an ironic and parodic sense of course!) sequence of the movie follows.

1700 – POLITICS

This sequence has Orlando as ambassador in Turkey. It projects the epitome of cinema as 'event', as haecceity, as 'becoming-woman'. Questions of love, integrity, sovereignty, honour, loss, ownership, possession, betrayal and origins (themes equally resonant in *The English Patient*, and thus connects with that movie in several ways) are highlighted, through the plane of organisation and metaphor in this most beautiful of desert scenes. But here, such 'meanings', elements of the 'molar' semiotics of the film, become part of the assemblage of 'event'. In other words, the very process of the film as movement-image bequeaths a material emotion to such concepts. They are imbricated within the process of the film's duration, to the extent that the film's beauty is created from the resonances of the film's materiality, in duration, not necessarily meaning construction. Here, quite literally East meets West, Turkey providing the literal 'territoriality' which is to be deterritorialised: a political 'interstitial' space. However, this is also an evolution of two separate elements of experience: the transcendent culture of Western civilisation and ideology, set in contrast with the forces of immanence; and Eastern philosophies of immanence, becoming, and the processual. East becomes West. In their imbrication, erupts the event of 'becoming-woman'. Quite literally, the becoming-woman functions as part of the semiotic construction within the narrative. Orlando really does 'change' here, in this sequence, from male to female. Boundaries are melded, merged, colluded and reassembled, producing a molecularity of sexualities, cultures and bodies. A series of 'becomings'.

The narrative trajectory shows Orlando as ambassador to Turkey, for the King of England, but Orlando functions outside the role of 'character'. As Deleuze indicates, 'what matters . . . is not the opinions held by the characters, in accordance with their social types and characteristics, but rather the relations of counterpoint into which they enter, and the compounds of sensations that those characters either themselves, experience, or make felt, in their becomings and visions'.[13]

The relations of counterpoint into which Orlando enters are imbricated with those 'energies', 'intensities' and 'singularities' of the Khan (Lothaire Bluteau). As a result, a melding, another space, another 'zone' is discernible which takes from both Western and Eastern philosophies, cultural values, ideologies and libidinalities, and offers another 'in-between' state, the 'aparalletic evolution' of Western and Eastern, masculine and feminine, transcendence and immanence. Both 'characters' might be male: the irony is that we 'know' that Orlando is actually 'female' in reality, and narratively is both male and female, as androgyne. But he/she/ it functions within this sequence to distanciate that fixed subjective and gendered positionality. As Orlando states in the most beautiful sequence of the movie, 'same person, no difference at all. Just a different sex.'

Orlando arrives in Turkey, an honourable and respected member of the British establishment, dressed in ludicrous regalia of Georgian style: lace, velvet and adorning wig. This symbol of Englishness is totally out of place in the Eastern ambience of pure simplicity, gentleness, sincerity and fluidity. On a semiotic level, such signs function as cultural tropes. However, on a Deleuzian paradigm, we can understand this sequence in more resonant ways. Indeed, there is a 'becoming-other' of the two cultures, which is visually and haptically manifested. Here, the Khan greets Orlando. The scene is one of calm, stillness, warmth, esoteric beauty, swaying movement. The words the Khan utters, implicate, imbricate and oscillate this sense of immanence. 'To the beauty of women and the joys of love . . .' The ambience of the scene is modulated, as material emotion, through specific filmic devices. Specific, individual shots highlight the isolation of the two main 'figures': Orlando and the Khan. Their isolation and difference is exacerbated by their positionality in relation to the desert. They perform as 'figural' elements in a landscape of silence, of acceptance and acknowledgement. On a narrative level, there is no sense of judgement, power or confrontation, although the Khan's power is implicit. Rather an atmosphere resonates with 'becoming-woman'. The lighting is suffused; the gentle rhythms of the desert landscape with deftly and delicately wafting grains of sand evoke a gentle warmth. Flames of fire light up the desert during an evening's repartee; flames flicker in a 'becoming' with the notes and tones of the diegetic music. Harmonies and tones of voices meld in vocal discord, which is simultaneously a harmonious discord. An Eastern evocation of the molecular.

Complexity is formulaic here in that the sequence does show us a literal 'becoming-woman' when Orlando changes gender and yet the sequence also functions as the epitome of 'becoming-woman' of immanence. If we relate this to the forces of Western and Eastern beliefs, what emerges is a valorisation of the imbrication across those spaces. But, I feel there is much more resonant beauty in the immanence of the Eastern. In terms of 'sensation' two discrete and separate intensities are here felt in synthesis. An embrace, or a clinch, of two different states of being is evoked: a state of symbiotic energies. The singularities (see Part Two) of each state energise and collide. But there is also a form of 'forced movement', which, as Deleuze indicates, occurs when '. . . two contrary sensations draw apart, release themselves, but also now to be brought together by the light, the air, or the void that sinks between them'.[14] Both forms of sensation are manifest through the film style, a style which uses suffused lighting, long-shots of the desert-scape, gently swaying rhythmic move-ments resembling the wind and other natural elements, evoked through the flames of the fires. Through the aesthetic resonances of the film, the 'void' or the intransigence is 'felt' between the two elements of different cultures. A differential relationship.

There is a 'becoming-other' which is felt through the molecularity of the sound molecules; the way in which certain sounds are heard in synthesis with particular movement-images. For example, the body movements of characters become 'figures' within the landscape, oscillat-ing in rhythmical sway with the beauty of the desert. This is most preciently obvious in Orlando's relaxing into Eastern belief, style, posture and reclination. His 'figural' operates in a liquid, ephemeral and evocative pose, across the entire screen, a pose which displays the delicate, sensuous lines of curvature across the body, through to the stance, and position of his head. Orlando reclines, relaxes, throws back her/his head in a pose of tranquillity. The colours and the textures provide both a visual and haptic sense, engulfing the frame: delicate hues of white, ochre, greys blend with the suffuse lighting and soft focus. The still shot provides a tableau in itself. As a 'figure' rather than a character, Orlando functions to modulate the becoming of this entire sequence. As such it serves to provide a critical turning point within the narrative and diegetic trajectory. The posture of Orlando is echoed in harmony in the later sequence, 'Sex', where Orlando is making love with Shelmerdine. The desert sequence exemplifies the joy of becoming, through an Eastern landscape, which in terms of fluid semiotics proposes a philosophy of becoming: a philosophy of the immanent. This is further exemplified by the dress codes. The Khan of Turkey epitomises in style, grace and demeanour the very essence of 'becoming' and hence is sensually premised on the existence of processual feeling – no finality, no endings, no fixed orgasmic point of closure. Such sexuality scintillates in total flux: no ending, no consummation, no fulfilment of desire, but a desire in process. In comparison Orlando, dressed in garish, awkward clothes and long inelegant wig, looks awkward, overpowered with redundant garments. They jar with the melodic and desultory visuals of the desert landscape.

When the Archduke returns for Orlando's investiture, he finds him/her a 'changed' person. Ironically, we know that this change is almost a literal account of what happens to him. Of course, all that is gentle, fluid, rhythmic within the Turkish culture is also completely filled with resolute determination, power and control. In the Kahn's asking for English support in battle, Orlando is compromised and finds all her/his desire, feelings, emotions, contradictory and oscillating. When he/she discovers a dying man, his/her reaction is to help, regardless of the status of the enemy. Such actions might be read through essentialist feminist debates around gender qualities – female or male – but this is too binary a reading, too static and reductionist a model. Death, loss and decay are redolent of a Western cultural belief in transcendence, finality, a return to fixed originations and centres of inorganic being. The slow, pulsating music with delicate tones set in point-counterpoint play in harmony with the fluid camera shots. Water functions in this sequence to provoke a liquid perception of the movement-images. The 'image' of Orlando floats through the molecularity, like the 'trickster'. Our perception of this image is determined via a resonance of eye–brain movements. The eye–brain connects across several elements. An instant cerebellum efferent motor response is modulated, which in turn effects a disturbance felt at a deeper level than subjectivity. It is felt at a molecular level, in the proto-subjective. The image that we see of Orlando, in transition, in transformation, influences the body/brain/mind in synaesthetic ways, through the kinaesthetics of filmic techniques, and provides a newly defined notion of the beautiful in the sense of beauty as a time-concept or triage, and not a concern with form and space. Indeed the scene evokes a new and disturbing notion of the beautiful. How is this scene beautiful? Why is this scene beautiful? The beauty does not lie in the 'form' of the images, or the tones and colours alone, but in the movements, the various forms of motion (one instinctively is reminded of David Lynch's description of 'speeds' in his most resonant sequences), which have been scientifically proven to be more appealing and alluring to the eye–brain. Like the pathways of the butterfly as I mentioned earlier, the camera shots here oscillate and weave a visionary dance across the eye–brain. This makes the brain continually break and form, break and form, like a series of waves, breaking from any symmetry. It is the motion that locks and entrains the brain that creates the allure and resonance of the sensation in this sequence. Similarly, the lighting causes a flickering of the eye, a delicate and insouciant movement, providing an ecliptic experience. The camera shots trace movement, such that the 'image' is 'matter'.

The sequence ends with Orlando, now Lady Orlando, travelling across the desert, away to the future, and back to the West, the transformation having been emanated through a literal 'becoming-woman'. Transcendence and immanence are binarily opposed and yet joined together: transcendence projecting a locus in an essential core, an inorganic sense of oneness in death; immanence reflecting the evanescence of life's ephemerality. In the 'in-between' spaces, where subjectivity is rendered subjectless, but not without feeling, and emotion, is the newly molecularised space. As a film, *Orlando* exemplifies this 'in-between' state in so many ways: the 'interstitial' states. Emotion is not thus totally negated and semiotics are not completely disregarded, but all are operative at a level of machinic assemblage, working at a level outside and beyond subjectivity.

Cut – to the second part of the movie with Orlando as female Lady Orlanda, in 1750s society. The 'image' of woman very clearly implied in the costume, dress and body language. Acting styles, performance style, the walking, gestures and body language of Orlando, epitomise the critique of masculine notions of femininity, and patriarchal conventions of female 'form'. Potter purposely uses such a style to present an ideological statement in the film. Once again, humour functions in this sequence to contrast and distinguish it from the previous sequence. Indeed, on a level of structuralist semiotics, the entire sequence 'Society' exemplifies a particularly static feminist stance.

Visually, the sequence is overly detailed and a variety of rich textures and colours, tones of blues, lilacs and whites, unites with the tactility of Orlando's dress. The beautiful white dress she wears is both a trope of those feminist debates, and yet is also an enigma, in its beauty. The carnivalesque, the masquerade, the simulacra are all pertinent to an understated beauty of the dress. Its colours, delicacy of frothy, white textures and sheer exuberance epitomise a desire to feel, in a sensuous tactile and visceral way, the experience of actually wearing it. (Of course now I will get a backlash from all sorts of feminist circles – who could possibly want to wear such a monstrosity? But who has not truly wanted to wallow in the finery of such rich 'costume' and 'display', to truly masquerade in simulation and seductive simulacra? The erotics of exhibitionism.[15]) The butterfly really does float through the gardens, here in the guise of Orlando. The hapticity of the image is one of sheer resonance. Texture and sight merge in fusion. As a 'figural' Orlando floats across the screen, quite literally, like a butterfly, evoking the pleasures of rhythm, movement and duration. As Virginia Woolf states, 'the sequence provides a bloc of ages, a block of epochs'[16] which are bound by the duration of linear time-scales. But the significance of *Orlando* (the movie) is that it reflects the formality and rigidity of a time-ordered set of beliefs and time-space sequentiality. Birth and death are reversed as 'orders of being' and life's evanescence is explored across the zones, across cultures, where connections and assemblages function in dichotomous arenas. Orlando 'acts' the figural, drawing together the movements, much like the Baconian figure of the triptych.

The fifth sequence, 'Sex' (1850), takes the narrative into Victorian England. Emerging from a maze in Victorian dress, Lady Orlanda falls to the ground. Piano concertos express the parody of the overt romanticism in this sequence. She falls at the feet of no other than Shelmerdine (a delicious and delirious Billy Zane), who emerges like an elusive romantic hero, replete with horse, from the 'mists of time'. What woman has not truly been in awe of such a figure (parodic or not? – romantic and Bovarian even? Such dishonesty!)? A sequence rich in a simultaneous parodic/pleasurable exploration of romantic and clichéd love, the scene serves to project Orlando into a 'future zone', where the infallibilities of love are distanciated through the beauty of a zone without 'gender'. The future looks blissful but paradoxically uncertain in a world in which the intransigencies of binary sexuality and power are diffracted through a landscape of aesthetically sensuous movements, speeds and nuances. A future of hopeful becomings, joyful cruelties and imperceptible zones.

NOTES

1. Deleuze and Guattari, *A Thousand Plateaus*, p. 255.
2. Deleuze and Guattari, *A Thousand Plateaus*, p. 294.

3. See Christian Metz, *Essais sur la signification au cinéma*; *Film Language: A Semiotics of the Cinema*; *Language and Cinema*; 'The Imaginary Signifier', in *Screen*; and *The Imaginary Signifier: Psychoanalysis and the Cinema*.
4. Deleuze and Guattari, *A Thousand Plateaus*, p. 266.
5. Carol Smith-Rosenberg, *Disorderly Conduct*, p. 291.
6. Virginia Woolf, *Modern Fiction: The Common Reader*, p. 189.
7. E. Cioran, *Anathemas and Admirations*, p. 4.
8. Deleuze and Guattari, *A Thousand Plateaus*, p. 277.
9. Deleuze and Guattari *A Thousand Plateaus*, p. 249.
10. Deleuze and Parnet, *Dialogues*, p. 92.
11. Deleuze, *Cinema 2*, p. 180.
12. Deleuze and Guattari, *A Thousand Plateaus*, p. 134, taken from Henry Miller, *Sexus*, p. 229.
13. Deleuze and Guattari, *What is Philosophy?*, p. 188.
14. Deleuze and Guattari, *What is Philosophy?*, p. 168.
15. See Dot Tuer, 'Pleasures in the Dark: Sexual Difference and Erotic Dev-iance in an Articulation of Female Desire', in *Cineaction*,
16. Virginia Woolf, *The Diary of Virginia Woolf*, vol. 3, p. 236 (Wednesday, 28 November 1928).

Chapter 7

The English Patient –
Deleuzian Landscapes of Immanence

we die, we die rich
with lovers . . . tastes we have swallowed,
bodies we have entered and swum up
like rivers,
fears we have hidden in

I want this marked on my body
where the real country is,
no boundaries or properties
of powerful men

that's all I ever wanted . . .
to walk in such a place with you.
With friends, an earth without maps.
. . . the light's gone out and
I am writing in the darkness.

Maps, mapping and rhizomes offer a creative and experimental panoply in the light of Deleuzian ideas, and yet maps also resonate across the narrative trajectory of the filmic experience in *The English Patient*. In this chapter I want to imbricate both a reading of Deleuzian mappings through the film and a reading of the film through Deleuzian ideas. A complete travesty it might be argued, given the post-humanism of his thinking, the coldness and cruelty of his rejections. A melding of two perspectives. What appears to be delirious and overindulgent narrativity is a serious inception to rethinking the trajectories of 'love' in a post-humanist vision. A map, not a tracing, suggests Deleuze, is how we experience existence, how we articulate and 'feel', albeit at a proto-subjective level, within the molecular structures of the autopoietic realms of our being, our 'becoming' with the world.

[T]he rhizome is altogether different, *a map and not a tracing*. Make a map, not a tracing. The orchid does not reproduce the tracing of the wasp: it forms a map with the wasp, in a rhizome. What distinguishes the map from the tracing is that it is entirely oriented toward an experimentation in contact with the real.[1]

In narrative terms to *The English Patient*, maps and mapping are essential elements within a plot which centres around the memories of a mortally wounded and burnt war veteran and map-maker, Count Almásy (Ralph Fiennes). On a level of structuralist language, and within a plane of organisation (as opposed to a plane of immanence – the molar rather than the molecular), the film juxtaposes elements of time, memory, place and identities through a variety of technical methods: specific forms of camera angling, fades, wipes, flashbacks and dissolves, all have a creative role to play in the relating of Almásy's narrative. The injured patient had been a member of the Royal Geographical Society, responsible for map-making prior to and during the first stages of the Second World War. The narrative juxtaposes his experiences and his tragic love affair with Katharine Clifton (Kristin Scott Thomas) both through, within and across the landscapes of war-torn Africa and Italy. Together with his colleague map-makers, Count Almásy quite literally creates 'maps' from their research into the terrain of the African landscape, searching and contextualising new discoveries from caves of repute to plateaus of metaphorical significance. The discoveries are both literal and metaphorical. Mapping the emotional and the relational as much as the spatial. Maps, then, per se, are profoundly significant both literally within the diegesis of the film and its narrative and ideological plateaux. Their purposes to both the Germans and the Allies within the movie become important elements within the plot, and Almásy's role within that.

But maps too readily speak of ownership, territory, possession, sovereignty, boundaries, containment and reclamation. The body, however, to refer us back to Katharine's dying words, is that which cannot, should not and will not be claimed, owned, possessed, just like the mind with which it is imbricated. Indeed it is the body without organs through which we can discern a sense of 'becoming' with the world, and Katharine's final words, resonant also in Almásy's words to her during one of their love sequences, direct an understanding of the exigencies of individual autonomy, freedom and 'becomings' beyond the confines of ownership through a collusion across subjectivities or identities between people. Becoming is beyond subjectivity: beyond any self/other relational. There is, through the processuality of 'becoming' and specifically becoming-woman, an autonomous, autopoietic level of existence through which life is lived and experienced at a molecular level, outside the exigencies of self to other relations, a purely viral and genetic evolution of life, in a truly biological or germinal sense: mind and body becoming with the world, in true autopoiesis. A vital sense of who and what we are (see Part Two).

Dialogue in the film provides an auditory 'map' through which we might connect with these ideas. Katharine's words become almost an ode to 'becoming-woman', where subjectivity is relinquished or subsumed to a sense of 'becoming' with the world itself, in a truly molecular sense. Obviously, what I am doing here, I have to acknowledge, is partially reading the film 'through' some Deleuzian ideas, across the auspices of filmic spaces, and I can detect voices of disapproval which will display horror at the thought of 'using' Deleuze in any way at all. I defend this by merely implicating and colluding with his ideas, across the molar readings of the film, through more ideological, structuralist, and metaphorical approaches. I want to discern the 'in-betweenness' of the molar and the molecular, to try to offer an innovative way of articulating the filmic experience, beyond the arenas of psychoanalysis, replete, as I have shown with a self/other relationship to issues of subjectivity and identity. This 'in-betweenness' both acknowledges and, yet, deterritorialises the molar elements of film 'readings' in a collaboration with the molecular and material elements of bio-aesthetics, sensation, affect and becoming-woman. A richer and more contingently textured expression of the 'haecceity' of filmic worlds.

I am not, of course, negating the significance of the film's semiotic and structuralist planes of being, the plane of organisation in a Deleuzian sense, through which we, as viewers, discern a specific set of narratives, played out through a group of characters, within and across a complex time/space zone. Neither am I suggesting that all those who view will necessarily discern the Deleuzian resonances throughout – such readings come with a required understanding and reading of the philosophy itself, or of course reading books like this! But one can excite, enrich, collide, indeed, meld with the other to open up new vistas of awareness and becoming. Deleuzian ideas, both in their philosophical explorations of becoming as the beyond of subjectivity and in explorations of the affective state as existing beyond any subjectivity, within the singularities of a proto-subjective state, enable us to consider the film as molecular body, in collusion with other bodies, creating a body without organs, an event, a haecceity.

I ask my reader, therefore, to go with my lines of flight, between, across and beyond the molar, and into the molecular, to both read Deleuze through film and film through Deleuze, as a form of film-philosophy, to discover a richer and more intense sense of the 'haecceities' of the filmic event and Deleuzian vitalism: an understanding of film aesthetics as the in-betweenness of a bio-aesthetic of sensation, and an event of 'becoming-woman'. A film, then, about map-making and literal territorialisation, nonetheless draws another 'map' in a vital (Deleuzian) sense; it connects, it melds and collides both the molar with the molecularity of 'becoming-woman' through immanence and a neo-aesthetic of sensation. That neo-aesthetic is premised on a biological notion of a pre-existing sense of existential integrities, outside of subjectivity, where indeed the brain is the subject itself. The brain is the centre of any sense of singularity outside a subjective state (see Chapter 4).

My exploration (and I purposely choose *not* to use the word 'reading' as this is too narrow a term) of the filmic event of *The English Patient* moves through the interstitial spaces of molar and molecularity. 'Becoming-woman' is a process of immanence, a description of the processual nature of affect, as opposed to subject. If 'becomings' are always specific movements, forms of rest, motion, speed, slownesses, such flows of intensity operate beyond any subjectivity, through the proto-subjective realm of an autopoietic state, through the 'unthought' or plane of immanence, which imbricates the material of the brain/body/mind at a deeper level than the subjective encounter. I write about *The English Patient*, then, from this 'in-between' or interstitial state.

Once again, I begin with endings. But the end is also the beginning. Katharine's dying words in the Cave of Swimmers provide a fundamental core to the affective spaces of *The English Patient*. Rich in a variety of tonalities, vibrations and syntheses with *Orlando*, the film's haecceity is expounded through both teleological and non-teleological elements. Love, death, sovereignty, ownership, possession, betrayal, loss and the exigencies of 'life' lived through 'becoming' connect across the visual, aural and the material pathways of the film, creating an architecture of encounter beyond representation, felt within the cellular structures of the brain's synapses and cellular structures, as much as within the emotions. I don't want to eradicate any conception of the emotional as having an important role to play in our experience of movies, but to suggest that there are other forces, within the biological make-up of our brain cells, that impinge on perception and consciousness.[2] What I am concerned with is affect, rather than emotion. The emotional might be discerned through the narrative structures of filmic events, in the sense of plot, for example. But as yet neuroscience has been unable to detect or explain how the emotions are triggered within brain patterns, as a result of specific experiences such as film.

Thematically, the film depicts a love story (ironies, of course, abound, since any notions of love premised on a self–other dichotomy, where subjectivity is premised as part of that binary relationship as we see in psychoanalytic discourse, are critiqued with Deleuzian resistance of such romantic and transcendent concepts). In Deleuzian terms, love might exist through finer, more deeply felt resonances of 'becoming' beyond any sense of self–other dichotomy, within, instead, the intensities of a processuality, a sense of evolution, a love of life's fuller, and finer, potentialities, its singularities: a 'different' love from the romantic, possessive self–other relational. In a sense, then, the film does explore, narratively, a romantic tale, but within that is the discernment of possessive love, ownership and 'territorialisation' through Almásy's relationship with Katharine. His words 'I hate ownership' are a response to her 'I hate a lie'; both are resonantly critical of clichéd 'romantic' love. Both, however, are caught up in a web of ownership, possession and lies in the intensity of romantic, adulatory and passionate love. In narrative terms, maybe their love is genuine, intense, profound and deeply mutual, and yet such a love brings with it lies and deceit, denials and regrets, pain and torment, as both Katharine and Almásy struggle with how to allow their love to have any resonance within the confines of a world confounded with binary moralities, fixed positionalities: no Spinozist ethics here! But at least Katharine tries to discern her love for Almásy as 'different': 'Here I am a different wife, in a different life.' Their affair, like all affairs outside the structure of monogamous and 'moral' confines, has to be doomed (this is a film after all) to tragic failure. This is what makes it romantic. The romance lies in the tragedy. The 'lie' is also of course to negate the potentialities of a richer self-love, of autonomy, of autopoiesis, which exist beyond the constraints of a self–other relation and yet enrich the experience of 'living' beyond subjectivity. That enrichment can of course feedback into relations with others, not just a self/other, in a truly Deleuzian vitalist sense. Katharine's first appearance in the movie foregrounds, through her words, the significance of different 'loves'. 'Romantic love, filial love, Platonic love. Surely not the same thing?' She seduces Almásy. The film narratively depicts the themes of love, impossible love, the boundaries of forbidden love, and the consequences of tragic love. The heart, suggests Hana in one sequence, 'is an organ of fire', and should have an acknowledgement within any sense of a beyond of the subjective. Where is the 'heart' within the finer molecular structures of singularities?

Set in 1939, the story unfolds of the disastrous, passionate and obsessive love affair between Count Almásy and Katharine Clifton, set within the confines of a world fascinated by, embroiled in and organised through 'territorialisation'. Map-making, sovereignty and ownership are highlighted through acts of sanctioning, sectioning and segregation across endemic moral codings. On a narrative and semiotic level (molar) the film offers a wealth of possibilities in terms of ideological readings: the auspices of political embroilment, through which the individual loses all sense of integrity, self-hood and autonomy.

We are taken into the movements and rhythms of the film through an opening shot which provides a Deleuzian sense of collusion at that point between the material and the sensation: 'The material is so varied . . . that it is difficult to say where in fact the material ends and the sensation begins.'[3] An artist's paintbrush is tracked across the screen from left to right, delicately tracing the liquidity of paint on to canvas (rock) of the screen, the imprints of colour, a rich, dark, crimson red; then it sweeps across the spectator's visual pathway from left to right. The processuality of such devices portrays the dynamic and processual beauty of *The English Patient* from the outset. This first sequence, together with the diegetic rhythms of Hungarian folk music, evokes a synaesthesia of colour/sound synthesised by the visual rhythms of the camera movements, which echo the former brush strokes, strokes which create tiny sculptured images: elongated shapes of swimmers, or maybe those in flight, across a spatial/time zone unknown, but foregrounded as a significant archaeological find. The elongated shapes of swimmers could also be flying, escaping across the rock/cave face/canvas across different time and spatial zones. Swimmers who take us, quite literally, in terms of the camera's directional movements into the movie, and simultaneously a flight through the depths of life's intransigencies, sexualities, death, love, betrayal and contradictions. *Orlando* collides already from the beginning of the movie.

The harmonies of the Hungarian folk music both echo and complement the possible Eastern origins. The melodic sounds counterpoint the diegetic rhythms and notes from the tinkling bells, birds and camels baying. A variety of tones and melodic intonations affect the nervous system of the viewer/observer/spectator at a neurological level. This neurological level exemplifies that intertwining of brain/mind and body which is the arena of an autonomous and autopoietic sense of self, the brain as absolute survey. Sounds impinge upon the body through the labyrinthine mechanisms of the hearing system, into the wave patterns within the brain's neurological make-up. These affect the nervous system as a vibrational force through the cerebral cortex, into the mind/body/brain through the molecularity of the body. In rhythmic synchronisation with these sounds, the camera pans from left to right . . . an aerial shot across the desert-scape revealing a plane, gliding across the frame. Chaos emerges in the proceeding attack. Visually, the desert landscape wavers with soft undulating curves, contrasting in dissonance with the harsh, clinical lines of metal, weapons, armoury – the cacophany of the war-machine of the previous sequence. The narrative offers a comparison of healing scenarios between the army's methods and those of the nomads. An eclecticism of camera angling in the military convoy sequence and usage of diegetic sounds contrasts with the Eastern voices and chantings of the Arabian healers, as the film cuts across the desert-scape. Slow, haunting chants and a delicate air of gentleness pervade the scene, and contrast therefore most resiliently with a painfully visceral image of the patient, burnt to the point of non-recognition (all identity deterritorialised – subjectivity distanciated). Already, the intensities and energies of the movie as 'matter' are effectuated through the hapticity of the movement-images. The smoke, flames and chaos of the Western war-machine are set in dissonant contrast with the lingering long-shots of the desert and its Eastern (immanent) resonations. The former is replete with harsh angles, eviscerating textures, discordant tones and sounds which collide and grate; the latter is smoother, undulating, gently rhythmical and flowing, synaesthetically drawn together by the resonant chanting. The sounds of tinkling bells, medicinal phials and drinking bottles collide with the shifting noises of camels baying. The camera movements work in symbiotic resonance, as an embrace, as a forced clinch of vibrations. The glistening jewel-like radiance of liquids, purples, pinks, rubies and emeralds contrast in forced movement with the sounds of the chanting and the haptic image of the 'burning' face. The close-up of Almásy's face, with the healing hands gently administering some sort of ointment, is painfully visceral.

Narrative action cuts to Italy 1944, and so the rest of the movie progresses through a series of flashbacks, between war-torn episodes of Almásy's past, and the present scenes depicting his death's progression in the monastery in Tuscany with Hana (Juliette Binoche), who nurses him through to his death. It is 1944, Italy; the patient is interrogated about his past, his position in the war, his nationality and identity. The flashback creates a structure which maps out the territory of resonances and intensities of affective experiences in the film. By contrast, and collision, the flashes are forced movements which resonate a harmonising rhythm to the entirety of the film's process. But movements and rhythms are imbricated with the stillness and silence of specific frames and shots.

For example, the death of Hana's friend, Jan. The sudden explosion of Jan's military truck as it overtakes the rest of the military convoy is a shock both intradiegetically and to the audience. Hana's immediate response is to run to Jan. She is restrained, and held closely by Hardy. Hana's stationary, fixed stance, set against the flat landscape, exaggerates the horror and desolation of the scene. This stillness, as opposed to the movements of 'becoming' throughout the film, is emphasised by the camera's long-shot, the desolation of the landscape created through the blocks of colour, in contrasting bands of green and blue: earth and sky. The 'in-betweenness' enervates the pain, shock and silence of the stillness in death. Exaggeration is created by stylistic means of such clashes, or vibrations. But a richer understanding of the film as 'experience' must bring together the 'in-betweenness' of molecular and molar elements, linking narrativity, linearity and molecularity of a neo-aesthetics premised upon neuroscience. 'But the results of these experiments give us powerful hints about the way in which the visual brain works. They provide compelling evidence to show that different processing systems take different times to reach their end-points, which is the perception of the relevant attribute. This in turn suggests that the processing systems are also perceptual systems, thus allowing us to think of several parallel processing-perceptual systems . . . By definition, perception is a conscious event.'[4]

The narrative, then, is part of the total assemblage of the film's movements. Hana, after Jan's death, says, 'I must be a curse; anybody who loves me dies,' as she looks towards the monastery, which is to become the resting place for Almásy to his death. Hana wanders up into the hillside to view the monastery. Contrasts, collisions and forced movements are epitomised by the dissonance of sequences here: the gory, bloody sequences of the hospital convoy are contrasted with Hana's walk through the minefield's landscape of both terror and silence. In further contrast, when Hana goes out to look at the monastery in the hills, we feel the delicate insouciance and silence of the wind's gently molecular movements across the wispy grasses, ferns and flowers: the rippling motion of the water with its reflections fibrillates a motion, a controlled motion which creates a tranquillity to the brain/mind/body of the viewer. This motion resonates with the colours, tones and textures of this sequence, beautifully climaxed, both visually and aurally, in Hana's discovery of the derelict monastery and the old piano – no dialogue, no diegetic music, pure cinema (in a Hitchcockian sense – that is, the very absence of sound is part of the drama). This is broken, or rather eclipsed, by the enchanting sound of Hana's piano playing; the celerity and timbre of the notes harmonise and, through the effectuation within the brain's cellular structures, simultaneously create an equal dissonance with the textures and colours of the landscape. Such colours are subsequently contrasted with the grey, subdued, cold, sultry tones of the monastery's interior; dusty, ancient frescoes gently meld with the emptiness of the room; echoes and distant ghosts pervade the ambience of the sequence. Slow, controlled panning of the camera projects the grey, white, pale and dusky-coloured marble textures of the monastery . . . in rich contrast with the earlier vital, and verdant, beauty of the natural world.

Sensuality pervades the ensuing sequence, not only visually and aurally, but within the performative actions of the actors, as 'figurals' across the canvas of the screen. Hana leans forward to feed her patient with rich, juicy plums. A close-up of fingers-into-mouth evocatively embraces a richness of texture, tactility and indeed taste. 'A very plum, plum,' states the patient. Such simplicity is captured by Hana's words, 'I don't know anything', in reply to Almásy's questions about history and Herodotus. Woman's body functions as 'figural'. Hana's body, in her movements as nurse to Almásy, in her dancing, in her playing the piano, in her relationship with Kip, in her innocent sense of awe and wonder at the frescoes in the Italian church, is paralleled with, and also contrasted to the quietly sedate, controlled, and yet erotic performativity of Katharine. Both women function as 'figurals' across the canvas, providing different but colluding resonances of 'becoming-woman'. Both women are part of the trajectory of a 'becoming-woman' of the movie. Indeed, the beauty of the female body is narratively foregrounded in the Herodotus extract spoken by Katharine, the tone, delicacy and rhythm of her words evoking the beauty of 'woman'. Katharine suggestively and seductively glances at Almásy, as he visually responds to the words from the Herodotus text. In this, Gyges, the King, loses his wife to Candaules, a suitor for the King's wife. Her 'body' becomes the catalyst and precursor to romantic and uxurious love, foregrounded in the film through Katharine's relationship with Geoffrey Clifton (Colin Firth), her husband, in contrast to her passionate, illicit love for Almásy. Woman's body is a symbolic territory within the movie, from the landscapes of the desert, and the 'shape of a woman's back' as Almásy describes some mountain formations, to the ethereal and fluid images in the Cave of Swimmers. It is woman's body, performing as 'figural', not as representative image, either through Hana or Katharine, which carries the movements of becoming throughout the movie. This is most apparent in both the dance sequences and the erotic love sequences. Such sequences function as contrasts in dissonance with the war/death sequences.

The entire film performs as a choreographed dance of memory: past, present and future. The female body performs as movement-image through several dance sequences. First is the dance at the luncheon club of the Royal Geographical Society, where Almásy first falls in love with Katharine. The intensity of their mutual passion is finely silenced in its illicitness, the passion all that more electric, through their first dance together. Looks, glances, silence and insouciance characterise the body language and patterns of looking between Almásy and Katharine. The febrile and delicious erotics of their movements are encapsulated by the circling camera movements and the rhythms of their dancing. The silence between them is all that more intense and vibrational.

Many of the desert sequences recall *Orlando*, providing links across the two films, thus providing a resonance and vibration of intensities across and between texts, which we can read together and in opposition. The first desert sequence introduces Katharine and Clifton into the narrative. The beauty of the movements of the camera provide a dissonant experience for the viewer, by virtue of the effects on the visual system of the cerebral cortex. A discussion about love, romantic love, filial love, Platonic love or uxorious love highlights a sequence which is then followed by rhythmical, undulating and sweeping camera movements of planes in flight, twisting and turning in tune to each other, with shot-reverse-shot camera actions between Almásy and Katharine hinting at an inferred romantic connection. The plane's flight patterns, the undulating lines of the sand dunes and the spatial expanses of the desert sequence evoke, through a neuro-aesthetic effect upon the brain,[5] a feeling of pleasure, through the processuality of the camera's movements. This is imbricated with the colours, which visually impact upon certain sections of the brain in particular pleasurable ways. The flight of the plane through the desert then evokes a becoming through its effects on the brain/body/mind. Certain sequences around the campfire collide with the earlier sequences in the desert in *Orlando*, reminiscent of Eastern resonations of immanence and becoming as opposed to Western vagaries of representation and being, in a transcendent sense. Such desert sequences occur in contrast and resonance with other sequences. For example, the medical convoy train is contrasted with the desert scene where the nomads tend Almásy. Shapes, colours, tones, lines, rhythms move in delicate contrast with the chaotic movements of the war scenes. Wherever there is a desert sequence, this is stylistically created with patterns of lines, tones, rhythms, shapes which contrast with both preceding and succeeding sections of the movie. The beauty of the desert contrasts with the horrendous death-like image of the burnt and dying body of Almásy in the monastery.

The desert sequences also contrast in resonance with the Tuscan landscapes of beauty. This is specifically apparent at the end of the film when Hana looks inspirationally towards a future, a new becoming, outside and beyond the confines of the war-torn Tuscan landscapes that she has experienced. Her future inspirational outlook is filmically conveyed through the intensity of the bright colours, blues, reds, greens, the camera's movements, the lighting, flickering sunlight projected through the trees, as she looks towards the young girl, an indication of the positivity of her unknown, but potentially joyful future. The joys of becoming-girl.[6] To follow a scene on the discussion of love with such a beautiful display of movements, tones, colours and processuality colludes two paradigms for the viewer, thus possibly impinging on the emotional, but through the affectivity and molecularity of the film's movements, speeds. What I mean here is that the flight sequences are quite beautiful to view and to feel (process not form), but following from the previous sequence, such affects resonate with the molar experience of the film's narrative and molar plane of organisation, characters, dialogue and so on. But there is an 'in-betweenness' which explains that space between the molar and the molecular. The viewer is affected in a neuro-aesthetic way, but also in an emotional (and the emotions have not yet been adequately explored within neuroscience to suggest that there is biological explanation for their behaviours) way. Thus the affective level through mind/body and brain functions alongside the emotional level imbricated through dialogue and narrativity. The 'in-between' space of the molar and the molecular evokes a richer engagement with the body of the film.

In terms of the haecceity of sensation the film works as a machinic opera, assembling consonant or dissonant rhythms, cadences as sequences which act as either vibration, resonance or a distension of forced movements. For example, colour operates as the modulator of such sensations. The desert and love sequences, which render the beautiful as processual, as movement, incorporate colour as a major element. Katharine, in all the erotic sequences, wears white, usually of a delicate texture, muslin, silk or some other 'feminine' evocation. In contrast, she wears red flowers and ornaments in her hair or on her dress (in one sequence, all that is red is symbolic both of the Christmas festivities and of her passion for Almásy). The silk texture of her stockings against her flesh and the silk underwear against her shoulders emphasise a romantic femininity, and their undoing is a delicious venture into the erotic.

Nothing blatant: febrile sensuality. Hana's blue floral dresses flow with a liquid movement across all her performances. Her dancing, with both Moose/David Caravaggio (Willem Dafoe) and Kip, and her running through the rain, complete with umbrella to the sounds of 'Heaven, I'm in Heaven', provide lines of intensity across the canvas of the screen which are inspirational and beautiful. The earlier scene where she cuts off her hair and changes from the military dress of war-time to more ethereal, fluid and colourful clothes provides a symbolic reversal of personae: from soldier to woman. Her dress becomes part of her, just as Katharine's is part of her. The colours, textures and flows of their clothes are part of the beauty of their movements.

As a triptychal structure, specific sequences evoke a forced movement across their three visual/aural planes. Aurally, the song 'Heaven, I'm in Heaven' links three such sequences, which are then read or at least connected together. First, the music is heard when Almásy is returning with Katharine following their second love sequence at his apartment; after a trip through the bazaar, Katharine returns to Clifton; second, a flashback through the intradiegetic music takes the audience back to Almásy, the patient, listening to the music in his room at the monastery . . . his memories and dreams having been fed through the present tense and present sounds played by Caravaggio. The third time this music is heard is in the sequence following the end of the war: both Caravaggio and Hana dance to 'Wang, Wang Blues'; the rain pours down, and Hana inspirationally leaps up with Kip, Hardy and Caravaggio to take Almásy, complete with bed, out into the refreshing rain. This sequence exudes with passion, exhilaration, and yet also a tenderness which is evoked through the recognition of Almásy's dying wish – to feel the rain on his face. Hana's body and her movements become part of a dance around the grounds of the monastery, thunder and lightning, and rain imbricating with the lyrics of the song. The lyrics of 'Heaven, I'm in Heaven' work as a form of aural intensity, across a triptych of sequences. The music connects the modulations as much as the colours and tones: the blues, purples, flashes of light, thunder and music together.

The seduction scenes function in a similar way, with colour, music and body language providing similar intensities. Harmonies of tone, line, rhythm colour and light figure across the three separate events of seduction. First, Katharine turns up unexpectedly at Almásy's apartment. The scene is back-lit, which highlights Katharine's pose, as she stands erotically in the doorway, wearing a provocative, transparent muslin white dress. Body language, warm tones of oranges, yellow, ochres and amber filter the textures of sunlit fabrics, gently flowing muslins and brocaded blinds. Slow-panning camera movements flow from the image of Almásy on his bed, to Katharine standing in the doorway. No dialogue, no music, but echoes from the Arabian market outside. Intense, erotic and sensual, Katharine and Almásy make love for the first time. They linger together, bathe and talk of personal loves, desire, fears and dislikes. It is here we discover Almásy's fear of possession and ownership and Katharine's dislike of lies. Both become embroiled with their own dislikes and fears.

As a sequence it preludes the following seduction scene, this time at the Christmas festivities. Again, Katharine wears white; similar colours and sounds pervade this scene, only here the seduction is much more forceful, more erotic, and its illicitness enhances its eroticism. The third love sequence is again in Almásy's apartment. Katharine this time stays the night; reclining in Almásy's bed, they discuss, again, ownership, possession, difference, as Katharine says, 'Here I am a different wife, in a different life.' to justify the seriousness of her infidelity, which is a paradoxical fidelity to Almásy. This difference reflects a closeness, an attachment outside the molar categorisations of monogamous marriage constraints. It is more of a molecular understanding of 'love' outside the constraining parameters of Western, transcendent ideals of love, ownership and possessiveness imbricated within a Western Christian theological tradition (emphasised by the Christian ritual of Christmas in this film). Eastern, immanent and anti-metaphysical concerns with love are freer, finer, more molecular. The eroticism of the sequence is manifested through subdued lighting, the camera echoing the lines of Katharine's feline-like and languid body: long, linear, ethereal lines are followed through and echoed by the camera's panning movements across the screen. Hungarian folk music provides an ambient air of Arabian-sounding vocals, as Almásy recounts a folk tale of love and ownership. Almásy himself professes to 'owning' part of Katharine's body. 'The Almásy Bospherous', he claims, is his. Similar resonances echo through *Orlando*, where Orlando claims Sasha as 'his' ('because I adore you') and for no other reason. The synaesthesia of sounds and the colours meld into a feeling of sensuality and calm. This provides a direct contrast and sense of dissonance with the sequence where Caravaggio is tortured and has his thumbs cut off, in the German-occupied village. War scenes are directly juxtaposed, through past memories and present scenes in the monastery, with Hana and Caravaggio. The most significant resonance of contrasted scenes is the wonderful liberatory scene of dancing through the rain, followed by the torture scene of Caravaggio. Both the seduction scenes and the dance sequences then function in juxtapositon and in dissonance, acting in vibration (see Chapter 5) with each other, but against the war sequences and the bomb-searching sequences (in these the camera movements work in a different way; they are much more chaotic, creating a 'busy' mise-en-scène of confusion and complexity). Visual elements such as colour, shape, body movements, tones and lighting effect the cerebral cortex of the viewer in a similar way in which sound acts on the labyrinthine mechanisms of both body and brain. A neuro-aesthetic works alongside the emotional elements of the film's narrative. The characters become elements within the aesthetic of sensation. They function as figurals, as we saw earlier with Hana and Katharine. Hana works as an inspirational figural across the sequences, joining them in terms of past and present and, as we detect in the final sequence, the future. All that is vital and natural in life is inspired and nurtured by her: she is seen feeding birds, tending to plants, cooking for and indeed caring for the patient. Her 'image' in the final sequence, as we have already seen, is an image which vibrates with layers of intensity, a 'graded richness, resolute with modulations of past, present and future'.[7] A movement-image, but also a figural within the aesthetics of sensation. Through Hana, we have an inspirational resonance towards the beyond of 'becoming-woman' into the girl; for ultimately 'It is not the girl who becomes a woman: it is becoming-woman that produces the universal girl.'[8]

> The body is stolen first from the girl, stop behaving like that. You're not a little girl any more, you're not a tomboy. The girl's becoming is stolen first, in order to impose a history, a prehistory, upon her. The boy's turn comes next, but it is by using the girl as an example, that an opposed organism, a dominant history is fabricated for him too.[9]

Deleuzian discussion of becoming-girl offers an understanding of how dominant structures of socialisation and culture have encouraged the loss of an essential core, an essential 'autopoiesis' or 'becoming' which is eradicated out of us through social processes. First, through constructions of gender, masculinity and femininity, the 'singularities' of the proto-subjective state are 'ordered' into a fixed sense of gender. The 'becoming-girl' is the means through which we can strive to resist such gendered categorisations of structured social processes. It is 'becoming-girl' which enervates a positivity in the joys of becoming, a vitalism and freshness, beyond any sense of gendered subjectivity. Indeed, 'becoming-girl' has nothing to do with the sexuality of a specifically biological girl but it is the autopoietic element of all who experience the joys of life lived through becoming – a vital life – sexuality outside of gender.

Of course, this exploration of the movie is using the film to explore some philosophical resonances in Deleuze, but I never said this was an impossibility; all possibilities collide through a Deleuzian assemblage which imbricates film and philosophy, into film-philosophy. Connections are made across, within and between the spaces of the film's diegesis, but also across other spaces, texts, into more complex 'bodies'. Various frames, sequences, as we have seen, resonate, bounce off each other, distort or divest each other. The elements of sensation are stylised through compositional elements like tone, line and colour. They are stylised through structures of contrasts, similarities and juxtapositionings. More than colour produces sensation. The eye engages with motion, process and movement, after it has connected to colour and form, but across different planes, and through different elements of the visual cortex. The central focus, left to right and top to bottom thresholds, as I explained earlier, demarcates the patterns in which the brain understands motion. Forms of motion that are alluring or beautiful or pleasurable to the eye–brain usually involve an equation of these different pathways. If we take the scene where Hana is taken to view the frescoes in the Tuscan church, we can discern how this processual beauty is understood through brain patterns, in a kinaesthetic visionary process. In this sequence camera angles follow the flight paths of Hana as she quite literally flies (by means of suspension from a rope hauled into position by Kip) across, through, besides, up and down, her face almost touching the representational faces of gods and saints in the frescoes. The colours and textures are dissipated through lighting, which emulates the torch-lit sequence. Hana swirls, sways and joyously wallows in the experience, feeling, touching, seeing and connecting with the Renaissance images. They become part of her reality. As spectators we collude with those resonances, through our brain's qualitative multiplicities (see Chapters 3 and 4); the brain is quite literally a 'subject in absolute survey'. Once again, contrast, through dissonance and vibration, is encompassed by the juxtaposition of this sequence with the following one, where Kip has to defuse a bomb found under a bridge, which is about to be crossed by demob-happy troops. In this sequence, the same music, 'Heaven, I'm in Heaven', resonates, thus linking, in a tryptichal way, earlier sequences, through an aural connectivity. Furthermore Hana's body works again as figural, but also as a nomadic force, or intensity.

[A] woman's body achieves a strange nomadism, which makes it cross ages, situations, places [as we saw in *Orlando*]. The states of the body secrete the slow ceremony which joins together the corresponding attitudes and develops a female gest which overcomes the history of men and crisis of the world.[10]

Deleuze continues, in *A Thousand Plateaus*, that the reconstruction of the body without organs, an anorganism of body, is actually inseparable from a becoming-woman or the production of molecular woman. Molecular woman is the 'girl' herself. Such ideas on the significance of the 'girl' in molecularity collide and resonate with my final chapter on *Leon* (and to some extent incorporate the 'child' through *Romeo and Juliet* and even Juliette Lewis's nymphette in *Strange Days* in the following chapters).

NOTES

1. Deleuze and Guattari, *A Thousand Plateaus*, p. 12.
2. Semir Zeki, *Inner Vision: An Exploration of Art and the Brain*. Zeki explains, in this text, how in fact the brain is the arena through which we make sense of the world. Vision is not a passive process but is an active engagement of the brain's molecularity, or as Zeki calls it modularity. Vision, for example, and seeing are effectuated at a biological or molecular level through various cellular operations at different parts of the brain. The actual act of seeing is carried through to the perceptual centres of the brain through areas which Zeki refers to as V1, etc., each of which is responsible for a particular element of the visual experience. Colour, form and motion therefore are effectuated in the brain through these cellular centres or molecular cells. Colour for example does not exist 'in the world' or in the 'image' we see but exists in the brain itself. This has a connection with the idea of the brain as the arena of the subject in 'absolute survey'; see Bains, 'Subjectless Subjectivities', in Massumi, *Canadian Review of Comparative Literature*, p. 511. It is the brain, and the functions of the brain itself, which enables perception of experiences. Such experiences, whether visual, auditory or tactile, exist in the brain formations, not out there in the world.
3. Deleuze and Guattari, *What is Philosophy?*, p. 166.
4. Zeki, *Inner Vision*, ch. 7, p. 67, and also p. 2, where he discusses what he means by neuro-aesthetics.
5. Zeki, *Inner Vision*, p. 131.
6. See Chapter 10 on *Leon*.
7. Polan, 'Francis Bacon: The Logic of Sensation', in Boundas and Olkowski (eds), *Gilles Deleuze and the Theatre of Philosophy*, p. 248.
8. Deleuze and Guattari, *A Thousand Plateaus*, p. 276.
9. Deleuze and Guattari, *A Thousand Plateaus*, p. 277.
10. Deleuze, *Cinema 2*, p. 196.

Chapter 8

Romeo and Juliet – Deleuzian Sensations

[O]f all things one feels, nothing gives the impression of being at the very heart of truth, so much as fits of unaccountable despair, compared to these, everything seems frivolous, debased, lacking in substance and interest.[1]

[T]his other plane [of immanence] knows only relations of movement and rest, of speed and slowness, between unformed, or relatively unformed, elements, molecules or particles borne away by fluxes.[2]

Two contradictory quotations: like the two contradictory houses of Capulet and Montague. How can we reconcile the sentiments of both, the integrities of both, the finesse of both those positions? Cioran's words seem to enthral with their respect for emotion, their respect for the finesse of life's truly important parts, the heart, the emotions, despair, the beyond of self-pity. Subjects relevant and pertinent to a tale of impossible and forbidden love and its tragic consequences. And yet, Deleuze's words seem to present, as we have seen through much of the book, a concern with the 'outside', with the 'immanent' and not with transcendent notions premised within a self–other relational, subjectivities dependent on another's dasein, another's integrity. Love of the self, through a narcissistic display of love of the other. Desire is replaced through Deleuzian ideas with the beyond of subjectivity, in becoming.

Romeo and Juliet is an interesting film to consider in the light of such contradictory or, rather, paradoxical positions and I want to take the reader back to Chapter 4, with its discussion of the proto-subjective state, where feeling resides in an existential integrity, outside of any emotional regime. Contradiction/paradox will abound in what follows. But paradox is sense and sense is paradoxical. Deleuzian philosophy, premised on Nietzschean belief in primordial indetermination and 'life' lived outside the exigencies of subjectivities, and self–other relationals equates 'becoming' with a 'worldly biological life'. The free mind, he argues, is built upon an autonomous and autopoietic realm, outside of any self–other relational. Life, rather, is experienced differently at each moment and each individual's becoming in the world is connected with his or her volitions with the natural world.

If we take this into thinking about the movie, *Romeo and Juliet*, then, at a narrative and ideological level, Deleuzian paradigms seem to discredit, and distanciate, affairs of the heart, affairs of romantic love, which is premised on a self–other relational, subjectivity being an important element of that, as we saw in psychoanalysis. But it seems that there is an interesting tension at work between a narrative which seems to parody romantic love, through a post-modern pastiche[3] style, and an aesthetic which articulates brilliantly an example of Deleuzian understanding of the beyond of desire through becoming and 'sensation' in the way that the film connects as a set of intensities, speeds and haecceities. This tension might be perceived as the space between the molar and the molecular, the space of the 'unthought'.

In this exploration of the movie, I want to suggest that despite the film's exemplification as a post-modern parody of romantic love (and of course we can suggest that the movie is a trendy, contemporary and colourful piece of MTV, produced to sell a commodity or a set of commodities – such reductionist views, albeit they may have some validity), it simultaneously valorises 'love' through a neo-aesthetic beyond subjectivity, through a becoming-woman, which is presented through a new consideration of the 'beautiful'. A different concern with love? What constitutes beauty through a variety of processual elements in the film 'becomes' an exemplification of love in an organic sense. The heart as an organ may indeed play a role in the biological field of proto-subjective states, despite Deleuzian ideas of the body without organs. Here is the contradiction: the heart as an organ, as part of a body without organs? Where is the heart? How does it function as a 'biological' organ? Or does it merely function in the arena of 'love' through chemical and hormonal effects distributed by the brain? Contemporary science seems set to argue that love only exists because certain neurotransmitters within the brain effect specific hormonal and chemical changes to the body: for example, serotonin or oxytocin produce, because of biological and evolutionary needs, the 'feelings' of love, warmth, connectivity, commitment even, as part of man's natural survival needs. Now there lies naivety!

A refreshing and tender, if somewhat sentimental and mythical, tale of courtly love, on a narrative level *Romeo and Juliet* gently disperses such post-human notions, and yet as I said it *is* also a parody of such

sentimental and courtly love,[4] ideas that are outside this book, but
nonetheless worth thinking about, given the parodic nature of the movie.
Is there a role for the organ of fire (heart) in a body without organs?
Indeed, C. Colwell seems to suspect that the organs of the body are part of
the proto-subjective.[5] I refer the reader back to Chapter 4 to the discussion on pathic events, or prehensive events. In the pre-personal state,
Deleuze's understanding of schizoanalytic subjectivities suggests that
experiences are 'felt' at a level deeper than the subjective, indeed at a
level of singularities. Singularities are points that produce effects of
transition, but they are not 'felt' by a subject. They are constitutive of
the self. Since multiplicities are defined as qualitative, duration, movement and process are intrinsic to them. Such qualitative multiplicities are
called 'events' or 'haecceities', effectuated through the processual, the
transitive and fusional intensity.[6] In other words, the 'processual' is
determined by qualitative multiplicities of proto-subjectivities. It is in
this autopoietic realm that we have a unity of mind/brain and body, prior
to any phenomenological field, or subjectivity.

Consequently, a movie like *Romeo and Juliet*, which works and
connects specifically through movements, processuality, duration, intensities and rhythms, expresses a Deleuzian sense of 'becoming-woman'
(whilst simultaneously evoking a concern with its narrative and ideological concerns with romantic love – such delicious duplicities!). Becoming-woman is that process of immanence, a description of a processual
experience of affect as opposed to subject. The molar and the molecular in
coagulation, in collusion. But I do want to remind the reader that, as yet,
scientific evidence is yet to be formulated which denies the role of
emotions within the brain's functioning. Any valorisation of a neo-
aesthetics or materialist aesthetic, which functions within the pre-personal realm of becoming, such as this book is presenting, does not need
totally to deny or distanciate an aesthetic premised on the emotions.
(Indeed, it should sit alongside all those other realms of film theory, as a
perspectival paradigm for film studies.) Indeed, where is the space
'between'? Perhaps that is what the future of film theory may develop,
and is one of the consequential possibilities of my research.

An imbrication then of the narrative molar level of engagement with
the film's diegesis, mise-en-scène, plot, its 'plane of organisation' is to an
extent constituted through a more fibrous molecularity: its aesthetic
configurations. Through its aesthetics, the body of the film works as a
'body' in collusion with other bodies. Its 'body without organs' might,
parodically, evoke an emotional concern, with love, in a post-modern
climate, which is both parodied and substantiated. A total complexity in

its denial and acceptance of the primordial world of 'unworded experiences' and a 'pre-linguistic insight into life'.

In exploring *Romeo and Juliet* through an aesthetics of sensation, I recall Deleuze's point in *Logique de la sensation*, conveyed here by Dana Polan, that,

> Beyond figuration and representation, then, sensation comes from a pure power that 'overflows all domains, and traverses them. This power is that of Rhythm, which is deeper than vision, audition etc.' . . . A logic of the senses, Cézanne said, that is non-rational, non-cerebral.[7]

Romeo and Juliet resonates with multiple rhythms. Its very visual display is rhythmical (I mean that the visuals themselves are effectively 'rhythmical' before any musical connection) with a variety of specular effects enhanced by a variety of different musical genres, in different tempos, cadences, modulations and melodies. The subjective encounter is indeed, hystericised beyond subjective spectatorial (gendered, cyborg,[8] oscillating or matrixial[9]) perspectives. The subjective is subsumed by forces of affect, through the elements of sensation: intensities, rhythms, flows of energy, lines of flight. Energy resonates vibrantly, passionately, incisively, through the scintillating score and visceral mise-en-scènes. This energy is most apparent through the musical elements in collaboration with the patterns of lines of longitude, latitude, and diagonals, much like the paintings of Mondrian or Kandinsky, traversing the frames of various sequences. A veritable moving canvas. Much of the film works like their paintings, with lines of flow, rhythmically moving across, through, above, within, and beyond the frame of the screen. These patternings of line are operative through specific sequences in the film and they function in contrast with and in vibration and resonance with the more fluid, gentler and softer sequences, where colour functions prior to line and dynamics. Semir Zeki, in his book *Inner Vision*, explains how, within the brain, there are five specific areas in the cortex, where the visual image, received by the ocular nerves, is translated differently, by virtue of specific cells within the cortical structure. He explains these as separate elements, from VI to V5, where colour, form and movement are differently discerned. He suggests that there is a range of varied signals which are related to colour, motion, depth and luminence. Certain cells which take signals which relate to different characteristics of vision are grouped accordingly in certain compartments. Different visual signals are sent to different visual areas I to V in the cortex. The visual brain therefore is a collectivity of multiple visual areas. These depend on the type of signal received. His argument is that vision is a modular system, that the brain handles different attributes of the visual frame in a variety of subdivisions. It is therefore seen as a parallel, modular system. Thus, he argues, aesthetics itself is modular. As a result of such processes, colour becomes a construction of the brain. Zeki argues that colour does not exist outside in the world, but in the brain's formations. It exists within the V4 area, whilst movement, for example, is detected in V5.[10] The 'subject' then is subsumed in the beyond of becoming, in sensation. The visual act of seeing ceases to be a merely organic activity, 'our eye . . . ceases to be organic, to become a polyvalent and transitory organ; objectively, it holds before us the reality of a body, of lines, of colours, liberated from organic representations'.[11]

This quotation is so specifically relevant to *Romeo and Juliet*. A vibratory facticity, a connection of sensations, vibrations and rhythms come together in the 'haecceity' that is *Romeo and Juliet*. Indeed, we should here remember Deleuze's quote that 'sensation contracts vibrations of the stimulant on a nervous surface or in a cerebral volume: what comes before has not yet disappeared when what follows appears'.[12] How then does the film exude such haecceities?

Baz Luhrmann's richly textured, erotic and visceral post-modern rendition of *Romeo and Juliet* takes the original Shakespearean text as its script, but fractures it through an exuberant choreography of dizzying visuals and auditory rhythms, tones, nuances: a veritable sensory delight! Contemporary popular music, classical music and opera create an eclectic pastiche of sounds which eclipses each and every visual moment of the movie. Indeed, the film was, on release, marketed and promoted through its soundtrack. Music 'performs' as a fibrous core through the text, creating a post-modern opera, through an assemblage of different sounds, diegetic and non-diegetic, evoking the concerns of love, sexuality (but a sexuality outside the confines of gender; the film is in its processuality very sexy!), death and tragedy. Indeed, sounds become gestures, which are also vocal, as Deleuze writes in *Cinema 2*,

> Where the visible body disappears . . . What is freed in non-desire is music, and 'speech', their intertwining in a body which is now only sound, a body of new opera. It is no longer the characters who have a voice, it is the voices, or rather the vocal modes of the protagonist (whisper, breathing, shout, eructation) which become the sole true characters.[13]

A very different film from either *Orlando* or *The English Patient*, nonetheless *Romeo and Juliet* takes as its thematic narrative a tale of romantic love and the ensuing tragedies. In the exploration of young romance lies a parodic and post-modern discernment of such concepts.

Death of the subject and the death of history also seem to relay the death of love.

The mise-en-scène is set within a contemporary American/Brazilian cityscape – in fact from the statue of Christ which looms out and provides an ambivalent icon of both love and death, we can see this is set in Rio de Janeiro (a Westernised Verona in several senses of the word). Here, Shakespearean lords and kinsmen are replaced with a sexy, colourful array of young popular dudes, straight and gay, transvestites, bisexuals, transsexuals, punks, bikers and sado-masochists. We are given characteristic emblems of the contemporary world of corporate finance (Paris) or else exotic, plumed and pulchral visions of excess and the carnivalesque (Mercutio). Romeo (Leonardo di Caprio) seems to fit somewhere inbetween, but his tendencies towards romantic love render him an innocent among such company! An innocent who nonetheless finds himself guilty of murder. Love and hate are yet part of the same equation of passion. However, that charming, witty and parodic post-modernism merely enthrals in its parallelism or repetition in difference of love, tenderly and sensitively enacted through the innocence of youth (Claire Danes as Juliet and Leonardo di Caprio as Romeo). The cynicism of parody is thus tinged with the proverbial delights of a 'neo-romantic' venture as a reply to the horrific renditions of a culture embroiled in the sometimes bereft despair and ugliness of irony, parody, deceit, critique and an all-pervading fear of the existence of 'love', or what that might mean in a *post*-post-structuralist climate! Fear of tradition, a disrespect for originations, a disdain for 'depth' and 'meaning' are ironically juxtaposed, becoming simultaneously a respect for a text and language that does speak with metonym and metaphor – a denial of everything Deleuze stands for. Such contradictions. The movie is both post-modern and yet *post*-post-modern in its forces, intensities and resonances of haecceity. Shakespearean language, taken out of its traditional literary context, becomes part of the 'energies' as it colludes and collides with contemporary sounds, diegetically and non-diegetically, through which the film impacts. Meanings, whether parodic or not, are actually not what concerns this Deleuzian exploration of the 'event', the 'haecceity', the 'becoming-woman' of the film.

There is across the movie a repetition-in-difference of all the various elements: generic characteristics such as character, plot, narrative, but also in terms of time and spatial zones. A difference-in-repetition across visual and aural 'affects' through 'becoming'. A neo-aesthetics, here, is explored through differential relations – unlike Freudian psychoanalytic ideas on pleasure (tied up with inorganic death originations) and 'bound excitation'. Deleuze refers instead to 'differential relations', differentiated forms of material and molecular elements of our make-up. So the generic characteristics no longer hold the only validity for understanding the impact of the cinematic event. Instead, other categories impose: colours and sounds fill the in-between spaces of the filmic text. The ways in which the colours clash, coincide, resonate, the dimensions of their tones and blurring of boundaries, the linearity across and within the frames, provide rhythms and movements across the screen, and this functions as sensation as opposed to 'pleasure'.

Rather than think of the movie as a filmic version of the famous romantic myth, I want to explore how *Romeo and Juliet* works as a rhythmical, processual and moving set of energies and intensities. It is an intensely rhythmical experience, set within a variety of different intonations of metre, timbre, pace, tone and voice. Certainly it does operate at the level of the molar, or semiotic, and the ideological and psychoanalytic readings could be a mechanism through which to explore its text. Such possibilities are inherent in the textual elements. (For example, the scene where Romeo and Juliet meet is replete with looks, gazes, returned stares between glass, screens and/or mirrors. Also, the Boschian-like party sequence[14] has some beautiful characters straight out of Freud's 'uncanny'.) However, the entire experience, as a two-hour event, works as a 'body' in connection with a rhythmical set of performances, resonant through a varied display of musical notations, scales, cadences, contrapuntal nuances, dissonances and lyrical patterns which collide and vibrate with both dialogue and visuals.

The music, I feel, provides the main structure to the film. We can discern a set of sequences, clearly defined across the different types of music. Through the music as an overall structuring fibre, we find a neo-aesthetics at work in this film. When our bodies absorb the movements of the screenic images, instead of reflecting them, our activity can be described as effort, or, as I have outlined in the book so far, as 'affect'. The 'affect' replaces or at least is simultaneous to representation. One of the most exciting films which epitomises the 'becoming-woman' of sensation, and performs as a body, in locomotion, as a concept-image-affect, *Romeo and Juliet* produces a theatricality of the cinema which is totally distinct from the theatricality of the theatre. As Artaud and the film director Carmelo Bene[15] suggest, the cinema can bring about a more profound theatricalisation than theatre. Here bodies embrace, entwine and intertwine, bodies which animate the scene, as Deleuze states, 'each body has both space and light, the body is also sound as well as vision, all components of the "image" come together on the body'.[16] We see this at work equally in Luhrmann's film *Strictly Ballroom* (1992). Other directors, like Scorsese, have also portrayed this 'gestural' or 'pathic' constitution of bodies in their films. I am thinking here of Scorsese's *Age of Innocence*, where the camera movements are a beautiful choreography through colour, texture, space and sounds, providing a bio-vital aesthetic which ennervates the emotionality of the film. Sounds and colours become attitudes of the body, gestures, categories constituting new bodies in neo-aesthetic consilience.

Any first viewing of *Romeo and Juliet* is set to blow the mind/body. Senses reel, distanciating any gendered subjectivity and fragmenting subjectivity beyond any sense of identity. The 'depth' of this neo-aesthetic experience is articulated through a sheer materiality and viscerality of the affect and sensation. This is accommodated through the many rhythms, spaces and interstices of the movie, as a 'body' very much relating to a wider body. But not the phenomenological 'lived body,' the corporeal human body, but a body at a deeper level, at a level of felt intensity. An intensity which is in and of itself, a material sensation. There is a 'non-commensurability' of the various images. What force enables, produces and evokes such intensities – a desire felt outside any positionality, outside any psychoanalytic, libidinal, semiotic or cultural formations of desire? Such force is felt within the depths of the body without organs, within the joyous realms of the processual, on the plane of immanence, not within any lived or phenomenological body. What is experienced is sheer nervous vibration. Here is the real 'becoming-woman' of the cinematic, where depth and processuality of the material emotion are emergent through a technologised body of the screen. That screen is also a facialised body.

The film quite literally begins with a small television screen, centre frame. A face (the screen is face, her face the screen) of a female presenter introduces us to the narrative of Shakespeare's *Romeo and Juliet*. From an instant image of a television screen displaying a face, we are carried into the spaces of the film's mise-en-scène. The face/screen becomes a body through a vibrant choreography of camera and cinematographic rhythms and cacophony of sound. The film displays a vast array of forces, sheer velocities and movements, which are dynamic, ecstatic and jouis-sancial[17] in their fluidity – a fluidity which is both static and dynamic. Take, for example, the opening shots of the movie. From the small television screen the camera pans out in vast sweeping gestures, as though carried on a helicopter, which then becomes part of the image.

We are carried, cinematographically, into the screen, on the helicopter, taking us into a contemporary Brazilian/American city/beach esplanade, juxtaposing sixteenth-century Verona, through sweeping rhythms of the camera, flying across, through, from all angles and positions, in a dizzying choreography of chaos. Still, blank screens with the words 'In Fair Verona' or 'A pair of star-crossed lovers' are juxtaposed with the action shots. The materiality of both sound molecule and the felt, haptic, experience of the visual collide to carry us outside of our fixed bodies, to the extent that we feel that we do actually move, fly, swim, with the camera, in a dizzying disorientation. The heart literally races (remember the definition earlier of the affect as an autonomic physical response) with the viscerality of this sequence. We really do, as Deleuze indicated, occupy the interstices of the edits, cuts, wipes and fades of the camera, becoming part of the cinematic body and constituting a wider 'body' of world/body connections.[18]

We feel the energy exacerbated through images of heat, death and destruction. A dramatic intensity proliferates the screen. Signifiers on billboards indicate contemporary destruction. Stills are framed in close-up shots, alongside wipes and fades. The Capulet Boys and the Montague Boys invade/seduce our space on the screen, parading their sexy, angular, Romanesque bodies through a palette of exuberance: cobalt, ultramarines, violets, blues, rich warm yellows, passionate and exotic reds. Flames engulf the screen in several places, creating a haptic scenario of passion and danger together. Textures of diamond-studded metal guns/swords, gleaming, feral, feline teeth, snarling, glowing bodies in armour seem to come straight out of a neo-western, replete with Sergio Leon-esque music. The hero's cowboy image is replaced with the majesty of the Roman centurion. Tybalt's erotic bodily display is matched by his equally intense and dynamic words, 'Peace, I hate the word . . .' His words act as a figural gest, in terms of the pitch, intonation and tone, as a cadence with the music, to present a poetic vibration with the diegetic musical sounds. The intensities of the movie are felt through its processual rhythms of colour, movement and sound. The flow and rhythm are so important to the diegesis of the film as are the feelings of openings, floating and flying, effectuated through diagonal, vertical and other lines of movement.

The performativity of the film is indeed very beautiful. But not in any romantic sense of the word 'beautiful'. The processuality of the film takes over the formality of the aesthetic form of narrative closure. Things just 'flow'. The eye of the spectator moves in a dance of its own, in matrixial ways, imbricating the tactile within the scopic, a haptic sense of 'relationality'. This relational space is at the interstitial space of the subject and object, the in-between as I mentioned earlier. Such eroticisation of the eye means that the spectator's gaze functions processually to incorporate a synaesthetic assemblage: a 'felt' experience. The beautiful, as Brian Massumi suggests, 'in this view of aesthetics, is the incipient perception of the vitality of matter, its dynamogenic strength or force. Its autopoiesis.'[19]

Post-modern in its eclecticism, pastiche and parody, the diegesis presents choreographed bodies, flying, dancing and elegantly displaying and performing, such that we experience the totality of the screen as a body in movement, constituted from several bodies in locomotion. Some of the most evocative scenes are the fight sequences, where guns/swords are projectile prostheses and become part of the owner's performance, deftly choreographed to the point of vibratory exhilaration (one recalls a similar erotic sword sequence in Terence Stamp's performance in *Far from the Madding Crowd* (1967)). Symphonies of classical music, Mozart's 25th Symphony and at times operatic music from Tristan and Isolde, drift into street style, bombastic rapper riffs and chords. Repetitious chords and riffs frisson through the body's depths. We are literally carried into the movie through sound as much as image. We 'become' part of the processuality of the film's movement, into a filmic body, as a whole harmonics of performativity. This sequence ends with the police warning the two houses of Capulet and Montague, of ensuing catastrophe in the light of their continued aggressions.

We cut to a more serene, calm and gently flowing camera action, as we follow the Montagues in their car searching for Romeo. The music of Radiohead (popular band of the 1990s) languorously drawls from their emotive lyrics: 'You want me . . .' Our first glimpse of Romeo is enhanced by the melancholy and soporific lyrics of Radiohead's music. Romeo is set against what looks like a mock cut-out image of an old dilapidated proscenium arch theatre in Sycamore Grove, which becomes a pastiched platform, as a theatrical stage: a stage, within a stage, within a world, for the setting of several sequences across the rest of the movie – most evocatively the death of Mercutio and the ensuing death of Tybalt. Here we have Romeo, his figure set in contrast with the splendour of the elements, stunning orange and apricot skyline set against threatening grey clouds, all encapsulated within the proscenium arch of a 'theatrical, dramatic stage'. This scene acts as a forced movement, the pace and rhythm of music, camera movements and edits, changing, as a contrast with the prior sequences. Images oscillate (for example, the hooker who erotically seduces those who merely stand and stare) in gentle, erotic, slow-motion rhythms to the sound of Radiohead, enhancing the distanciation and collisions with the prior sequence.

Comedy, and carnivalesque style, in the form of the Capulet mansion

sequence, works as resonance with the previous sequence. Suddenly we
are presented with a different film style. Camera movements echo silent-
cinematic techniques, where characters' movements are comedic and
farcical because of the stark linearity, awkwardness and sterility of the
body language. Juliet's mother beautifully epitomises this in her distraction and agitation. Repetition of Juliet's name, screamed at different
pitches and timbres, by both nurse and mother, resonates (in the Deleuzian sense of the word) with the actions to the point of delirium, providing
a contrast with the serenity and tenderness of the previous scene with
Romeo in distraction over unrequited love. The sound works as a pattern
across the accompanying images, effectuating a comic style. Such comedy
is beautifully counterpointed with classical music, colliding with the
images to present movement-images in patterns across the screen. Patterns of linearity and stark, harsh shapes, tones, colours and textures
create a 'malleable mass' of images, perceived as movement-images, 'the
whole is no longer the logos which unifies the parts, but the drunkenness,
the pathos which bathes them and spreads them out. From this point of
view, images constitute a malleable mass, a descriptive material loaded
with visual and sound features'.[20]

Juliet's mother, for example, displays a classical masquerade as Cleopatra, replete with exotic dark wig, but parodied by her prior parading
around, dressed and made up like some clown out of a pantomime. In
contrast with this, she splendidly leaves the room, elegant and monu-
mental in gold-sequinned dress, tightly bound by breath-taking (literally)
corsets, hair and dress enhanced with feathers, with the following words,
'Juliet . . . ugh!' A moment of pure delight. She performs as some sort of
figural action, rather than as a character.

Cut to different music . . . 'Angel', a gently rhythmical piece, augmen-
ted with a stunning colourful mise-en-scène, brightly highlighted with
fireworks of purples, pinks, turquoise and gold at Sycamore Grove. This
is followed through with the move to the party scene, following Romeo's
scene with Mercutio where they both indulge in drugs. Mercutio's speech
to Romeo on 'love' in its lyricism, rhythm and volatility designates an
hysterical madness, whilst performing as an intensity, a volition within
the patterns of sounds, resonating and bouncing off from the previous
music. What follows is a beautifully choreographed and colourful drug-
induced hallucination: Catherine wheels swirl in colourful resonation in
rhythm with the camera movements, circular tracking shots, which
provide a reeling motion. This action, together with the primary colours,
impinges on the brain/eye movements in specifically pleasurable ways;
there is nothing fixed, nothing angular. All is rhythmically and beautifully

choreographed providing a processual experience. Colour is experienced before form, movement before form.[21] But only ever so gently mediated, that the process is almost instantaneously 'felt'. The variation of rhythms in the sequences contrast, complement and disrupt others, or else they work as prosthetic assemblages.

The highlight of the party sequence is Mercutio's erotic display of cross-dressing, resplendent in white-sequinned corset and stockings (contrasting with the deep purple of the other dancers), white wig resonating against the masculinity of his moustached and dark, passionate, rich features.[22] A delicious delirium of erotica. He descends the staircase to the vibrant sounds of Kim Mazelle's 'Young Hearts' (parody intended of course). His/her dance is part of different dance modes in the film.[23] In contrast with the earlier frenetic displays of flying bodies, his musical sequence gives a gentler swaying and creatively sculptural quality to its bodies and to the body, the wider 'body' constituted by both film, spectator and world. Bodies weave, collide, connect, oscillate and interrelate through a diegesis of 'malleable images'. Visions of excess, tactility, sensuality and the frisson of sexual exorbitance and transgression are visualised and hapticised (from the word 'haptic') through shapes, colours and tones moving in time, but also dislocated from time. Demons, angels and whores become tropes from mythical fables and fabulations. Cleopatra to Caesar are masqueraded within the vibrance of the mise-en-scène and seem to come out of Freud's 'uncanny'. This is, of course, all a hallucinatory dream, induced by drugs, but as a film it works on the brain, as a form of altered state.[24] Just as drugs work on the brain in chemical ways which affect the synaptic and neuronal mechanisms of the cellular structures, so too film as matter works on the brain in similar ways. Thus, such images are not purely 'images' (yes, of course they do also operate 'as' image seen by the eye, but the eye/I is not a passive vessel of visual stimulants). Images are not merely representations, for interrogation, but 'elements of sensation', as the 'stuff' of matter, or brain formations. The colours, movements and oscillations generate/compose the brain's active processes. The act of 'seeing' is not a passive thing, neither is it only an eye/I relational of psychic manifestations (although of course there is still a role for psychoanalysis and the more recent uses of psychoanalysis through the work of Bracha Lichtenberg-Ettinger; see the Bibliography for details of her work). I am not trying to suggest we should deny this, but to suggest other frames in which film works on the brain. The brain actively creates the perception through molecular and cellular actions. Percept and affect form as a block of sensation. The 'aesthetic composition . . . agglomerates in the same transversal flashes, the subject and object, the self and other, the material and the incorporeal, the before and the after . . . in short, affect is not a question of representation and discursivity, but of existence'.[25] Indeed, it is this rich body of percepts and affects that displaces any fixed idea of identity and thus makes room for richer creative tendencies, accommodated through the imbrication of brain/mind and body, in collusion with the wider molecular and cellular body of life.

Juliet is introduced through her angelic costume, virginal white and delicately textured, marking the ethereality and chastity of her innocence. This works both as parody and yet is in its symbolism, tenderly sincere. Metaphorically and metonymnically then, the film does have many resonances. But in a Deleuzian sense, the film impacts as matter, as a processual 'event' in ways outside of representation, metaphor or imagery. It connects; it constitutes a 'worlding' process. It is a total worlding of experience of molecular forces through a materialist aesthetic.

The party mood is counterpointed by Des'ree singing the popular track 'Kissing You', with its romantic, soft and delicate rhythms and intonations, romantically bringing Romeo and Juliet together for the first time, but distanced through the screens of a vast aquarium. The languorous liquidity and fluidity of the colours and tones lend a sensuality to the mood and feel of the sequence. The swaying rhythms of the music are echoed through the movement-image as liquid perception in the image of the fish, swimming and wafting in the rippling water. Water provides again one of those molecular ways in which matter effectuates brain mechanisms. Pleasure is evoked by the gentle fluidity of rippling effects. Colours – greens, turquoises, blues, opals, lavenders – are painted across a canvas which fades and wipes into a liquidity of sensuality and sensation. Dissipated lighting and rippling shades enhance the transience of the scene, highlighting the ephemerality and processuality, not only of this sequence, but the very image-concept-affect of 'love'. This is further enhanced by a display of camera movements, in a different dance structure: a swirling set of bodies, which reflects a charming and tender pattern of gazes, glances, looks, gestures, smiles and eye contact, with matrixial patterns of looking across and between Romeo and Juliet, as Juliet dances with Paris. (Remember the dance sequence between Almásy and Katharine in *The English Patient*, which has similar resonances.) The dance itself is a gentle, romantic, slow, delicate and controlled action of bodies and faces, close and apart, resonances of ambiguities, sensibilities and sensitivities across two bodies which are eloquently apart – interestingly one looking, the other looked at! The depth of material emotion is part of the same canvas as romantic love. Of course, one might argue that this is all parodic in intent, pastiched to the point of ridiculing the convention of romantic love. Such cynicism is justly valid, and yet it could be argued that this view is naively resistant of an understanding of love, and the realities of love in a wider sense.[26] Such cynicism perhaps fails to engage with the depth of emotion felt in the primordiality of the body's and brain's physical experience of sexual encounter. Yes, of course, bodies collide, and resonate, chemically and hormonally effectuated, or not, but maybe, just maybe, there is something deeper, felt within the depths of a primordial state. Why else is there discrimination and distinction? It cannot all be merely biological. There is a connection at a primordial level. Everything connects. Only connect. Is it just *Howards End*? But, it depends on the two bodies/brains/minds in collision (that is, discrimination and distinction). The film works on a multidimensional level. It literally engages the technologised body (the act of watching a film is a technologised experience, an altered state as much as sex or drug taking) in assemblage with the sensual, the pathic and the intellectual, as much as the arena of sensation.

The famous balcony sequence offers much in the way of vibrant movements, oscillations of lines, rhythms and resonances. A haptic sense of vision is created through the liquidity of the images, and the tactility of textures. The curtains sway eloquently, softly evoking haptic sensuality. The two bodies literally collide, resonate, and force each other apart here, swimming under water, and exhilaratingly in and out of each other's consciousness. Again, reflection, colours, tones and movements work together to create the undulating sensuality of the scene. The bodies in the water modulate, through both movement and colour, a liquidity of perception, where the perceived image is diffused into vibrations, so that the liquid movement goes beyond itself into a material, energic element (see Chapter 5). The formation of the 'image' is defined by molecularity, not by visual representation. Sensation is accommodated through this molecularity.

The lyricism of Shakespeare's words works in delicate contrast to the post-modern parody of a 1990s pastiche. The film continues to impact through the 'unthought' interstitial spaces, through the molar and the molecular. Juliet's initial speech, the famous 'Romeo, Romeo . . .' speech, works as a lyrical musical refrain, setting in counterpoint, the flickering, visual movements of the camera. It also works as a delicate parody, given the humour and comedy of the acting styles here – comic, awkward, angular and farcical at times. Romeo continually falls over, colliding into things. The sequence ends with Romeo rushing off to Father Lawrence's, to the track, 'You and Me, Always, and Forever', a light-hearted and uplifting lyrical piece.

Music continues to provide the fibrous tissue for the film's diegesis and impact. In the rest of the movie, the variety of tones, lyrics and melodies of the musical notation provides vibrational contrasts across and between sequences. The marriage of Romeo and Juliet is played out to the track 'Everybody's Free to Feel Good'. But the following death of Mercutio and Romeo's revenge on Tybalt are set in counterpoint and resonance with the marriage sequence by the dramatic operatic music. Romeo's ensuing madness and banishment are further enhanced through the musical score, with intradiegetic music effecting its force upon our experience of the movie. Flash lightning, chaotic camera angling, uncontrolled fits of passion and despair from Romeo's words (first when he realises the severity of his killing of Tybalt and echoed again when he hears of Juliet's death) vibrate through the sound molecules of the soundtrack, all in contrapuntal collision with the earlier, delicate and joyous sequences. But such resonances (and I use the word resonance here in the Deleuzian sense) don't merely provide diegetic elements to a narrative. In Deleuzian paradigms of the 'beyond of desire' they impact with the molecularity of the brain to provide the processuality of the beyond of subjectivity, the becoming-woman of the cinematic, the aesthetics of sensation. In terms of my overall argument, then, the cinematic experience is something beyond the purely representational. If film theory has located debates within representation, semiotics and theories of desire premised on some sort of visual encounter with identity and subjectivity within that scenario, then to date such film theory has omitted to consider the wider impact upon the minds/brains/bodies of those who experience film. It works as sensation, as an experiential event of becoming. The becoming is modulated through the processes of brain/mind/body formations in collusion with the visual and aural elements of the textual format.

The final sequence of Romeo and Juliet's romantic death effuses bright colours: blues, golds and silver and sensual lighting is diegetically created within the mise-en-scène through candlelight. Such colours collude, vibrate with the musical score, with the notational elements of the music, within the synapses of the brain's functioning processes. Of course, the emotional nuances also impinge (or maybe they are created) through the totality of the experience, a commingling of sensation, and total imbrication of molar and molecular elements. Indeed, scientific research has not yet been able to totally explain the ways in which emotion is effectuated within the brain's cellular functioning patterns. It is within the molar and the molecular perhaps. Consequently in rethinking any aesthetic within film studies, it might be pertinent for us to engage with this imbrication of ideas – not opposing, but conjoining perspectival views.

A neo-aesthetics of sensation or a neuro-aesthetics (Semir Zeki[27] refers to a new perception of aesthetics as neuro-aesthetics) then is premised, as we have seen here, on affect and sensation, rather than a subjectivity. Such a neo-aesthetic works through the molecularity of matter. Within its modulational elements, colour, as I have explored above, is specifically significant, and is the first impact within the brain's cellular functioning. Colour is extremely resonant in *Romeo and Juliet*, and it operates across the canvas of the film as a certain energy expenditure, conceived through certain cellular activities. Visual experiences are not necessarily premised on the mechanisms of the eye as such, or on seeing. Sensation is accommodated within the brain's functioning. Norseen's description of the instant cerebellum efferent responses is specifically appropriate to the party sequence described above.[28] The various forms of motion, which are referred to as processual, and therefore pleasing to the brain's mechanisms, are prevalent throughout the movie. Gyrating wheels, circular camera movements, circular tracking shots echoing spinning wheels, swirling bodies, heads, arms, legs, shapes in collusion with the sounds are molecular elements of sensation.

Post-modern parody it may be, but *Romeo and Juliet* operates as a veritable 'becoming-woman' through its forces of sensation. In some ways these patterns are also discernible, but differently so, in the next film under discussion, Kathryn Bigelow's *Strange Days*.

NOTES

1. Cioran, 'Meetings and Movements', in *Anathemas and Admirations*, p. 148.
2. Deleuze and Parnet, *Dialogues*, p. 92.
3. Pastiche here is defined as a conscious imitation. Pastiche incorporates the knowledge that the imitation is enjoyable, but understood for what it is: enjoyable cliched imitation. This enables fun to be poked at romantic love while also inviting us to enjoy it.
4. To each his or her own reading.
5. 'Pre-personals exist as a kind of field of different forces or intensities, wills to power, that resonate with one another, that interact in ways that produce effects on one another. Sexual drives, the surface of bodies, aggression, one's internal organs, emotions, experiences, sensations are all pre-personal' (C. Colwell, 'Deleuze and the Prepersonal', in *Philosophy Today*, p. 18).
6. Deleuze relates Bergson's definition of qualitative multiplicity as follows. 'A complex feeling will contain a fairly large number of simple elements; but as long as these elements do not stand out with perfect clearness, we cannot say that they were completely realised and as soon as consciousness has a distinct perception of them, the psychic state which results from their synthesis will have changed for this very reason'; see Deleuze, *Bergsonism*, p. 42.

7. Dana Polan, 'Francis Bacon: The Logic of Sensation', in Boundas and Olkowski (eds), *Gilles Deleuze and the Theatre of Philosophy*, p. 240; his reference is to Deleuze, *Francis Bacon: Logique de la sensation*, p. 31.
8. See Cyborg spectatorship in B. Kennedy, 'Post-feminist Futures in Film Noir', M. Aaron (ed.), *The Body's Perilous Pleasures*.
9. Matrixial is a word which has current purchase in contemporary film theory. It has been theorised by several film and art theorists, for example Bracha Lichtenberg-Ettinger in her insightful work beyond Lacan. See Lichtenberg-Ettinger's work 'Matrix and Metamorphosis', in *Differences, A Journal of Feminist Cultural Studies*.
10. Semir Zeki, *Inner Vision*, ch. 9, esp. pp. 59, 83.
11. Polan, 'Francis Bacon', in Boundas and Olkowski (eds), *Gilles Deleuze and the Theatre of Philosophy*, p. 241; Polan translates here Deleuze, *Francis Bacon: Logique de la sensation*, p. 37.
12. Deleuze and Guattari, *What is Philosophy?*, p. 211.
13. Deleuze, *Cinema 2*, p. 191.
14. As in Hieronymus Bosch's paintings of the underworld.
15. Bene, according to Deleuze, is closest to the work of Artaud. Deleuze discusses Bene's work in *Cinema 2*, p. 191.
16. Deleuze, *Cinema 2*, p. 191.
17. Jouissancial is a French term which refers to orgasmic bliss and pleasures felt through specific experiences. See B. Kennedy, 'Post-feminist Futures in Film Noir', in *The Body's Perilous Pleasures*.
18. Deleuze, *Cinema 2*, pp. 191–223.
19. B. Massumi, 'Deleuze, Guattari and the Philosophy of Expression', in *Canadian Review of Comparative Literature*, p. 16.
20. Deleuze, *Cinema 2*, p. 158.
21. Zeki explains how the brain responds to colour prior to form or movement, but so acutely close are these mechanisms, that they seem almost instantaneous. In fact, they are not. Colour is recognised as primary to form. (See Zeki, *Inner Vision*, ch. 7, p. 58–69).
22. Antipodean cinema in the 1990s has shown a love of parody, pastiche, cross-dressing, and masquerade. Films such as *Strictly Ballroom* and *Priscilla, Queen of the Desert* (1994) are fine examples. Both are dynamic and visceral films.
23. Dance often functions in film as a way of distanciating any fixed or gendered spectatorial positioning. It articulates a matrixial space, or a matrixial gaze, where gendered identity is unfixed and oscillates. See descriptions of *Basic Instinct* (1992) and *Romeo is Bleeding* in B. Kennedy, in 'Post-feminist Futures in Film Noir', in M. Aaron, *The Body's Perilous Pleasures*.
24. See Anna Powell, *Transformations: Altered States in Film*.
25. F. Guattari, *Chaosmosis*, p. 93.
26. There has been a whole arena in feminist theory which has reconsidered and valorised the notion of the 'romance' and its validity as a reality of life.
27. Zeki, *Inner Vision*.
28. John Norseen, 'Images of the Mind: The Semiotic Alphabet'.

Chapter 9

Strange Days – Deleuzian Sensations

> Things fall apart; the centre cannot hold;
> Mere anarchy is loosed upon the world,
> The blood-dimmed tide is loosed, and everywhere
> The ceremony of innocence is drowned;
> The best lack all conviction, while the worst
> Are full of passionate intensity.[1]

> There is a pure plane of immanence, univocality, composition, upon
> which everything is given, upon which unformed elements and materials
> dance that are distinguished from one another only by their speed, and
> that enter into this or that individuated assemblage depending on their
> connections, their relations of movement.[2]

What could Yeats have meant when he talked of the worst being full of
'passionate intensity', when in a Deleuzian sense, intensities are the very
essence of becoming-woman through sensation? Should passionate
intensity denote negativity, as it seems to in Yeats's poem, or is there
an intensity which, in its very passion, is full of positivity, life, hope and
new beginnings? This is the sort of intensity that vitally courses through
the diegetic veins and body of Kathryn Bigelow's *Strange Days*, a violent
and visceral movie by all accounts. But through that violence flows a
dynamic and emphatic resurrection of life's positivities, energies, becomings – a terrible beauty? In the chaos of imagery and a mise-en-scène
which is disturbingly violent lies a rich, effusive and contagious confirmation of hope, life's volatility and germinal possibilities. Life continues and evolves, despite and indeed because of the horrors, and
pleasures, of the diegetic imagery. Certainly Yeats's very Catholic poem
was an apocalyptic vision of the Second Coming, the end of a Christian
era, brought about by an increasingly secular world, replete with greed,
selfishness, materialist pleasures and a denial of the spiritual. But what

relevance do such words offer in today's vision, a secular world which has managed through science to prioritise the secular and the natural, to question anything outside of a real and natural existence, and to dissipate the world of transcendent values? The joyful cruelty of becoming and a valorisation of immanence as opposed to transcendence. Transcendence is replete with teleological endings, with sources of origination premised in some other zone of being, for example, a spiritual zone – desire effectuated through a need to return to that original inorganic moment. A desire premised upon some sense of satisfaction and containment through endings and satiation. The realm of immanence offers no teleological endings, no satiation, no concerns with original sources or inorganic origins, through which the death instinct is connected to desire. The realm of immanence is in and of itself a processual effectuation of transition and creative evolution. It is a continual evolution of life's positivities, possibilities and becomings. A denial of the spiritual need not negate the positivity and joyfulness of life's evolution, life's becoming. Indeed, the plane of immanence is a continuum of forces of desire, as Deleuze argues, existing as speeds, intensities, fluxes, outside any teleological end points, and outside any psychoanalytical frameworks and their notions of subjectivity.

Writing this chapter only days before the actual (real time) as opposed to virtual millennial celebrations (seen continually on television and the internet) and experiencing the cultural euphoria and endemic exhilaration at this very moment of watching/writing, I don't want to offer any ideological readings of apocalyptic doom (such visions are obviously apparent throughout Bigelow's movie) premised on such effete and, indeed, well-known forebodings, such as the end of the world, the beginnings of a new form of Enlightenment. Such ideas are still of course redolent of a culture premised on origins and endings, on linearity, on goals, on psychoanalytic versions of the unconscious, on Oedipal configurations of desire; no process, no beauty of processuality, ephemerality and becoming. Although I intend to look at this movie as a haecceity, as an 'event' of movement and becoming, rather than as a text with a meaning, through Deleuzian aesthetic frameworks premised on processes of becoming-woman, as a body without organs, I have to first acknowledge that as a text, there is a powerful molar politics at work within Bigelow's film; and any experience of the film as 'event' or 'haecceity' imbricates an awareness of the molar within its molecular resonances. Psychoanalysis still has its role to play in any analysis of textual formations, and I don't wish to deny those possible interpretations of a movie as text. I aim merely to offer different paradigms for engagement. The film is indeed a violent movie, textually. But critiques of the aestheticisation of violence fail to consider how the film impacts, vibrates and connects through its aesthetic resonances, as a powerfully moving (emotional, psychological, biological and literal) canvas, and indeed body, outside its representational images. Bigelow's film offers an experience of a neo-aesthetic engagement which impacts on the consciousness through brain/mind/bodily assemblages, as a newer body, into a potentially political frame. The affective spaces, as new enunciative processes of the film, contaminate and thus might effectuate change in mentalities. Guattari's belief in *Chaosmosis*, as we saw in Chapter 1, establishes a new concern with aesthetics as a way of re-engagement with the world, outside of any molar political programmes. Certainly, through the plane of organisation of the film, one can discern a powerful and moving condemnation of a racist American culture which brought us the horrors of the Rodney King killing, emblematic of a history of racist, white, imperialist intransigence, ironically formulated within a so-called 'Christian' and interestingly thus 'transcendent' ethic. The death of such history is a welcome beginning for a new millennium. If read through a framework of ideology and representation, Bigelow's movie does much to bring home the horrors of contemporary racism, and indeed sexism, as it pervades our culture still, and I don't wish to deny those reductionist but still important textual 'readings' of the film. A basic, reductionist, structuralist and semiotic reading of the film is replete with metaphorical displays of degradation and torment, providing vibrant analogies of a racist, sexist,[3] oppressive culture. But what I am suggesting is that those very political reverberations are to some extent effectuated through a plane of consistency, through the elements of sensation that resonate through the 'event' of the film as experience, not merely as representation.

Contemporary movies display a diversity of narratives depicting apocalyptic visions, nightmare scenarios of death, destruction, despair, negativity and repulsion. From *Twelve Monkeys* (1995), through to *The End of Days* (1999),[4] Hollywood seems to provide familiar horrific future visions: the end of time, the end of history; but that end of history, projected through post-modernist discourse, is merely a blip in a time loop which is eternally returning, in gyration, in vortical movement and in processual becoming – a time outside 'time' in any diachronic sense, a synchronic time which is different at every moment of its being, in continual processuality. The volatility and creativity of *Strange Days* lies in its 'becoming-woman' and sensation, in its processuality and its terrible beauty: a beauty which pertains to a process of time, not to form.

A very different film from *Romeo and Juliet*, nonetheless *Strange Days* works through similar patterns and vibrational resonances to impact upon both the brain/mind and body. Like most of Bigelow's films, there seems to be an overt theatricality of thrillingly visceral action-packed visions.[5] My choice of the film has been disturbingly ironic, ambivalent and confrontational for my own consciousness, given that I am trying to position a neo-aesthetic which might become a pragmatic move towards a change in consciousness outside of any politic, but through an aesthetic. I purposely chose *not* to position a specific genre. But to look at a cross-section of different film genres. Films like *Orlando* and *The English Patient* quite obviously offer more 'peaceful' diegeses, whilst *Romeo and Juliet*, in its post-modern delights, is refreshingly innocent. How can a violent movie like *Strange Days* effectuate a similarly transformational framework for humankind's future becomings, resonances and creativities? This, therefore, is a difficult rhizome to explore, which must take on board the imbrication of molar regimes, like psychoanalysis, like semiotics and textual understandings and more interestingly, in my opinion, the molecular.

Narratively the film is set just before the end of the millennium party celebrations (Y2K) in Los Angeles (for Los Angeles, of course, read all those analogies of the death of history, the death of 'man' and the death of the subject redolent in post-modernist discourse – the death of the real, and the exigencies of the hyperreal, of which Baudrillard[6] so effectively makes us aware). In this Baudrillardian sense the film is very much 'not real' but hyperreal in its graphic depictions of chaos. It is in this post-modern Los Angeles, two days before the final catastrophe/euphoria of Y2K, that the plot unfolds. Ralph Fiennes plays ex-cop Lenny Nero, who makes his living selling 'clips', or miniature recordings of experiences, which can be played back through the 'SQUID' (super conducting quantum interference device) devices placed on the head. Man/woman is quite literally 'wired' for 'life', usually a piece of somebody else's life! The narrative makes a neat and clever (although this does not justify for one moment, I feel, such viscerally violent and pornographic images as the rape scene, which I describe below) analogy for philosophical considerations of the constructions of consciousness: the realm of the actual versus the virtual, the ways in which the mind might be disturbed, refracted, re-created, by a variety of technological energies and wavelengths through the cerebral cortex's transpositions by means of electrical impulses to synaptic tissues and cellular matrixes, not to mention the role of subjectivities or singularities within the auspices of consciousness. (It is a matter of fact, now well substantiated scientifically, that drugs like LSD have had similar liminal effects on the brain's mechanisms, its cellular structures and synaptic mechanism.) The very realm of fantasy becomes mind-blowingly (literally) real, in the possibilities for mind distortion and virtual engagement beyond and outside the exigencies of the real. The techno-euphoria of cyberspacial virtual reality (teledildonics with head set and data gloves) and video playback are taken one step further and played through the direct mainlining of the cerebral cortex, rather than the computer or TV screen, as hardware. The cerebral cortex becomes the body, becomes the machine, fed by the arteries/cerebral tissues, which operate as channels, tuned into the drug-like contamination of the software clips, played through a miniature play-back device, as small as a computer mouse. Drugs through cyberspatial technologies – a literal on-line source.

However, in one violently disturbing sequence, a rapist has his victim wear a SQUID device, thus enabling her to see and feel someone actually experience her own fear, as she sees and feels the experience 'through' that of her rapist/killer, as he perversely records the experience for 'play-back' – 'black-jack clips', snuff movies taken to even more sadistically disturbing extremes.[7] The rapist thus feeds gratuitously off his victim's fear, heightening his own vile, sadistic pleasure in her vulnerability, fragility and weakness. Who 'owns' the experience? Is there any mutual experience? Has she been psychologically, and emotionally, raped and violated (we could of course argue that this is possibly the felt experience of those who view) as much as physically violated? A total violation of her personae. Whose experience is this, the killer's or the victim's? An intensely chilling, and disturbing scene – viscerally as well as psychologically and morally nauseating. (The perpetrator is justly punished in the course of the film's narrative trajectory.)

How can a film with such representations hold any experience which is inspirational and transformative? How can this film exist as haecceity, and becoming? Is there a terrible beauty at work? I ask the reader to try to open up the 'mind' to the wider scenarios outside the representational to consider the aesthetic resonances for the film as a framework for transformations. But I don't negate the horror of the disturbing mysogynistic scenes which are part of the molar frame of the film's plane of organisation. This is not to justify such scenes, but to acknowledge them *as* disturbing whilst simultaneously part of the very critique that is generated through an 'in-between' state of the molar and the molecular.

The whole moral and ethical questioning about mind-control and perversion of consciousness is interestingly apparent though visually disturbing and problematic. Lenny's peddling of such pornographic software[8] ironically leads him into the search for the killing of Jericho 1, a black activist leader, and his friend, by two white cops – obviously a direct reference to the Rodney King killings. With the help of his friend, Macey (Angela Bassett), he becomes ensnared in the underground sado-masochistic and fetishistic world of Philo Gant (who, it transpires, is behind the surveillance and killings of black rap stars like Jericho 1) and his ex-lover Faith (Juliette Lewis). Ironically Lenny is a romantic and innocent lover, who cannot relinquish the unrequited love he feels for Faith (symbolic?). Sexuality, love, death and the perverse resonate across a diegesis about racial and sexual tension and social disintegration.

> *Dancing to P. J. Harvey's music, Faith sings . . . 'I can hardly wait . . . I can hardly wait' . . . waiting, within . . . without, in circular, spiralling ecstasies of technic modalities. She sways, swirling, synthetic, spiralling synergistic energies of molecular sexualities. In her hot, white, erotic and visceral movements, she collides in and against time, through time, rhythmically immanent, to the ebb and flow of the waves: the sound of the music colludes with waves of vision: the surface of the sea slowly becomes transparent, rippling, relaying, reverberations, until . . . slowly . . . her melting rhythm slowly fades to the earthy particles of the lotus, locust, locus . . . locomotion . . .*

According to Deleuze, waves are vibrations, shifting borderlines, inscribed on a plane of consistency. *Strange Days*, set then in 1999, the apocalyptic euphoria of the end-of-the-century party provides, as I have explained, a narrative of politico-racial tensions, exacerbations and questionings. A film which disorientates and distanciates the gaze of spectatorial identifications and representations, simultaneously, as we have seen, accommodates a neo-Marxist critique of late-capitalist pomo-distillation and disintegration. The neo-noiresque mise-en-scène provides a panorama of techno-furious culture, enhanced, encased and endangered within its own techno-euphoria. Mind, memory and matter meld in a set of discursive patterns of techno-post-modern angst. But such descriptions purely explain the film through a plane of organisation – an ideological paradigm. Kathryn Bigelow's style presents a different panoply for consideration. *Strange Days* creates a rhizome, or a cartography, of visionary dances. Forms, subjects, identities, representations merely replicate ideological structures and molarity. Molar lines or strata of segmentarity confine us to the ideological entrapments of State Apparati, filial, conjugal and gendered hierarchies: a Cartesian/Hegelian framework within which our bodies/minds are enshrined in ideological encasement.

But Deleuze suggests we should destratify; we need to open up beyond seeing our 'selves' as 'identities' as 'subjectivities' entrapped within the molar prisms of a capitalist, phallocentric world, the world which main-stream Hollywood dictates. Instead, molecularity enables a destratifica-tion beyond the processes of gendered or ideological subjective readings. We can connect, instead, through a mind/consciousness meld, with the molecularity of the film. Film as haecceity and sensation, rather than representation only. Film as abstract machine, as an assemblage of molecularity within and across a plane of consistency. *Strange Days* is not just a tale of apocalyptic visions, a narrative of filiative regimes of family, class, religion or race, or a set of symbolic and metaphorical analogies of post-structuralist or post-modern discourses. (It is, of course, all of those things.) It is rather, and more creatively, a process of 'becoming', an apparatus of capture, a modulationary experience of neo-synaesthesia and hapticity of consciousness. 'Becoming' is not about 'forms' and 'objects' or narrative, it is constitutive of immanence. Where, then, in the film are such resonances, such 'becomings' effectuated? The borderlines between the molar and the molecular.

Visually and aurally, the film exudes a mise-en-scène which vibrates and resonates in a variety of contrasting rhythms. The pace of the entire movie oscillates and sets up a resonance with the body and mind of the spectator. Sequences of total disintegration and chaos are created through an exciting array of camera movements, trajectories, lighting and use of colour. The opening sequence takes us into the mind-set of a 'clip' performing the (disturbing) fantasy of a violent robbery. Erratic camera angling, tracking shots, panning and hand-held camera techniques are evident here, as the camera tracks one or other of the robbers. Colours and lighting are subdued and dour: no intensity, no warmth, complete coldness and cruelty. The scene is reminiscent of the opening of *Nikita*. Cut to Lenny ripping off the SQUID device, leading us into the narrative – we learn that this was a fantasy peddled to punters as on-line, mind-set drugs. Cut to street-life culture, with images of chaos, destruction and havoc – burnt-out cars, muggings, killings, and general mayhem – set to regular rapper-style music. Contemporary musicians like Tricky and Massive Attack provide much of the soundtrack, thus effectuating a contemporary resonance of political and racial tension to the film's aesthetic. This is the night before New Year's Eve 1999. The camera pans from right to left, taking us across a panoply of devastation. Swirling camera actions track helicopters from a variety of angles, as in *Romeo and Juliet*, the sound of the blades becomes part of the intradiegetic cacophony. Chaotic and erratic illogical cutting gives way to slow-motion superimpositions – Santa Claus is mugged! Complete denial of the fantasy, the origin, the legend. Costume, uniform, personae are defused from reality, diffracted into a hallucinatory dreamscape. LA city police-cars (and men) become evanescent, surreptitious movement-images which float across the entire frame of the movie, almost pervading every sequence, performing as a figural movement-image. Whilst not acting as 'representational' symbols, they perform across the synaesthetic scopic matrix into the depths of a liminal space in our consciousness.

Early on in the film, we witness Iris, flying through the frames, erotic dark-blue sequinned outfit transiently displaying a masquerade of fe-tishistic glamour, a creature out of *Bladerunner*, trying to escape the threat of the cops as they hound her. (We later learn that they are anxious to retrieve a SQUID of a killing for which they are responsible.) The chase sequence has the camera floating, running alongside, changing speed, direction and angles of vision continually as it tracks Iris; we witness the effect from her point-of-view shot. Bigelow adeptly and chillingly conveys the terror, but beauty of a stillness, in contrasting resonance with the cacophony of the chase, at the subway station, through the aesthetic modulations. Vibration and resonance are effec-tuated through a variety of techniques here. Following the ecstatic and dynamic camera tracking of Iris, we are taken into the subway. The diegetic music stops; the cameras slow down to a state of febrile tension. That febrility is felt in the depths of a body without organs, through matrixial spaces, natal and pre-Oedipal, and within a primordial state beyond any 'subjectivity'. A frame of the subway shows the cold, stark, angular grey platform and train, in stillness, in silence. The shot is held for a couple of tense and meaningful seconds. Suddenly Iris lurches across the frame and shoots, like a liquid effusion of paint or light, into the train. Visually she functions as a literal shot of liquid blue across the still, grey, insipid canvas of the platform. A veritable liquid perception. This is eclipsed by the following shots which frenetically display Iris screaming hysterically in the train carriage with the police in violent pursuit. Such terror, noise, colour and action vibrate resonantly with the preceding shots of the silent subway platform.

Later in the movie, one of the same cops accused of murder drags his shackled body across the frame and lunges to shoot Macey – a beast straight out of Yeats's poem 'The Second Coming' . . . slouching towards Bethlehem? Indeed, the very slouching movement of his body language contrasts in a Deleuzian sense, as a vibration, with the earlier movement-images of Iris, Faith and Macey (interestingly 'woman' and not 'man') which float, run and dance across the diegesis. This black/white and striped phenomenon (policecar/man) performs a lively dance throughout the script, engaging us in a subconscious submergence.

Lenny, meanwhile, drives nonchalantly amidst such fantasies, simultaneously talking on his mobile to possible clients. The mise-en-scène is both reality and fantasy conjoined. Vibrant colours, reds, blues and yellows splatter our visual senses, imbricated with a montage of nondiegetic opera, and diegetic rap and rock music, all of which disorientate our sensory equilibrium. The mind/body/brain is already in a state of disorientation this early on in the movie.

Bigelow thus paints a visually and aurally rhythmical moving canvas, which provides a mind-blowingly chaotic mise-en-scène all the way through the movie, through a vibrant display of erotic costumes, jouissancially delightful but simultaneously dangerously deranged. The fetish club, where Faith performs her erotic dance, is perhaps the most significant of these sequences. Faith's performance is scintillatingly erotic and beautifully choreographed, her body swaying through undulating curvatures and circular motions in tune to the crystalline lyrics of P. J. Harvey's 'I Can Hardly Wait'. Dressed in exotic chain-mail dress, which seductively clings to her body, she functions in a haptic sense, not so much as 'woman' but as 'force' as 'the anomalous' as Mona does in *Romeo is Bleeding*.[9] Later she performs a similar dance, both violent and gentle, in contradistinction and contrapuntal nuances, with the lyrics 'You're not rid of me . . . no you're not rid of me . . .' similarly providing a contradictory erotic and disturbing figural across the film's diegesis. She performs as an anomalous 'figural' and 'outsider' modulating the haecceities of the music into and across the various rhythms of the film. She performs and becomes a contrasting, vibrational line of flight from those of Macey, and yet, in doing so, she enables such lines taken by Macey to effectuate change and positivity. Life's positivity, force and vitalism are aesthetically modulated through the circularity of camera angling around Faith's dancing, and indeed her general bodily movements within the rest of the film (for example, when she seduces Lenny). Such movements are resonated in complete contrast with Macey's static, electrifying, angular movements, latitudinal and longitudinal, in self-defence action sequences. Macey's body functions in martial combat, a terrifying machine, a black line, but a different black line from the white police/men/cars, quite literally figuring across the canvas in synchronisation with Faith's delicacy and evanescence. A bold contradistinction to the black line of the policecars and cops which weave and collide throughout the mise-en-scène. The bodily performativities of both Faith and Macey, one in circularity, the other in linearity, act as lines of movement, as movement-images which evoke, through the molecular, the sensations created through resonance, vibration and forced movements across and within the screen. Cleverly patterned fight sequences enhance the linearity and Pollockian definition of such scenes. A Pollockian canvas come to life, as it were – a body which assembles through its body without organs, with the bodies/minds/brains of those who view.

In several sequences, specifically the fetish club scenes, neo-fetishistic costumes straight out of cyberpunk fictions, and aberrant styles of sado-masochistic delights and desires, infuse our visual space, visually and haptically stunning in their textures of silks, leathers, satins, metals and a variety of tropes of erotica. As fantasy, they effect the brain's visual spaces through colours and tactility. The music resonates with such visuals to vibrate, and disorientate both brain and body at a molecular level. On this affective level, the brain/mind is overloaded with data to the visual cortical area: colour, motion and sound collide in sequence. In this way, what is 'representationally' disturbing can at the same time be rhythmically quite beautiful (for example, the mugging of Santa in tune to operatic crescendos) and perform as liquid perception within the brain. One is here reminded of Scorsese's beautifully choreographed boxing sequences in *Raging Bull* (1980), which far from being violent (although of course they are violent on a visceral level) render a terrible beauty in their rhythms and flows, a beauty which serves through vibration to highlight the emotional traumas of his personal life and inner conscious-ness. In this way, the molecularity of the film as 'event' merges with the film's molar trajectory – its characters and their narrative.

In this way, *Strange Days* similarly 'connects' right through its diegesis, rather than 'means'. It can be thought of as an event of experience, rather than a text as such. In Bigelow's movie, this imbrication of disturbing images with a processual beauty serves to offer a creative connection for the viewer, which might just disturb enough to affect mentalities in a Guattarian sense – could this be new enunciative processes at work? This is especially apparent and exemplifed in the very touching and beautiful sequence where Macey's young son dances innocently to the gentle ballad rhythms, swirling and enjoying a poetic autoeroticism in his unacknow-ledged pleasure as he floats his sparkler through the darkness. The sparkler leaves traces of its own (but not his own as it is the brain's formation) colour and light (can we remember such fascinations as a child: how a hand-held sparkler, when moved through the dark space of the night, leaves traces of purples and lilac molecules, the brain's own creation of movement-images?). Movement and colour within the brain's cortical mechanisms effectuate a stillness, a calmness and serenity. Any

'form' that is simulated from such cortical configurations quickly disperses into the ether. As a sequence this innocence and beauty, capturing
affect and becoming, counterpoints the violence and degradation of the
rape scene and the violent killing of the black activist leader. The horror
of both the rape and the killings is effectively enhanced and distanciated
by a process of forced movements within the scene centring on Macey's
son. Whilst the innocence of childhood is effectuated through a resonance
of colour, movement and rhythms, Lenny, in the background, concen-
trates on the visuals of the clip in which the black activist is murdered.
Counterpoint and distanciation effectuate an aesthetics of transformation. A new enunciative process of aesthetics effectuates a change in
mentality for the viewer. A micro-politics and ethics. A vibration is at
work across these two scenes. The killing of the black activist Jericho 1,
which Lenny replays whilst Macey watches her son (imbricating the
resonances across three positionalities), is set within a mise-en-scène of
detritus and squalor. Two white cops humiliate and degrade, their bodily
performativities erect, violent, upright, horrific and intransigent, against
the subservience of the kneeling activists. Subservience, truth and justice
are raped by a cowardice parading as strength and virtue. Weakness
becomes strength in its annihilation. Visually the scene exudes horror, in
terms of chaotic camera movements, the sound of the voices and screams
in relation to gunshots and non-diegetic music. The figurality of the cops
in uniform presents a line of annihilation and horror both here and across
the entire canvas of the movie; this line is counterpointed by the more
sensual and gentle rhythms of the dance we see from Macey's child – the
creativity, positivity and germinality of becoming-child.[10] The comparison of these two sequences on a neo-aesthetic level determines a true
micro-politics at work, a pragmatics of becoming.

In Macey's delightful vision of her son, Macey's vision is also our
vision. The pattern of gazes across and between Macey (her son is quite
oblivious, however, to her gaze, thus enhancing the autoeroticism and
delicate beauty of the scene) and her son, his movements, are beautifully
choreographed through the camera's swirling back to Macey's subjective
point-of-view shot. This creates a choreography and matrixial web of
gazes, which becomes part of the processuality of the film's haecceity –
and through that haecceity and sensation a molecular politics is discernible. A pragmatics of becoming.

But on a narrative level, ironically, the synaesthetic delights of the fetish
club and similar sequences of sado-masochistic pleasures highlight the
disturbing, suspect sexual and racial politics which permeate the movie.
Bigelow, I feel, is both parading and yet questioning those pleasurable

and dangerous spaces of the erotic. This is not a condoning, but a creative immersion. In a Chekovian way, Bigelow presents, she does not judge, or comment. She offers up a panoply of life's exigencies. Like Cronenberg,[11] she take us into our own mind/brain/bodily zones, frighteningly and chillingly confronting the contradictory spaces of fantasy, reality, and the erotic – where they combine and where they disperse, where they meld and where they assemble – rhizomatically evoking a confrontation with one's own ghosts. Psychoanalysis might well provide some exploration of the erotic and the exotic in the movie. But the aesthetics at work in the mind/brain, whilst 'felt' at a level beyond subjectivity, at the point of the microtubular, can also invoke, prosthetically, mechanisms which lure the emotions into play – the space 'between' the subjective encounter and the non-subjective space of pre-verbal singularities, the 'depth' of that primordial sense of aliveness – autopoiesis.

NOTES

1. W. B. Yeats, 'The Second Coming', in *The Collected Poems of W. B. Yeats*.
2. Deleuze and Guattari, *A Thousand Plateaus*, p. 255.
3. I am of course taking a simple approach to the issue of sado-masochism. The film's depiction, at a narrative level, of sado-masochistic life styles is of course both problematic and yet simultaneously liberating. Debates abound around the discourses of sexuality, and the possible liberatory discourse within sado-masochistic depictions and dangerously erotic imagery has been well written about in feminist film theory, e.g. Barbara Creed, *The Monstrous Feminine*, Carol Clover, *Men, Women and Chainsaws*, Michelle Aaron's collection on *The Body's Perilous Pleasures*. I don't want to engage with those debates here, but merely to acknowledge the breadth of theory around such filmic imagery.
4. It is interesting to note that Kathryn Bigelow's film well precedes the accolade accorded to this most recent Arnold Schwarzenger film and did not receive the acclaim it deserved at the time. Female directors continue to be perceived differently from their male counterparts.
5. See for example *Near Dark* and *Blue Steel*.
6. See Baudrillard's *America*.
7. Thankfully Bigelow has us spared the explicitness of the physical violence, but it is still nonetheless very disturbing, specifically from a woman director, and I personally have had problems in defending this sequence.
8. Ironically, the same software which produces the degradation and violence of pornography has also enabled the entrapment of the two racist murderers. A problematic irony in the technology's potentialities for good or evil. The technology alone is innocent. It is, of course, those who use the technology who produce the manifestations of its possibilities.
9. In Peter Medak's film *Romeo is Bleeding*, Mona is the third line of flight outside the lines of Natalie, the faithful wife, and Sherry, the mistress. Mona's disorientational activities confirm her action as figural and anomalous, and outsider – a monstrous force for change and disorientation.
10. Deleuze writes that the beyond of becoming-woman is becoming girl. Through a becoming-girl we reach the vortex of processuality and becoming through that

which has not yet been Oedipalised or hierarchised through social or gender structures.

The following film, *Leon*, attests to a becoming-girl through the expedience of becoming which distanciates the violence and horror of the narrative and teleological level of the film's plane of organisation.

11. See Cronenberg's *Videodrome* (1982) or *Crash* (1996).

Chapter 10

Reconfiguring Love . . . A Deleuzian Travesty? *Leon* and a Molecular Politics via the Girl and the Child

AN EXPLORATION OF *LEON*

OUTLINING THE STRUCTURE – DEFINING THE 'GIRL'

Knowing how to love does not mean remaining a man or a woman: it means extracting from one's sex the particles, the speeds, and slownesses, the flows, the sexes that constitute the girl of *that* sexuality. It is Age itself that is a becoming-child, just as Sexuality, any sexuality, is a becoming-woman, in other words, a girl.[1]

[B]ecoming-woman or the production of molecular woman is the girl herself. The girl is certainly not defined by virginity: she is defined by a relation of movement and rest, speed and slownesses, by a combination of atoms, an emission of particles: haecceity. She never ceases to roam upon a body without organs. She is an abstract line, or a line of flight. The girls do not belong to an age group, sex, or kingdom: they slip in everywhere, between orders, acts, ages, sexes; they produce *n* molecular sexes on the line of flight in relation to the dualism machines they cross right through.[2]

In terms of a post-feminist politic, *Leon* (1994), like other films such as *Nikita* (1990),[3] offers new spaces and representations of woman as 'war-machine' (the image of woman as strong, assertive and autonomous, a rather reductionist and binary explanation of visual imagery). But, of course, 'representation' has never been my major concern for writing about film in this work. However, what I want to do in this chapter is to explore a molecular politic, to take a 'tangential' move away from Deleuzian ideas on 'sensation' to some extent, and I emphasise the proviso 'tangential', to explore the Deleuzian concept of the 'girl' in relation to 'becoming-woman'. Of course there is in a way an ironic twist, in that Deleuze himself rejects metaphor and metonymy and there is, perhaps, an audacity and irony in utilising metaphor in imbrication with

Deleuze. But I am only doing that which Deleuze himself does in his exploration of literature and art; paradoxically developing a rhizomatic format of creativity, which connects and imbricates works through machinic assemblage.[4] This is not about analysis, but about assemblage: film as an experience, as event, as consciousness formation, not purely a text. But the text is and has to be part of that machinic body.

However, in this chapter, as opposed to those so far under scrutiny, I use those very elements (metaphor and metonymy) of narrative play to explore some Deleuzian thoughts. I ask the reader therefore to abandon molar critique, and to explore creatively *Leon* in a somewhat different way from those above. To move, but only tangentially so, 'outside' the earlier chapters of this book which have framed the 'haecceity' and 'event' and to some extent to move back into frameworks of textuality, metaphor and metonymy. Abandon the machine, to present a more heterogeneous machine. However, it is important not to revert (binarily!) into those arenas without the hindsight of 'haecceity'. Having read Chapters 6, 7, 8 and 9, which deal more specifically with the haecceity, these should heterogeneously collude with this chapter. On the contrary, this exploration will not dispense with my argument of a neo-aesthetic at work in the experiential element of film, and I intend to show how this imbrication of a neo-aesthetic alongside an analysis or reading of the movies through the notion of the Deleuzian 'girl' can offer creative and refreshing understandings of the impact of such films, working as a 'body' in a molecular sense. A true 'in-between' of representation and haecceity. A molecular politic and a post-feminist pragmatic methodology which re-establishes aesthetics as a possible micro-political arena.

So far, then, I have considered how we might utilise Deleuzian ideas on the beyond of subjectivity and the beyond of desire, through sensation, affect and becoming-woman, as ways in which to consider film as an event, as a 'haecceitas' formation, and I have looked at how we might analyse the ways film modulates and connects through those spaces of Deleuzian philosophy. What I want to do in this chapter is slightly different but it projects an interestingly conclusive development out of the work done so far.

In this concluding chapter I shall take the Deleuzian concept of the 'girl' and its place in 'becoming' to read the film. Deleuze discusses becoming-girl as an abstract concept within his arsenal of ideas on becoming. It is part of the same assemblage as becoming-woman. It does not refer to any literal image, or definition of an actual molar girl, just as becoming-woman is not about real, molar women as such. Rather, becoming-girl is the ultimate molecular becoming of woman, in an abstract conception of those terms. However, in an ironic way, I *am* using an actual image of the girl, within the film (in the case of *Leon*, the character of Mathilda, and in *Nikita*, of course Nikita, a very different girl from Mathilda) to focus and develop an understanding of the abstract concept of 'girl'[5] in its Deleuzian sense, but in a way which enables a micro-politics to emerge. That micro-politics is in fact premised on both the molecularity of 'becoming-girl' but also the neo-aesthetics of the films. I don't want to lose a sense of what the book has so far argued, that film 'works' as a machinic assemblage, as a molecular body with other 'bodies'.

Rather than losing that argument, and backtracking into theories of representation and the molar, what I am doing is actually taking that argument further, to open up fresh possibilities for film theory. It must not be forgotten that I am also reading the film through an appreciation of the neo-aesthetics of sensation, to see how the aesthetic reverberations and molecularities enable and stimulate the molar reading. What should emerge is an example of that 'interstitial' space, which Deleuze argues is truly the molecular space of creativity and 'involution'. In the 'in-between' spaces of molecularity and molarity is an aparalletic evolution[6] of two sensations. This does not suggest a hybridisation of perspectives, but a continual machinic evolution between perspectival ideas. 'The only way to get outside the dualisms is to be between, to pass between, the intermezzo.'[7] First, I shall provide an exploration of the film through a molar reading, and second, in relation to aesthetic molecularities.

We should therefore be able to discern a micro-politics at work, which, as I argued in Chapter 1, might enable a reconnection with the political, through the aesthetic. So, in a sense, this chapter functions as a 'coming-together', 'becomings', but in a machinic way, not in a hybrid way, of molarity and molecularity, as a way of arguing for a new assemblage of enunciation to take us into micro-political and pragmatic considerations. The aesthetic, the pragmatic and the micro-political are conjoined through the film's assemblages.

Such micro-political questions, in *Leon*, are highlighted around violence, and its opposite: ideas of fixity, transition, change, stability, mobility, and ethical frameworks of love, validation, integrity and worth. What appears to be a film replete with violence and images of death, sadistic pleasures and horrific brutality (Gary Oldman as the DEA cop, Stansfield, presents and performs a horrific trope of all that is evil, menacing and sadistic, yet also that which is delicious and seductive!), *Leon* actually works to assuage those very negative elements of experience, in validation of the positivity of life's becoming, life's joy and germinal possibilities in 'becoming' rather than a desire locked into teleological and psychological frameworks of conclusions, endings and satiation. This 'becoming' is effectuated as processuality through the idea of the machinic elements of 'girl'. Like Hana, in *The English Patient*, like Juliet in *Romeo and Juliet*, like Sasha in *Orlando*, like Faith in *Strange Days*, *Leon*'s heroine Mathilda works as a female, child, character (as representational image) but also as a figure or figural – a 'movement-image' – within the haecceity of the film's assemblage. It would be simple in the extreme to suggest that Mathilda 'represents' a girl and what I want to develop from that, through the aesthetic modulations of the movie, is how 'girl' functions as an abstract concept. She functions as movement, as a molecular 'body' in machinic connection with other bodies, within the diegetic patterns of the narrative (on the plane of organisation and transcendence) but also through haecceitas formations, on a plane of immanence and consistence. This complex route away from, but including, the 'represented image' is sustained by my argument that subjectivity is rendered subjectless, and thus the experiences 'felt' in this movie are 'outside' any fixed positionality. They exist in the proto-subjective states of the brain/body/mind assemblage. All three come together, as Deleuze indicates, in the brain itself – in autopoiesis.

In a brief aside for a moment, how can we begin to understand Deleuze's abstract concept of 'girl?' As I argued earlier, 'becoming-woman' is, for Deleuze, the first element in a processuality of 'becoming' which operates differently and beyond a desire premised on satiation. It is 'becoming-girl' which is essentially the molecular woman and 'haecceity' itself. Let's look, first, at how Deleuze connects his ideas on immanence and haecceity, which we saw in earlier chapters and evinced in the films *Orlando* and *Romeo and Juliet*, to the 'girl': 'There is a mode of individuation very different from that of a person, subject, thing, or substance. We reserve the name haecceity for it.'[8]

Deleuze, with Guattari, indicates that we pass from one plane (organisation) to another (consistency or immanence):

> [W]hy does the opposition between the two kinds of plane lead to a still more abstract hypothesis? Because one continually passes from one to the other by unnoticeable degrees, and without being aware of it, or one becomes aware of it only afterward. Because one continually reconstitutes one plane atop another, or extricates one from the other.[9]

This is vitally important to my argument, because whilst I am arguing and positioning a concern with cinema as experience, as event and as material capture, there is a way in which the molar and the plane of organisation of the movie, its narrative forms, its characters, its diegesis, its molarities of sound and image, are also part of the 'event' itself. A denial of the plane of organisation would negate the concept of machinic heterogeneity – a machinic assemblage which occurs through the heterogeneities of the molar and the molecular, between the spaces of the plane of 'immanence' and plane of 'organisation'. All the elements which constitute those planes will dance, mingle, coalesce and 'become' across any fixed or even hybridised positionality (since hybridisation is still too fixed, too static) . . . a dance of the atoms.[10] This space of the inexplicable, which resides outside of hybridisation, is a fugitive space, the space of the 'girl'.

> What is a girl, what is a group of girls? Proust at least has shown us once and for all that their individuation, collective or singular, proceeds not by subjectivity, but by haecceity, pure haecceity. 'Fugitive beings'. They are pure relations of speeds and slownesses and nothing else. A girl is late on account of her speed.[11]

Deleuze explores how social and cultural forces actually 'rob' the literal girl of her own 'body' as it were, by virtue of the fact that socialisation processes force her to behave in specific, appropriate and acceptable ways. 'Stop behaving like that, you're not a little girl any more.'[12] And so I have to keep telling myself, especially when I fall in love!

The autopoietic, non-gendered, proto-subjective and non-subjective forces, energies and volatilities are in fact socialised out of her by the time she has to become a woman. Her 'becoming' is thus stolen, first, from her, in order for her to be 'culturally and ideologically positioned' as 'woman'. She thus loses the vitality of the pre-symbolic state. The boy's turn comes next, as his socialisation is premised upon acknowledging his 'desire' for the other, where the girl becomes an object of desire for the boy. The girl is 'robbed' of her body without organs, and so needs to reconstitute that as inseparable from a process of 'becoming-woman'. In order to reconstitute the body without organs, that abstract concept which imbricates volatility, vitality and processuality, in order to live through 'becoming' and not transcendent notions of desire, the *anorganism* of the body needs to be accommodated. In other words a molecularity of being needs to be effectuated: to reclaim those intensities, energies, lines of flight, velocities of 'girlishness'. I use the word 'girlishness' here as a similar word to 'thisness', which comes from Duns Scotus's – and thereafter, Deleuze's – definition on haecceity. Scotus takes the word 'haecceity' as premised upon the Latin word 'haec', which means 'this thing'. 'Girlishness' then is similarly derived as a 'thisness of girl'. As Deleuze and Guattari indicate, it is 'doubtless, the girl becomes a woman in the molar sense, or organic sense. But conversely, "becoming-woman" is the "molecular-woman", IS the girl herself.'[13] It is certain, asserts Deleuze, that molecular politics proceeds via the girl and child. This is why, in this final chapter, I want to take this abstract concept of the 'girl' through which to position a molecular politics; a politics of heterogeneity, beyond hybridity but through a machinic heterogeneity of aesthetic modulations in relation to film. Molecularity enables a micro-politics which is evidenced through a neo-aesthetic. Deleuze and Guattari refer to the writer Trost, who painted a picture of the girl as 'linked to the fate of revolution; her speed, her freely machinic body, her intensities, her abstract line of flight, her molecular production, her indifferences to memory, her non-figurative of desire. Joan of Arc? The special role of the girl in Russian terrorism, the girl with the bomb, guardian of dynamite?'[14]

THE 'BECOMING-GIRL' IN *LEON*

In *Leon* as much as *Nikita*, the 'girl' is quite literally, the machinic, post-human image of locomotion. This is perhaps more evident in *Nikita*, where Nikita quite literally becomes an assassin, a killing machine of the first order. She is *l'étranger*, the anomalous, the threshold, the borderline. Like the 'girl' in *Leon*, she functions as force, affect and movement-image, as a veritable figural across the texts. Deleuze writes,

> [T]he movement of the infinite can occur only by means of affect, passion, love, in a becoming that is the girl, but without reference to any kind of 'mediation'; and that this movement as such eludes any mediating perception because it is already effectuated at every moment, and the dancer or lover finds him- or herself already 'awake and walking' the second he or she falls down, and even the instant he or she leaps. Movement, like the girl as a fugitive being, cannot be perceived.[15]

Once again, this is relevant to my argument, that the in-between states of the molar and the molecular of the filmic experience reside within the 'girl', within the fugitive spaces of her becoming. We cannot discern a totality of 'meaning' from either/or positionality from the plane of immanence or the plane of organisation, but a space which is somewhere else, and not somewhere else, because it is a fugitive place: a 'girl'.

Narratively, *Leon* explores the story of a New York hitman of Italian origins, Leon (Jean Reno), a rather simple, uneducated, but a physically strong and dedicated guy. He befriends a young twelve-year-old girl,

Mathilda, recently orphaned as a result of the murder of her family by DEA personnel (Gary Oldman leading the team) in a case of drug-dealing and police retribution. The drug-ridden and violent streets of Little Italy provide a chaotic, dangerous, but exciting mise-en-scène, within which the relationship of Leon and Mathilda poignantly and sensitively evolves.

But how can 'sensitivity' be operative in a Deleuzian frame of non-human prescriptions? What do we mean by sensitivity here? It does not function as a romantic notion. What I want to explore is how we might think of 'sensitivity', love,[16] as a state-in-process, not 'of being', an acceptance of a non-satiable space of 'desire'. Desire in process, not in finality or satiation. This processual state is accommodated through the body without organs of the proto-subjective state, and exemplifies the 'girl' of 'becoming-woman'. It is created through aesthetic resonances, through 'sensation' in a Deleuzian sense, as much as through the diegetic narrative, characterisation and generic elements of the film's plane of organisation. *Leon*, like *Strange Days*, is violent and replete with horrific 'representations' deriving from a diegetic scenario which tells the tale of love, a valorisation of joy and vitality, through an understanding of innocence, naivety, fragility and a strength within that fragility.[17] Non-fixity: in other words, process. Neither fragility nor strength but an in-between or an aparalletic evolution of the two states and a paradoxical understanding of the strength within fragility, and fragility in strength. The film nonetheless also functions in a micro-political way, through its aesthetic, in collusion with the plane of consistency, to present an inspirational understanding of the vitality of 'Life'. A different under-standing of the concept of 'love'.

Whilst Mathilda functions as a girl, as a 'character' in a narrative, with relationships across the text of the movie, the idea of the 'girl' in a Deleuzian sense enables us to consider the intensities of that concept, as an abstract concept. What I want to do is to elide these two perspectives to see if we can discern an aesthetic which rests upon abstract terminology and yet also uses an 'actual' image, or rather a movement-image, of a 'girl' through which to think through that abstraction. That abstraction is premised upon characteristics of vitality, dynamism, movement, joy, exuberance, and a sense of germinal and positive forces emanating from an autopoietic sense of aliveness and existential singularities. Whilst it seems a travesty to discuss 'love' in a Deleuzian landscape, in fact this abstract concept of the 'girl' comes very close to a reconsideration of love. Deleuze offers different perspectives. This is a love outside the exigencies of romantic, sexual or self/other relationals, subjectivity premised on a valorisation of the self in relation to the Other and the forces of psycho-analytic regimes. It is the 'molecular love' accommodated through a body without organs, the awareness of 'Life' as force, vitality and becoming. Deleuze himself refers to this, as we see in the first quotation at the beginning of the chapter. This philosopher of monstrosity and the post-human actually enables a reconfiguration of love through abstract concepts such as the 'girl'.

How then is this concept both an abstract concept and an actual molar image functional across the diegetic scenario of *Leon*? And how do the elements of sensation work to bring about this notion of the 'girl'? I shall explore several sequences of the movie, and discuss them through the abstract concept of the 'becoming-girl' but also taking on board the notion of sensation, as it is accommodated through the three modes: vibration, resonance and forced movement. By establishing how the sequences relate in juxtaposition, how they move through frame-by-frame choreographies, how certain molar elements like 'characters' can function in molecular ways as figurals, lines and forces, then we can discern how 'sensation' in the Deleuzian sense is operating through the rhythmical movements of the sequences, either in contrast, comparison, or in juxtaposition with each other.

This interrelationality enables us to consider the abstract concept of 'becoming-girl' because it echoes those characteristics of 'vitality, dynamism and energy' emblematic of 'girlishness'. It is the interrelationality of styles in the movie which creates a rhythmical and processual notion of the beautiful; but it is a different type of 'beauty': beauty as a 'process' and not an aesthetic premised upon 'form'. This different and neo-aesthetic definition of beauty (as opposed to romantic notions of beauty, which are premised on form, tone, shape, colour and so on) is determined by the concept of 'time' in terms of the sequentialities, movements and intensities working across, between and through the different sequences. Beauty, therefore, pertains to a time-factor, a temporal notion, a processual 'opening out' into another space, another moment, in the future, before the present has actually become the past, so that past, present and future are, as it were, contained in the one movement. As Deleuze indicates in *Cinema 2*, the notion of time does not exist as a linear projection to or from specific points, which have beginnings, middles and ends. All moments of time are moments in collision:

> indifferently divisible and possibly connectable, as if laid out on a single surface of availability, indeterminate until a contingent encounter makes one moment stand out or fall. Beauty pertains to a process that takes

empirical precedence over existing formed things and their narratively closable coursings.[18]

The consciousness perceives this process before form, because this is how the brain accommodates the world around it.[19]

I want to begin by exploring the film in a textual way, but I shall develop from this to expose how these textual elements work, in terms of Deleuzian aesthetics of sensation. The establishing shots of the movie in many ways echo those of *Romeo and Juliet*. Except here gentle violin music accompanies an aerial shot across Central Park, the camera zooming into centre frame, into the diegesis of the narrative's mise-en-scène: Little Italy, the heart of New York. Narrative cut to Leon and Tony. Eyes, faces, the hands and the look become significant elements in the relationship between Leon and his Mafia boss, Tony, as the camera oscillates across and between the gazes of each in a pattern of disconcerting effects.

Fragmentary shots of Leon are all we have in the following sequence. Drug-peddling gangsters are warned off through Leon's threatening assault, but already we can establish an identification with Leon, because of the way in which he has been introduced. His 'alien' or 'loner' characteristics are clearly exemplified through his concealment of identity – the dark glasses concealing the eye from any close encounter. So we actually see Tony reflected in Leon's glasses in a close-up shot. An innocence and gentleness is acknowledged because of his style and body language: his lack of English, his inability to read, his doleful eyes (both threatening and simultaneously innocent and reflective), his trademark glasses, and woolly hat, his long, dark overcoat and his angular and awkward gait.

Leon and Mathilda first encounter each other when Leon returns to his apartment, following his recent 'cleaning job' (contract killing). The camera slowly tracks Leon. We then have a sequence of images, which through controlled camera movements, made in time to non-diegetic delicate riffs from guitar and xylophone, modulate the abstract concept of 'becoming-girl'. How is this done? The camera pans from a still image of Mathilda's right foot, swinging gently, to reveal both feet, centre frame, clad in huge, brown, leather boots, swinging in contrapuntal time to the music. (In several frames in the film, this pair of feet is centrally located within the frame, in contradistinction to Leon's, with significant reverberations of contrast, dissonance, and similarity-in-difference.) Their cumbersome look is paradoxically gentle and awkward because of the way in which the sound and vision are here edited. The next frame shows the camera tilting (a shot reminiscent, it will be detected by film students, of similar craning shots from *Citizen Kane*) upwards over Mathilda's body, her clothes, white lacy bolero, velvet choker and pink patterned leggings, textually and evocatively 'feminine' in their tactility and colour-ful tones. All is belied by the cigarette so naively but eloquently held from Leon's view at arm's length. An interesting and paradoxical trope of eloquence, sophistication and maturity disguised by her innocent exter-ior. Non-fixity, complexity, a multiplicity of personae. It is this multi-plicity, together with Mathilda's function as figural, and vitalism (as we see in later sequences), which disorientates Leon's apparent masculinity (so obviously represented by his physique, which is muscular, robust and totally fit as he carefully follows a regime of fitness exercise to maintain his stamina) and resilience, thus establishing his 'becoming-girl'. The following shot cuts to Mathilda's face, framed and yet contained behind the intricacy and delicacy of the lace-patterned wrought-ironwork. Her pale face is part of the rhythmical swirls in the wrought-iron patterning. The angle of her face is pietà-like, in its angelic and Madonna-esque nuances, as she inclines gently to the right, an innocent and sympathetic and paradoxical expression of hope, and forlorn anxiety. But also provocation. This provocation is in no way Lolita-esque, and I don't read the film as sexual in a molar way at all. Its sexuality is purely in its molecularity. That 'thousand tiny sexes', which Deleuze relates in *A Thousand Plateaus*. The provocation is less 'sexual' than 'molecularly sexual'. It is replete with singularities of 'girlishness'. This innocence/maturity is evoked by the still frame: the camera maintains this shot for three seconds. This is followed by a shot which is held for six seconds, of her face, and hair, emphasising the intricate and balanced movements, through close-up of her eyes, nose and delicate mouth. The beauty lies in the processuality and hapticity of those movements, not in the form itself. It is the body and facial movements, the hand which becomes face, the eye which becomes nose, becomes mouth, which modulate the 'girl' in the abstract sense, evoking the vitality, and joyousness of her 'becoming'. She surreptitiously hides the cigarette, while the camera pans up, from a low angled shot, and from Mathilda's point of view, up to Leon's face. Thus follows a close-up shot of Leon and Mathilda, with intricate and prolonged shots and close-ups of eyes, to eyes, shot-reverse-shot edits. Eyes and head movements, micro-movements, modulate a 'rhythmical beauty' (in the processual sense of the word beauty) across the screen. The sequence ends with a close-up centre-framed shot of Mathilda, then Leon, significantly followed by the first image of Stansfield (Gary Oldman), the DEA cop with, yet again, a close-up of feet introducing the macabre and evil character. Consequently, the cut to the following sequence conveys the cacophony and chaos of Mathilda's home apartment, highlighted when Stan erupts, threatening her father.

Leon already shows signs early on in the film of being a loner, but with a sensitivity which belies his macho and gangster-like image. The film conveys this through specific shots, for example, of the plant which Leon tends with affection and regularity (he tends to his weapons with equal care and affection), moving it into the light or out on to the ledge for air. It becomes a trope of life, growth and germinality throughout the movie. This is seen for example in another sequence. Leon watches Mathilda, punched and kicked by her father, following his own abuse at the hands of Stan and his colleagues from the DEA. The image cuts from this scene to Leon's plant, providing a contrasting connection across the two types of behaviour. The mise-en-scène of Leon's room is sparse, but carefully tended, white flowing curtains waft in the air, as he moves the plant out into the sunshine. He slowly and purposively folds his clothes: neat, folded, organised. Static, slow, controlled and angular body movements. No dialogue, no voice-over, but a non-diegetic symphony of classical music, violas and other strings crescendo with a beautiful shot, held for three seconds, of Leon taking a shower. His body angle, the gentle expressions of delicate insouciance, the angle of his head against the wall (echoing Mathilda's earlier pietá look), the gentle rhythm of his arm movement across his body, the movements of the water flowing across his body, work in tune, rhythmically to the music, and in paradoxical contradistinction with the images of him wiping his weapons, cleaning his guns and that static controlled movement of purposive order and functionalism.

This scene exemplifies a Deleuzian hapticity of movement-image and liquid perception: in other words, the feeling of being able to touch and see at the same time. To feel a specific tactility, to want to reach out and feel with the hand, within the movements in the image itself. The fluidity of the shot is evoked through the liquidity of water flowing in tune with the music's tonalities. Sound and image in total imbrication, through a liquidity of perception. In molecular terms, the brain's acknowledgement of what it sees and hears is first activated across the cerebellum and efferent motor responses of the brain, by the movement, the process, then the sound and image. It is the liquidity of the movements which creates the notion of the 'beautiful' here. The brain, as Norseen argues,[20] perceives such movements in a specific way which impinges upon the cerebellum in pleasing formations. It is this processuality, premised on 'time', of things 'flowing', the feeling of experiencing the 'now' when the 'past' has not yet disappeared, the micro-movements of Leon's body (and the shots by the camera) and the 'hapticity' of the 'movement-image', which effectuates a beautiful gentleness. This continues in the shot of him ironing his clothes. A gently rhythmical movement across the ironing board, a right to left movement, which takes the eye across and through the scene. The very stature of his body is itself fluid, and flowing; there is a distinct rhythmical line across the contours of his body, into iron, into the clothes he irons. One begins where the other ends: processuality. This gentleness pervades Leon's overt, stereotypical masculinity and the sequence provides a Deleuzian sense of 'sensation' in its vibration and resonance with other sequences, as I shall exemplify below. It is these elements within Leon which connect him through Mathilda's 'girlishness', into something which ennervates them both. The 'becoming-girl'.

This 'becoming-girl' is further evident in the following sequence, where we see Leon in his apartment the next morning. Cut from his apartment to Mathilda's: Leon exercising contrasts through edits with the violent sister who batters Mathilda, phone ringing, TV blaring, and general mayhem. Mathilda talks to her headmistress of her mother, and thinking of herself, says 'She's dead.' Her pain and the pain epitomised by the close-up shot and music here are diametrically contrasted with the previous sequence of tranquillity and the rhythmical beauty of Leon. He leaves the apartment, to walk down the street.

The narrative cuts to a close-up central-framing shot of Leon's face: a static vibrational shot as it is in contrast with the previous sequence. His eyes are staring, mouth smiling, at some off-screen stimulus. He turns his head ever so slightly and innocently to the right, as the diegetic music from the film he is watching, 'Love has made me see things in a different way . . .' pervades from Gene Kelly in *Singing in the Rain*; Leon's 'becoming-girl' is envisioned through this close-up shot. This 'becoming-girl' is effectuated through the film's technical and aesthetic processes in the following edits. The scene proceeds with a luminously fluid dissolve, effectuated as much through the music as the tones, shapes and lines of the visuals, from Kelly's flowing movement left to right of screen, pure movement, pure processuality, into a right to left aerial shot, which tracks Leon up the apartment stairway. Here he finds Mathilda crying: he gives her a tissue. She continues the gesture of friendship and leaves to buy Leon his milk.

On her return, she encounters the DEA cops, and the killing and decimating of her apartment. Gently, in slow-motion camera movements, from right to left of screen, Mathilda floats towards Leon's door. Her delicacy, fragility and vulnerability are aesthetically created by the camerawork. She looks pathetically innocent and fragile as she is positioned, a tiny creature, centre frame, knocking at Leon's door. And yet the music belies that stature. Rather it presents a magnificent gesture of strength, hope, courage and belief; utter positivity, from Mathilda. She looks upwards; the camera shows a full frontal close-up of her, but from a high camera angle, thus emphasising the paradoxical vulnerability. A long-shot, behind her, down the corridor points to the place of violence from which she is trying to escape. Her vulnerability is highlighted, and yet simultaneously denied (and this is an example of the idea of sensation operating through resonance; two elements, one the visual track, one the soundtrack, work together and bounce off each other) by the music, which crescendos with a simultaneous full key lighting effect as Leon finally opens the door, emblematically both saving her and providing the way forward to both his own 'becoming-girl' through her influences, and Mathilda's own progression towards maturity.

The scenes between Leon and Mathilda continue to epitomise the 'becoming-girl' of Leon. The first time in his apartment, Mathilda, crying and bleeding, is shown with a close-up of her face, as she looks down. Shot-reverse-shot follows, with Leon similarly tilting his head lower to echo, as a choreography across the two, his and Mathilda's facial expressions. Her words become as tender and evocative as her image, here operating in vibration, rather than resonance, with the image: 'They killed my little brother . . . he was only four years old . . . all he wanted to do was to cuddle.' A close-up of Mathilda's face shows her changing moods when Leon begins to cajole her with games and comic gestures; he tenderly plays a game of puppets, using his oven cloth as a 'pig' which Mathilda watches in earnest: her smile, eyes and countenance change accordingly. That discrete movement of different facial intonations exemplifies the forced movement. Close-up shots convey the intensities of these micro-movements in her facial expressions. She stares, open-eyed, at Leon, as she responds with 'Cute name'. The words belie the innocence of the image. The edits create lots of eye contact across the two; slow camera movements collide with classical music, as a gentle connection is evidenced between them. A gentleness counterpointed by the discussion of weapons, guns, and his job as a 'cleaner'.

The most tender of all sequences between Leon and Mathilda is the one in which the soundtrack is Björk's 'Venus as a Boy', itself a melodic and plangent refrain, the lyrics of which can be read alongside the images we see, in productive ways. For example, sings Björk, 'He believes in beauty . . . Venus as a boy . . . he believes in beauty . . .' This plays as non-diegetic music, whilst the screen gives a series of actions and movements that cement a bonding between Leon and Mathilda. In a sequence with hardly any dialogue, Leon teaches Mathilda about weaponry and in return Mathilda cleans and helps Leon with his reading and writing. 'Pure' cinematic technique again: image and no dialogue. They exercise in unison: they work in unison. The camera pans from right to left, following Mathilda's gait as she slowly teaches Socrates to Leon. Their closeness is then cemented when they play a series of masquerades: Mathilda dresses and sings as Madonna, and as Marilyn Monroe – Leon innocently fails to recognise these. (I could provide a whole range of intertextual readings around these images, in another context 'Mathilda–Madonna–Monroe' – emblematic of a distanciating and cajoling notion of femininity upon the stature of masculinity.) He does, of course, recognise Gene Kelly when Mathilda sings, 'I'm singing in the rain . . .' Leon tries to play John Wayne (now there's an image of masculinity!), his body movement exaggerated to the point of parody. Contradiction, and paradoxes, abound.

BEYOND SUBJECTIVITY – TO HAECCEITIES OF SENSATION – THE AESTHETIC OF SENSATION

However, to explore the notion of 'becoming-girl' the analysis so far has been largely premised upon style, semiotics and technicalities, which formal film theory has always enabled to a certain degree, and certainly psychoanalysis developed upon those textual elements of film theory to provide more sophisticated ways of understanding subjective readings, or the perception of a subjectivity created by the film's visual elements. I have purposely used a descriptive, semiotic and textual reading, so far, to exemplify the 'becoming-girl' of Leon, at times ennervated by the Deleuzian elements of sensation. But how has Deleuze enabled a different way of understanding film and such stylistic elements to become part of a 'haecceity' or an event? To think about film as an experience, an event, not as a representation. To move away from subjectivity and desire. Indeed, that very haecceity of the experience of a movie, *is* also part of the 'becoming-girl'. This is because 'becoming-girl' is predicated on heterogeneities, not hybridities, movements, intensities, energies, volatilities, which are elements of processuality, fundamentally within the brain's processes. Processuality is a description of the 'movements' which make up what I referred to earlier as 'qualitative multiplicities'. Those qualitative multiplicities are part of the beyond of subjectivity. They function as a continual processuality outside of subjectivity. Qualitative multiplicities operate beyond the subject of any phenomenological notion of subjectivity. They exist within the singularity of a multicomponential state, that pre-subjective, or proto-subjective state, in the very molecular movements of microtubular action: that is, within the brain itself. The brain's own sense of itself (what Deleuze refers to as absolute survey or true form) is operative in creating qualitative multiplicities. Thus there is subjectless subjectivity which is premised on movements, things flowing, and moving, at a deeper level than subjective awareness. Affective awareness is thus not necessarily a psychic state. The 'feeling' lies beyond any subjective awareness. Haecceity rather than subjectivity. Thus the film impacts as a modulation of haecceities, rather than through subjectivities.

What I want to explain now is how these sequences, whilst evoking the 'becoming girl,' work in this way because of certain elements of sensation, premised upon states of singularity and subjectless subjectivity (through a plane of immanence and consistency) alongside any reading premised on the plane of organisation that we have seen above. They work as a concerto of rhythmical voices or bodies, as 'sensation', the haecceitas beyond of any subjective encounter, which is effected through the brain/ mind and body meld, in the Deleuzian sense. In other words, these sequences function in three major ways: as vibration, resonance and forced movement. These three elements bring about 'sensation', the beyond of subjectivity, as the energies are effectuated through the brain's (of the viewer) cerebral activities and through those regions of the non-subjective state: the proto-subjective or the 'non-subjectified affect' in the auspices of singularities. Here, processuality is effectuated through micro-movements of molecularity in the multiplicities which make up those singularities (see Chapter 4 for clarification). Perception of the movie is dependent upon the micro-molecular movements within the brain's functioning as much as the mind and the body. Those movements are of course assemblaged into motion by the modulations of the film's style. Therefore, the aesthetic and the affect might be 'felt' but they are felt beyond the realm of a subjective encounter. The encounter is beyond subjectivity, in 'sensation'.

First, then the element of vibration, as Deleuze describes it in sensation, works as a 'power that overflows all domains, and traverses them. This power is that of rhythm.' [21] How then does the film Leon work as a rhythmical event? Its rhythms are evinced through the differential relations across sequences. For example, the scenes described above between Leon and Mathilda are juxtaposed in a rhythmical way with sequences which vibrate or resonate through their intense differences in technicalities, visual aesthetics and sounds. An example of these more violent scenes is where Mathilda's family are murdered, and the scenes towards the end of the movie, where Leon is hounded by the 'feds' (FBI). More significantly, the scenes in which Oldman plays the cruel cop Stansfield, a sadistic, evil and menacing creature who takes pleasure in destroying innocence, and terrifying the vulnerable, exemplify vibration. An example of this is the scene in the DEA toilets, where he threatens Mathilda with the horror of his vocal cruelties. Consequently when we watch the 'images' of each sequence, rather than merely seeing them in a rational or cerebral sense, as images through our subjectivity, we actually experience those images as part of something wider. They participate in a tapestry of vision and sound which 'hystericises' subjectivity. Subjectivity is subsumed through 'intensities, energies'. The eye actually becomes a polyvalent organ. Therefore, the colours, shapes, tones and lines help to compose those 'images' within the brain in a different way, so that they don't actually 'represent' any form. They exist as 'vibratory facticity'. The brain itself is an active participant and is responsible for the sensation. But what constitutes the sensation? The very 'sensation' happens in the brain which assembles this amorphous set of colours, shapes, tones and lines. The brain reacts to movement before form for example. The brain acknowledges 'malleable images' through a 'temporal state'. What 'comes before has not yet disappeared when what follows appears'.[22] In other words 'an amorphous mass or a malleable mass' as Deleuze indicates. This is why Deleuze refers to movement-images as opposed to images. So a 'vibration' occurs at the moment of oscillation of different colours, tones, lines and sounds. It is premised on difference in intensity and collision.

So the sequences where we see Leon showering, and also the one watching the Gene Kelly movie, and returning to his apartment (described above), 'vibrate' with the scene depicting a horrendously cruel attack on Mathilda's family. This 'vibration' is modulated through differential relations: collision, difference, oscillation of a variety of aesthetic elements (lines, colours, tone, body movements, music). For example, non-diegetic violin music is interspersed with the sound of drum rolls, and a close-up frame as the cops come into view from a long-shot of the corridor. The first one, front camera angle, backward motion, brings in one cop, then another; body language is synchronised to the rhythms of the music. Then a climactic shot of Stansfield (Oldman). His body movements, angular, erratic, almost insect-like in their febrile energies, convey a movement-image which disturbs. He swallows a pill, and the very micro-movements which he performs are in themselves insect-like, animal-like – a veritable Gregor of Kafkaesque fantasy. He throws back his head, makes a horrendous crack as he bites the tablet, which he swallows with an equally alarming noise. Facial expressions, squirms and menacing eyes penetrate into our consciousness staring back from this strangely static 'moving-image'. What is specifically disturbing are Oldman's dance-like jerky rhythms of walking. He dances/walks holding out quivering arms and fingers, evoking the insect again, as he chatters feverishly, 'I love these calm little moments before the storm' with Beethoven (again, this operates in vibration with the sounds of his voice) as non-diegetic music. Such static, jerky, angular and animal like gestures 'vibrate', and 'resonate', in contradistinction, like Oldman's voice, with those beautiful modulatory and linear shots of Leon as he showers, his body movements differently rhythmical, eloquent, refined. Leon emits a 'becoming-girl' which Stansfield could never emulate, appreciate or evoke. But nonetheless there is something strangely scintillating and pleasurably dangerous about Stansfield, which is created through the vibrational and thus contrasting (with Leon) elements of the performance aesthetics. This 'becoming-animal' of Stansfield is later evidenced when he screams at the 'feds' to bring out everyone to find Leon. He turns his head ever so gently to the left, cranes up his neck and screams, 'I said *everyone*'. The sound, tone and timbre of his voice are both terrifying and, simultaneously and paradoxically, scintillatingly pleasurable. That in-between space of pleasure and danger. Rather than operating as a mere 'character' in a narrative however, Stansfield thus functions in a figural and haptic way (in the Deleuzian sense) and as a dynamic refrain, in a musical sense. His insect-like body, voice and movements provide a vibrational symphony, and an expression of 'forced movement' across other sequences, with those of Leon and Mathilda. But his image is one which exudes a feeling of 'an impulsion to touch' because of his very rhythmical, dance-like gestures (especially where he quivers his hands and fingers – an exquisite performance). As a figural this movement-image ennervates a disturbing effect across our affective responses which we carry throughout the rest of the film. In terms of 'forced movement' again it is the sequences which have both Leon and Stansfield, both opposite and similar, in paradoxical distinction. Near the ending of the film is a beautiful shot of Leon, slowly and lugubriously moving, in delicate anticipation of the freedom, exemplified, technically by the vibrant lighting and uplifting music. Suddenly the camera angle displays a disturbed, Caligarian[23] juxtapositioning of diagonal, and off-centred position. We discover that this subjective viewpoint comes from Leon. He has been shot; but the beauty of the camera movement, evincing the delicacy and tragedy of Leon's death, simultaneously and ironically show Stansfield's final victory. A victory only to be annulled in the final retribution – an apocalyptic vision of death, through the grenade/body of Leon. In finality, it is Mathilda who epitomises the vitality and becoming-girl of the movie, and the final moment sees her strong, independent, resilient and emancipated: a fragility and vulnerability colluding and imbricating with an inner strength and joy in 'life' and its vital possibilities.

ENDING OR BEGINNINGS? JUST PROCESS . . .
AN AESTHETICS OF FUTURE POSSIBILITIES

How then, do we begin to discern some sense of significance to this collusion between philosophy and film theory? The final chapter, specifically, in an exploration of *Leon*, has, as I have established, shown how the molar elements of film theory can work alongside newly created ideas developing from Deleuzian ideas, a molecular paradigm. The earlier chapters display a more apparent location of sensation, a concern with the intensities and energies of modulation, force and the beauty of those. But I don't foresee this use of both the molar and the molecular as in any way a new binary distinction. Rather, the 'in-between' space of the molar and the molecular may be compared, though not identified, with the space of cyborg-becoming,[24] a space which has no boundaries within boundaries, a place which is not a strictly hybridised space, but a space of continual motion, movement and becoming. A neo-aesthetics of sensation, as I have explored, enables this consideration of how film impacts, how it ennervates and engages as a material capture, as an event, as a processuality. With such a new vocabulary in film studies, those earlier concepts of beauty, feeling, movement and sound can take on different meanings, different equations in our perceptual processes. That new mind-set of concepts can help us to redefine desire and its relation to the filmic experience. Vision and sound are not purely experienced through representation, through the visual and the aural, but through the materiality of a whole range of 'bodies', from a deeper engagement of body/brain and world, bodies which are human, non-human, technologised and machinic. What is most creative is that this refreshing conceptualisation of aesthetics takes film studies back into the realm of cinema as art, and reclaims the aesthetic, but a bio- and neo-aesthetic, from those ideological, sociological and libidinal restrictions which have emerged in film theory for too long. Post-structuralism, and its manifestation within a post-feminist pragmatics, has enabled this kaleidoscopic and multiperspectival approach to language perception, thus enabling a merger with philosophy towards rethinking the 'event' of the cinematic, outside those debates contained within early feminist film theory. Perhaps in this way we can delight in the dance of the atoms; we can feel, become and energise through those wonderful cinematic experiences. As Deleuze indicates, film 'spreads an "experimental night" and a "luminous dust"; it affects the visible, with a fundamental disturbance, and the world with a suspension which contradicts all natural perception. What it produces is the genesis of an "unknown body".'[25]

And so, it is a delightful, energised and vital sense of the dynamism in life that enables these insights into new collusions and collisions across film and philosophy, new spaces of the interstitial, new engagements with an aesthetics which becomes a 'tiny thousand sexes', and, I hope, the suggestion that disciplines of knowledge need not be rarefied to the boundaries of their own volitions. Academia would do well to take note of the emergence of aparalletic evolution. My own journey, ironically very non-Deleuzian in its subjective encounter, through those spaces has been deliciously schizophrenic, and at times brought painfully back, in more ways than one, to the psychoanalytic. However, that aparalletic evolution with the beautiful stranger enabled creative volitions which I know can only evolve further through a 'becoming-girl'. I close with these words from the poet-artist Pessoa,

For a Moment

For a moment
Upon my arm
In a movement
Less of thought than
Of weariness,
You laid your hand
And withdrew it.
Did I feel that
Or didn't I?

I don't know. But
I have, still feel
Some memory,
Steady, solid,
Of you laying
Your hand that had
Felt what it did
Not understand,
But so lightly! . . .

This is nothing,
But on a road
Such as life is
There is something
Not understood . . .

Do I know if,
When your hand felt
Itself lying
Upon my arm
And a little
Upon my heart,
There was no new
Rhythm in Space?

As you, not
Intending to,
Touched off in me
Without a word
Some mystery,
Sudden, divine
That you did not
Know existed.

Likewise the breeze
In the branches
Without knowing
Muttered something
Vague but happy . . .[26]

. . . in a fugitive place, just a 'girl' . . . B.

NOTES

1. Deleuze and Guattari, *A Thousand Plateaus*, p. 277.
2. Deleuze and Guattari, *A Thousand Plateaus*, pp. 276–7.
3. We might also add *The Assassin* (1993), the American version of *Nikita* (1990).
4. See especially Deleuze and Parnet, *Dialogues*, chapter on literature, and Deleuze and Guattari, *Kafka: Toward a Minor Literature*. See also David Musselwhite's work on Deleuzian readings of Victorian literature, *Partings Welded Together: Politics and Desire in the Nineteenth-Century English Novel*, and Ian Buchanan and John Mark (eds), *Deleuze and Literature*.
5. I would argue that any abstract concept, like a cliché, is to some extent premised on a literal meaning. So that the concept 'girl' does in some ways develop out of characteristics of 'girlishness': innocence, naivety, weakness, frailty, ethereality, fluidity, complexity, etc. All of course are redolent of social and cultural positioning. An 'essential' descriptor of the girl is premised on these stereotypical characteristics.
6. Aparalletic evolution is a term which Deleuze and Guattari use to explain the 'in-betweenness' of things. They express the concept of 'aparalletic evolution' as the becoming that exists between two contrasting matters: as an example, from *Dialogues*, 'There are no longer binary machines: question/answer, masculine/feminine, man/animal, etc. This could be what a conversation is, simply the outline of a becoming. The wasp and the orchid provide the example. The orchid seems to form a wasp image, an orchid-becoming of the wasp, a double capture, since "what" each becomes, changes no less than that which "becomes". The wasp becomes part of the orchid's reproductive organs at the same time as the orchid becomes the sexual organ of the wasp. One and the same becoming, a single bloc of becoming, "aparallel evolution" of two beings which have nothing whatsoever to do with one another.' See Deleuze and Parnet, *Dialogues*, p. 2.
7. Deleuze and Guattari, *A Thousand Plateaus*, p. 273.
8. Deleuze and Guattari, *A Thousand Plateaus*, p. 261.
9. Deleuze and Guattari, *A Thousand Plateaus*, p. 269.
10. See paper on cyborg-becoming by Francisco Javier Tirado, 'Against Social Constructionist Cyborgian Territorializations', in Angel J. Gordo-Lopez and Ian Parker (eds), *Cyberpsychology*.
11. Deleuze and Guattari, *A Thousand Plateaus*, p. 272.
12. Deleuze and Guattari, *A Thousand Plateaus*, p. 272.
13. Deleuze and Guattari, *A Thousand Plateaus*, p. 272.
14. Deleuze and Guattari, *A Thousand Plateaus*, p. 277.
15. Deleuze and Guattari, *A Thousand Plateaus*, p. 281.
16. This is not love in the romantic sense, but love as an accommodation of volatilities and energies which are positive and can be mutually energising; Mathilda's resonances upon Leon are beautifully positive, vital and energic, but not romantic in any sense of the word 'love'. Indeed, Deleuze indicates that learning to 'love' is nothing to do with being a man or a woman in the molar sense.
17. Interestingly, Deleuze refers that in order to become truly capable of loving, 'one has to first become the fool'. 'To become the real lover, magnetiser, and catalyser . . . one has to first experience the profound wisdom of being an utter fool.' (See Deleuze and Guattari, *A Thousand Plateaus*, p. 134.) An imbrication of innocence and profundity?

18. Brian Massumi, 'Deleuze, Guattari and the Philosophy of Expression', in *Canadian Review of Comparative Literature*, p. 746.
19. Semir Zeki, *Inner Vision*, pp. 62–7.
20. See J. D. Norseen, 'Images of the Mind: The Semiotic Alphabet'.
21. Deleuze quoted in Polan, 'Francis Bacon: The Logic of Sensation', in Boundas and Olkowski (eds), *Gilles Deleuze and the Theatre of Philosophy*, p. 240.
22. Deleuze and Guattari, *What is Philosophy*, p. 211.
23. I refer here to 'Caligari' from the German movie *The Cabinet of Dr Caligari* (1919), which was an important example of German Expressionist cinema in the 1920s, its characteristics being multiple camera angles which create a sense of disorientation, angst and an undercurrent of fear, death and the perverse.
24. See Tirado, 'Against Social Constructionist Cyborgian Territorializations', in Gordo-Lopez and Parker (eds), *Cyberpsychology*, where he collides notions of cyborg consciousness, with Deleuzian notions of becoming, a cyborg-becoming, is a way of describing that unfixed space, not a hybrid place, but a processual plane of consistency, a becoming.
25. Deleuze, *Cinema 2*, p. 201.
26. Pessoa, 'For a Moment', in *A Centenary Pessoa*, p. 45.

Bibliography

Aaron, M. (ed.) (1999), *The Body's Perilous Pleasures* (Edinburgh: Edinburgh University Press).

Adams, P., Brown, B., and Cowie, E. (eds) (1984), *m/f: a feminist journal*, no. 9, (London).

Allison, D. B. (ed.) (1985), *The New Nietzsche* (Massachusetts: MIT Press).

Andrew, D. (1978), 'The Neglected Tradition of Phenomenology in Film Theory', in *Wide Angle*, 2.2, pp. 45–6.

Ansell Pearson, K. (1997a), *Deleuze and Philosophy: The Difference Engineer* (London: Routledge).

Ansell Pearson, K. (1997b), *Viroid Life: Perspectives on Nietzsche and the Transhuman Condition* (London: Routledge).

Ansell Pearson, K. (1999), *Germinal Life: The Difference and Repetition of Deleuze* (London: Routledge).

Bains, P. (1997), 'Subjectless Subjectivities', in B. Massumi, 'Deleuze, Guattari and the Philosophy of Expression', in *Canadian Review of Comparative Literature*, vol. 4, September, p. 519.

Baron-Cohen, S., and Harrison, J. E. (1997), *Synaesthesia: Classic and Contemporary Readings* (Oxford and Massachusetts: Blackwell).

Barthes, R. (1972), *Mythologies*, trans. A. Lavers (New York: Hill and Wang).

Baudrillard, J. (1983), *Simulations*, trans. P. Foss, P. Patton and P. Breitchman (New York: Semiotext(e)).

Baudrillard, J. (1988), *America*, trans. C. Turner (London: Verso).

Baudrillard, J. (1990), *Seduction*, trans. B. Singer (London: Macmillan).

Baudrillard, J. (1994), *Simulacra and Simulation*, trans. S. F. Glaser (Ann Arbor: University of Michigan Press).

Beck, U., and Beck-Gernsheim, E. (1995), *The Normal Chaos of Love*, trans. M. Ritter and I. Wiebel (Cambridge: Polity).

Bell, D., and Kennedy, B. M. (eds) (2000), *The Cybercultures Reader* (London and New York: Routledge).

Benhabib, S. (1995 [1990]), 'Feminism and Postmodernism: An Uneasy Alliance', in L. Nicholson (ed.), *Feminist Contentions: A Philosophical Exchange* (New York: Routledge).

Bennett, J. (1984), *A Study of Spinoza's Ethics* (Cambridge, London, New York, Sydney, Melbourne: Cambridge University Press).

Benvenuto, B. and Kennedy, R. (1986), *The Works of Jacques Lacan: An Introduction* (London: Free Association Books).

Bergson, H. (1911), *Creative Evolution*, trans A. Mitchell (New York: Holt).

Bergson, H. (1991), *Matter and Memory*, trans. N. Margaret Paul and W. Scott Palmer (New York: Urzone).

Bergstrom, J., and Doane, M. A. (eds) (1989), *Camera Obscura: A Journal of Feminism and Film Theory*, nos 20 and 21, September (Baltimore: John Hopkins University Press).

Bogue, R. (1989), *Deleuze and Guattari* (London: Routledge).

Bogue, R. (1996), 'Gilles Deleuze: The Aesthetics of Force', in P. Patton (ed.) (1996), *Deleuze: A Critical Reader* (Oxford and Cambridge, MA: Blackwell), pp. 257–70.

Boorman, J., and Donohue, W. (eds) (1974), *Projections 3* (London: Faber and Faber Ltd).

Boundas, C. V., and Olkowski, D. (eds) (1994), *Gilles Deleuze and the Theatre of Philosophy* (London: Routledge).

Braidotti, R. (1994a), *Nomadic Subjects: Embodiment and Sexual Difference in Contemporary Feminist Theory* (New York: Colombia University Press).

Braidotti, R. (1994b), 'Toward a New Nomadism: Feminist Deleuzian Tracks; or, Metaphysics and Metabolism', in C. V. Boundas and D. Olkowski (eds) (1994), *Gilles Deleuze and the Theatre of Philosophy* (London: Routledge), pp. 157–87.

Braidotti, R. (1996), 'An Anti-Oedipal Tribute', in *Radical Philosophy*, 76, pp. 3–5.

Braidotti, R. (1997), 'Meta(l)morphosis', in *Theory, Culture and Society*, 14:2, pp. 67–80.

Broadhurst, J. (ed.) (1992), *Pli: Deleuze and the Transcendental Unconscious* (Coventry: University of Warwick).

Brooks, P. (1977), *Freud's Master Plot*, vols 55 and 56, pp. 290–1.

Buchanan, I. (1997), 'The Problem of the Body in Deleuze and Guattari, Or, What Can a Body Do?', *Body and Society*, 3.3, September, pp. 73–91.

Buchanan, I. (2000), *Deleuzism: A Metacommentary* (Edinburgh: Edinburgh University Press).

Buchanan, I., and Colebrook, C. (eds) (2000), *Deleuze and Feminist Theory* (Edinburgh: Edinburgh University Press).

Buchanan, I., and Marks, J. (eds) (2000), *Deleuze and Literature* (Edinburgh: Edinburgh University Press).

Burgoyne, R., Flitterman-Lewis, S., and Stam, R. (eds) (1992), *New Vocabularies in Film Semiotics* (London and New York: Routledge).

Butler, J. (1990), *Gender Trouble: Feminism and the Subversion of Identity* (New York: Routledge).

Butler, J. (1993), *Bodies That Matter: On the Discursive Limits of Sex* (London: Routledge).

Butler, J. (1995a [1991]), 'Contingent Foundations', in L. Nicholson (ed.) (1995), *Feminist Contentions* (London: Routledge).

Butler, J. (1995b [1993]), 'For a Careful Reading', in L. Nicholson (ed.) (1995), *Feminist Contentions* (London: Routledge).

Camus, A. (1946 [1942]), *The Outsider*, trans. Stuart Gilbert with intro. by Cyril Connolly (Middlesex: Penguin).

Cashmore, E., and Rojek, C. (eds) (1999), *Dictionary of Cultural Theorists* (London, New York, Sydney and Auckland: Arnold).

Cassirer, E. (ed.) (1945), *Rousseau, Kant and Goethe*, trans. James Gutmann (Princeton: Princeton University Press).

Cioran, E. M. (1992), *Anathemas and Admirations*, trans. Richard Howard with an intro. by Tom McGonigle (London: Quartet).

Cixous, H. (1975), 'Sorties', in La Jeune Née (Paris: Union d'Éditions Générales, 10/18).

Cixous, H. (1976), 'The Laugh of the Medusa', in *Signs*, 1, pp. 875–99. Quoted in Marks and de Courtvron.

Clover, Carol (1992), *Men, Women and Chainsaws* (Princeton: Princeton University Press).
Colwell, C. (1997), 'Deleuze and the Prepersonal', in *Philosophy Today*, Spring.
Connolly, W. E. (1995), *The Ethos of Pluralisation* (Minneapolis: University of Minnesota Press).
Conrad, J. (1973 [1902]), *Heart of Darkness* (Middlesex: Penguin).
Cornell, D. (1995a), 'What is Ethical Feminism?', in L. Nicholson (ed.) (1995), *Feminist Contentions* (London: Routledge).
Cornell, D. (1995b), 'Rethinking the Time of Feminism?', in L. Nicholson (ed.) (1995), *Feminist Contentions* (London: Routledge).
Cowie, E. (1984), 'Fantasia', *m/f*, pp. 70–105.
Crary, J. (1992), *Techniques of the Observer: On Vision and Modernity in the Nineteenth Century* (Cambridge, MA: Massachusetts Institute of Technology Press).
Crary, J., and Kwinter, S. (eds) (1992), *Incorporations* (New York: Zone).
Creed, B. (1993), *The Monstrous Feminine: Film, Feminism and Psychoanalysis* (New York and London: Routledge).
Deleuze, G. (1981), *Francis Bacon: Logique de la Sensation* (Paris: Editions de la Différence): vol. 1 contains Deleuze's text; vol. II contains reproductions of Bacon's paintings.
Deleuze, G. (1986), *Cinema 1: The Movement-Image*, trans. H. Tomlinson and B. Habberjam (London: Athlone and Minneapolis: University of Minnesota Press); (1983), *Cinéma 1: L'Image-mouvement* (Paris: Editions de Minuit).
Deleuze, G. (1989), *Cinema 2: The Time-Image*, trans. H. Tomlinson and R. Galeta (London: Athlone); (1985), *Cinéma 2: L'Image-temps* (Paris: Editions de Minuit).
Deleuze, G. (1990), *The Logic of Sense*, trans. M. Lester with Charles Stivale (New York: Colombia University Press).
Deleuze, G. (1991), *Bergsonism*, trans. H. Tomlinson and B. Habberjam (New York: Urzone).
Deleuze, G. (1994a), *Critique et Clinique* (Paris: Minuit).
Deleuze, G. (1994b), *Difference and Repetition*, trans. P. Patton (London: Athlone).
Deleuze, G. (1995), *Negotiations, 1972–1990*, trans. M. Joughin (New York: Colombia University Press).
Deleuze, G. (1997), 'Immanence: A Life', in *Theory, Culture and Society*, 14:2.
Deleuze, G., and Guattari, F. (1984), *Anti-Oedipus: Capitalism and Schizophrenia*, trans. R. Hurley, M. Seem, and H. R. Lane (London: Athlone); (1972) *Capitalisme et Schizophrénie tome 1: l'Anti-Oedipe* (Paris: Editions de Minuit).
Deleuze, G., and Guattari, F. (1986), *Kafka: Toward a Minor Literature*, trans. Dana Polan (Minneapolis: University of Minnesota Press).
Deleuze, G., and Guattari, F. (1987), *A Thousand Plateaus: Capitalism and Schizophrenia*, trans. B. Massumi (London: Athlone); (1980), *Capitalisme et Schizophrenie tome 2: Mille Plateaux* (Paris: Les Editions de Minuit).
Deleuze, G., and Guattari, F. (1994), *What is Philosophy?*, trans. G. Burchill and H. Tomlinson (London: Verso); (1991), *Qu'est ce que la philosophie?* (Paris: Les Editions de Minuit).
Deleuze, G., and Parnet, C. (1987), *Dialogues*, trans. H. Tomlinson and B. Habberjam (London: Athlone).
Diprose, R. (1994), *The Bodies of Women: Ethics, Embodiment and Sexual Difference* (London and New York: Routledge).
Doane, M. A., Mellencamp, P., and Williams, L. (eds) (1984), *Revision: Essays in Feminist Film Criticism* (Los Angeles: University Publications of America).
Doel, M. (1999), *Post-structuralist Geographies* (Edinburgh: Edinburgh University Press).

Eisenstein, S. M. (1943), *The Film Sense* (London: Faber and Faber).

Ferguson, R. (1991), *Henry Miller* (London: Hutchinson).

Forster, E. M. (1910), *Howard's End* (London: Edward Arnold).

Fox Keller, E. (1983), *A Feeling for the Organism: The Life and Work of Barbara McClintock* (New York: W. H. Freeman).

Fraser, N. (1995a), 'False Antitheses', in L. Nicholson (ed.), *Feminist Contentions* (London: Routledge).

Fraser, N. (1995b), 'Pragmatism, Feminism and the Linguistic Turn', in L. Nicholson (ed.), *Feminist Contentions* (London: Routledge).

Fraser, N. (1997), 'Feminism, Foucault and Deleuze', in *Theory, Culture and Society*, 14:2, pp. 23–7.

Freud, S. (1957 [1922]), *The Standard Edition of the Complete Psychological Works of Sigmund Freud, Beyond the Pleasure Principle, Group Psychology and Other Works, 1920–1922*, vol. 18, trans. and ed. James Strachey (London: Hogarth).

Friedberg, A. (1993), *Window Shopping: Cinema and the Post-Modern Condition* (Berkeley and Los Angeles: University of California Press).

Friedberg, A. (1994), 'Cinema and the Postmodern Condition', in L. Williams (ed.) (1994), *Viewing Positions* (New Brunswick, New Jersey: Rutgers University Press).

Gardner, W. H. (1953), *Gerard Manley Hopkins* (Middlesex: Penguin).

Gatens, M. (1996a), *Imaginary Bodies: Ethics, Power and Corporeality* (London and New York: Routledge).

Gatens, M. (1996b), 'Through a Spinozist Lens: Ethology, Difference, Power', in P. Patton (ed.) (1996), *Deleuze: A Critical Reader* (Oxford and Cambridge, Massachusetts: Blackwell), pp. 162–88.

Giraud, P. (1975 [1971]), *Semiology*, trans. George Gross (London: Routledge and Kegan Paul).

Gledhill, C., and Williams, L. (2000), *Re-inventing Film Studies* (London and New York: Arnold).

Goethe, J. W. von (1945), 'Theory of Colours', in E. Cassirer (ed.) (1945), *Rousseau, Kant and Goethe*, trans. James Gutmann (Princeton: Princeton University Press).

Goodchild, P. (1996), *Deleuze and Guattari: An Introduction to the Politics of Desire* (London: Sage).

Gordo-Lopez A. J., and Parker, I. (eds) (1999), *Cyberpsychology* (London: Macmillan).

Griggers, C. (1997), *Becoming-Woman: Theory Out of Bounds* (Minneapolis: University of Minnesota Press).

Griggers, C. (2000), 'Goodbye America (The Bride is Walking . . .)', in I. Buchanan and C. Colebrook (eds) (2000), *Deleuze and Feminist Theory* (Edinburgh: Edinburgh University Press).

Grosz, E. (1990), *Jacques Lacan: A Feminist Introduction* (London and New York: Routledge).

Grosz, E. (1994a), *Volatile Bodies: Towards a Corporeal Feminism* (Bloomington: Indiana University Press).

Grosz, E. (1994b), 'A Thousand Tiny Sexes: Feminism and Rhizomatics', in C. Boundas and D. Olkowski (eds) (1994), *Gilles Deleuze and the Theatre of Philosophy* (London: Routledge), pp. 187–213.

Grosz, E. (1995), *Space, Time and Perversion: Essays on the Politics of Bodies* (London: Routledge).

Grosz, E., and Probyn, E. (1995), *Sexy Bodies: The Strange Carnalities of Feminism* (London and New York: Routledge).

Guattari, F. (1984), *Molecular Revolution: Psychiatry and Politics*, trans. Rosemary Sheed (Harmondsworth: Penguin).

Guattari, F. (1989), *Les Trois Écologies* (Paris: Galilée).

Guattari, F. (1995), *Chaosmosis: An Ethico-Aesthetic Paradigm*, trans. P. Bains and J. Pefanis (Sydney: Power Publications); (1992), *Chaosmose* (Paris: Editions Galilée).

Gunning. T. (1989), 'An Aesthetics of Astonishment: Early Film and the Incredulous Spectator', in *Art and Text*, 34, pp. 31–45.

Haar, M. (1985), 'Nietzsche and Metaphysical Language', in D. Allison (ed.) (1985), *The New Nietzsche* (MIT Press).

Hansen, M. (1993), 'Early Cinema, Late Cinema: Transformations of the Public Sphere', in *Screen*, 34: 3, Autumn, pp. 197–210.

Haraway, D. (1991), *Simians, Cyborgs and Women: The Reinvention of Nature* (London: Free Association).

Haraway, D. (2000 [1991]), 'A Cyborg Manifesto; Science, Technology and Socialist Feminism in the Late Twentieth Century', in B. Kennedy and D. Bell (eds) (2000), *The Cybercultures Reader* (London: Routledge).

Hardt, M. (1993), *Gilles Deleuze: An Apprenticeship in Philosophy* (Minneapolis: University of Minnesota Press).

Hegel, G. W. F. (1975), *Hegel's Aesthetics: Lectures on Fine Art*, trans. T. M. Knox (Oxford: Oxford University Press).

Horner, A. and Keane, A. (eds) (2000), *Body Matters: Feminism, Textuality and Corporeality* (Manchester and New York: Manchester University Press).

Houlgate, S. (1986), *Hegel, Nietzsche and the Criticism of Metaphysics* (Cambridge: Cambridge University Press).

Hughes, J. (1997), *Lines of Flight: Reading Deleuze with Hardy, Gissing, Conrad, Woolf* (Sheffield: Sheffield Academic Press).

Irigaray, L. (1974), *Speculum de L'autre femme* (Paris: Minuit).

Irigaray, L. (1976), 'Women's Exile', interview in *Ideology and Consciousness* (May 1977), pp. 62–76.

Irigaray, L. (1980), 'When the Goods Get Together', in E. Marks and Isabelle de Courtivron (eds) (1980), *New French Feminisms* (Brighton: Harvester).

Irigaray, L. (1985), *This Sex Which is Not One*, trans. C. Porter with R. Burke (Ithaca, NY: Cornell University).

Irigaray, L. (1986), *Amante Marine de Friedrich Nietzsche* (Paris: Minuit).

James, H. (1963), 'The Figure in the Carpet', in *The Complete Tales of Henry James* (London: Rupert Hart-Davies).

Jardine, A. (1984), 'Woman in Limbo: Deleuze and his (br)others', in *Substance*, 44/45, pp. 46–60.

Jardine, A. (1985), *Gynesis: Configurations of Woman and Modernity* (Ithaca, NY: Cornell University Press).

Kafka, F. (1961 [1916]), *Metamorphosis*, trans. Willa and Edwin Muir (Middlesex: Penguin).

Kant, I. (1929), *Critique of Pure Reason*, trans. Norman Kemp Smith (London: Macmillan).

Kant, I. (1982), *Critique of Judgement*, trans. J. Creed Meredith (Oxford: Clarendon Press).

Kaplan, E. (ed.) (1980), *Women in Film Noir* (London: British Film Institute).

Kaplan, E. (ed.) (1990), *Psychoanalysis and Cinema* (London: Routledge).

Kennedy, B. M. (1999), 'Post-feminist Futures in Film Noir', in M. Aaron (ed.) (1999), *The Body's Perilous Pleasures* (Edinburgh: Edinburgh University Press).

Klossowski, P. (1997), *Nietzsche and the Vicious Circle*, trans. Daniel W. Smith (Chicago: University of Chicago Press).

Kristeva, J. (1974), 'La femme ce n'est jamais ça', in *Tel Quel*, 59, pp. 19–24.

Kristeva, J. (1984), *Revolution in Poetic Language*, trans. M. Walter (New York: Columbia University Press).

Kristeva, J. (1986a), *Desire in Language: A Semiotic Approach to Literature and Art*, ed. Leon S. Roudiez, trans. Alice Jardine and Leon Roudiez (Oxford: Blackwell).

Kristeva, J. (1986b), *Powers of Horror*, trans. L. S. Roudiez (New York: Colombia University Press).

Kristeva, J. (1980), 'Woman Can Never be Defined', in E. Marks and Isabelle de Courtivron (eds) (1980), *New French Feminisms* (Brighton: Harvester).

Lacan, J. (1977a), *Ecrits: A Selection*, trans. A. Sheridan (London: Tavistock).

Lacan, J. (1977b), *The Four Fundamental Concepts of Psychoanalysis* (London: Hogarth Press).

Lecercle, J. J. (1985), *Philosophy through the Looking-Glass: Language, Nonsense, Desire* (La Salle: Open Court).

Lechte, J. (1990), *Julia Kristeva*, (London and New York: Routledge).

Levinson, J. (1998), *Aesthetics and Ethics: Essays at the Intersection* (Cambridge: Cambridge University Press).

Lichtenberg-Ettinger, B. (1992), 'Matrix and Metamorphosis', in *Differences, A Journal of Feminist Cultural Studies*, 4:3, p. 176.

Lingis, A. (1994), *Foreign Bodies* (London: Routledge).

Lucie-Smith, E. (1996), *Visual Arts in the Twentieth Century* (London: Lawrence King).

Lyotard, J. F. (1971), *Discours, Figure* (Paris: Klincksieck).

Lyotard, J. F. (1984), *The Postmodern Condition: A Report on Knowledge*, trans. G. Bennington and B. Massumi (Manchester: University of Manchester).

McMahon, M. (1997), 'Beauty: Machinic Repetition in the Age of Art', in B. Massumi (ed.) (1997), *Canadian Review of Comparative Literature*.

McWilliam, E., and Taylor, P. (eds) (1996), *Pedagogy, Technology and the Body* (New York, Washington, Berlin, Paris, Vienna, Berne, and Baltimore DC: Peter Lang).

Marks, E. and Courtivron, Isabelle de (eds) (1980), *New French Feminisms* (Brighton: Harvester).

Massumi, B. (1992), *A User's Guide to Capitalism and Schizophrenia: Deviations from Deleuze and Guattari* (Cambridge, MA: MIT Press).

Massumi, B. (1996), 'The Autonomy of Affect', in P. Patton (ed.) (1996), *Deleuze: A Critical Reader* (Oxford and Cambridge, Massachusetts: Blackwell), pp. 217–40.

Massumi, B. (1997), 'Deleuze, Guattari and the Philosophy of Expression', in *Canadian Review of Comparative Literature*, vol. 4, September.

Mayne, J. (1993), *Cinema and Spectatorship* (London: Routledge).

Merleau-Ponty, M. (1962), *Phenomenology of Perception*, trans. Colin Smith (London: Routledge and Kegan Paul).

Metz, C. (1971, 1972), *Essais sur la signification au cinéma*, vols I and II (Paris: Klincksieck).

Metz, C. (1974a), *Film Language: A Semiotics of the Cinema* (New York: Oxford University Press).

Metz, C. (1974b), *Language and Cinema* (The Hague: Mouton).

Metz, C. (1975), 'The Imaginary Signifier', in *Screen*, 16(2) Summer.

Metz, C. (1982), *The Imaginary Signifier: Psychoanalysis and the Cinema* (Bloomington: Indiana University Press).

Miller, H. (1965), *Sexus* (New York: Grove Press).

Modleski, T. (1991), *Feminism Without Women, Culture and Criticism in a 'Postfeminist' Age* (New York and London: Routledge).

Moi, T. (1985), *Sexual/Textual Politics* (London: Methuen).

Mouffe, C. (ed.) (1996), *Deconstruction and Pragmatism* (London and New York: Routledge).

Mullarkey, J. (1997), 'Deleuze and Materialism: One or Several Matters?' in Ian

Buchanan (ed), *A Deleuzian Century: Special Issue of the South Atlantic Quarterly*, 96.3 (Summer), pp. 439–63.

Mulvey, L. (1989), *Visual and Other Pleasures* (London: Macmillan).

Musselwhite, D. (1987), *Partings Welded Together: Politics and Desire in the Nineteenth-Century English Novel* (London and New York: Methuen).

Nicholson, L. (ed.) (1990), *Feminism/Postmodernism* (London: Routledge, Chapman and Hall).

Nicholson, L. (ed.) (1995), *Feminist Contentions* (London: Routledge).

Nietzsche, F. (1954a), *Werke I* (Munchen: Carl Hanser Verlag).

Nietzsche, F. (1954b), *Werke II: Die Fröhliche Wissenschaft* (Munchen: Carl Hanser Verlag).

Nietzsche, F. (1954c), *Werke III* (Munchen: Carl Hanser Verlag).

Nietzsche, F. (1968), *The Will to Power*, trans. T. Kaufman (New York: Vintage).

Nietzsche, F. (1969), *On the Genealogy of Morals*, trans. Walter Kaufmann (New York: Vintage Books).

Nietzsche, F. (1982), *Daybreak: Thoughts on the Prejudices of Morality*, trans. R. J. Hollingdale, with intro. by M. Tanner (Cambridge: Cambridge University Press).

Nietzsche, F. (1998), *Twilight of the Idols*, trans. with intro. and notes by Duncan Large (Oxford: Oxford University Press).

Norseen, J. (1996), 'Images of the Mind: The Semiotic Alphabet', in *American Computer Scientists' Association*.

O'Connell, S. (1997), 'Aesthetics: A Place I've Never Seen', in *Canadian Review of Comparative Literature*, September, p. 486.

Ondaatje, M. (1993), *The English Patient* (London: Picador).

Patton, P. (1994), 'Anti-Platonism and Art', in C. Boundas and D. Olkowski (eds) (1994), *Gilles Deleuze and the Theatre of Philosophy* (London and New York: Routledge), pp. 141–57.

Patton, P. (ed.) (1996), *Deleuze: A Critical Reader* (Oxford and Cambridge, Massachusetts: Blackwell).

Penley, C. (1989), *The Future of an Illusion: Film, Feminism, and Psychoanalysis*. (Minneapolis: University of Minnesota Press).

Penrose, R. (1997), *The Large, the Small and the Human Mind* (Cambridge: Cambridge University Press).

Pessoa, F. (1995), *A Centenary Pessoa*, ed. by E. Lisboa and L. C. Taylor, trans. poetry by K. Bosky, prose by B. McGuirk, M. Lisboa and R. Zenith, intro. by O. Paz (Manchester: Carcanet).

Polan, D. (1994), 'Francis Bacon: The Logic of Sensation', in C. Boundas and D. Olkowski (eds) (1994), *Gilles Deleuze and the Theatre of Philosophy* (London and New York: Routledge), pp. 229–55.

Pollock, G. (1988), *Vision and Difference: Femininity, Feminism and Histories of Art* (London: Routledge).

Powell, A. (2001), *Transformations: Altered States in Film* (London: Flicks Books).

Prigogine, I. (1989), 'The Philosophy of Instability', in *Futures*, no. 396, p. 400.

Rodowick, D. N. (1991), *The Difficulty of Difference* (London and New York: Routledge).

Rodowick, D. N. (1997), *Gilles Deleuze's Time Machine* (London: Duke University Press).

Root-Bernstein, R. (1997), 'Art, Imagination and the Scientist', in *American Scientist*, 85, pp. 6–9.

Ropars-Wuilleumier, M. C. (1994), 'The Cinema, Reader of Gilles Deleuze', in C. Boundas and D. Olkowski (eds) (1994), *Gilles Deleuze and the Theatre of Philosophy* (London and New York: Routledge), pp. 255–61.

Rosset, C. (1993), *Joyful Cruelty: Towards a Philosophy of the Real*, trans. and ed. by D. F. Bell (Oxford and New York: Oxford University Press).

Ruyer, R. (1952), *Neo-finalisme* (Paris: PUF).

Sandoval, C. (2000), 'New Sciences: Cyborg Feminism and the Methodology of the Oppressed', in B. M. Kennedy and D. Bell (eds) (2000), *The Cybercultures Reader* (London: Routledge).

Saussure, F. (1974), *Course in General Linguistics* (London: Fontana).

Schact, R. (ed.) (1993), *Nietzsche: Selections* (New Jersey: Prentice-Hall).

Shaviro, S. (1993), *The Cinematic Body* (Minneapolis: University of Minnesota Press).

Shiach, M. (1991), *Hélène Cixous* (London: Routledge).

Silverman, K. (1996), *The Threshold of the Visible World* (London: Routledge).

Smith, D. (1996), 'Deleuze's Theory of Sensation: Overcoming the Kantian Duality', in P. Patton (ed.) (1996), *Deleuze: A Critical Reader* (Oxford and Cambridge, Massachusetts: Blackwell), pp. 29–57.

Smith-Rosenberg, C. (1985), *Disorderly Conduct* (Oxford: Open University Press).

Sobchack, V. (1992), *The Address of the Eye: A Phenomenology of Film Experience* (Princeton, NJ: Princeton University Press).

Sobchack, V. (1994), 'Phenomenology and the Film Experience', in L. Williams (ed.) (1994), *Viewing Positions* (New Brunswick, New Jersey: Rutgers University Press), pp. 36–59.

Stam, R., Burgoyne, R., and Flitterman-Lewis, S. (eds) (1992), *New Vocabularies in Film Semiotics, Structuralism, Post-structuralism and Beyond* (London and New York: Routledge).

Stern, D. (1985), *The Interpersonal World of the Infant: A Review from Psychoanalysis and Developmental Psychology* (New York: Basic Books).

Stone, R., Allucquere (2000 [1992]), 'Will the Real Body Please Stand Up', in B. M. Kennedy and D. Bell (eds) (2000), *The Cybercultures Reader* (London: Routledge).

Studlar, G. (1988), *In the Realm of Pleasure: Von Sternberg, Dietrich, and the Masochistic Aesthetic* (Urbana and Chicago: University of Illinois Press).

Tirado, F. J. (1999), 'Against Social Constructionist Cyborgian Territorializations', in A. J. Gordo-Lopez and I. Parker (eds) (1999), *Cyberpsychology* (London: Macmillan).

Tuer, D. (1987), 'Pleasures in the Dark: Sexual Difference and Erotic Deviance in an Articulation of Female Desire', in *Cineaction*, 10.

Valadier, P. (1985), 'Dionysus versus the Crucified', in D. B. Allison (ed.) (1985), *The New Nietzsche* (Massachusetts: MIT Press).

Virilio, P. (1994), *The Vision Machine* (Bloomington: Indiana University Press).

Wartenberg, T. E., and Freedland, C. A. (eds) (1995), *Philosophy and Film* (London and New York: Routledge).

Williams, L. (ed.) (1994), *Viewing Positions: Ways of Seeing Film* (New Brunswick, NJ: Rutgers University Press).

Wilson, E. O. (1998), *Consilience* (London: Little, Brown and Company).

Woolf, V. (1925), *Modern Fiction: The Common Reader* (London: Hogarth Press).

Woolf, V. (1925–30), *The Diary of Virginia Woolf*, vol. 3 (London: Hogarth Press).

Woolf, V. (1928), *Orlando: A Biography* (London: Hogarth Press).

Woolf, V. (1943), *The Waves* (London: Hogarth Press).

Woolf, V. (1992 [1925]), *Mrs Dalloway* (Harmondsworth: Penguin).

Yeats, W. B. (1977 [1933]), 'The Second Coming', in *The Collected Poems of W. B. Yeats* (London: Macmillan).

Zeki, S. (1999), *Inner Vision: An Exploration of Art and the Brain* (Oxford: Oxford University Press).

Filmography

Age of Innocence (1993) Martin Scorsese

The Assassin (1993) J. Badham

Basic Instinct (1992) Paul Verhoeven

Battleship Potemkin (1925) Sergei Eisenstein

Bladerunner (1982) Ridley Scott

Blue Steel (1990) Kathryn Bigelow

Blue Velvet (1986) David Lynch

The Cabinet of Dr Caligari (1919) Robert Weine

Crash (1996) David Cronenberg

End of Days (1999) Peter Hyams

The English Patient (1996) Anthony Minghella

Far from the Madding Crowd (1967) John Schlesinger

Howard's End (1992) James Ivory

Leon (1994) Luc Besson

Metropolis (1926) Fritz Lang

Near Dark (1987) Kathryn Bigelow

Nikita (1990) Luc Besson

October (1928) Sergei Eisenstein

Orlando (1992) Sally Potter

Priscilla, Queen of the Desert (1994) Stephan Elliott

Raging Bull (1980) Martin Scorsese

Romeo is Bleeding (1993) Peter Medak

The Sheltering Sky (1990) Bernardo Bertolucci

Sliver (1993) Phillip Noyce

Strange Days (1995) Kathryn Bigelow

Strictly Ballroom (1992) Baz Luhrmann

Strike (1925) Sergei Eisenstein

Twelve Monkeys (1995) Terry Gilliam

Videodrome (1982) David Cronenberg

William Shakespeare's Romeo and Juliet (1996) Baz Luhrmann

The Winter Guest (1997) Alan Rickman

Index